ARC OF UTOPIA

ARC OF UTOPIA

THE BEAUTIFUL STORY OF THE RUSSIAN REVOLUTION

LESLEY CHAMBERLAIN

REAKTION BOOKS

Published by Reaktion Books Ltd
Unit 32, Waterside
44–48 Wharf Road
London N1 7UX, UK
www.reaktionbooks.co.uk

First published 2017
Copyright © Lesley Chamberlain 2017

Printed and bound in Great Britain
by TJ International, Padstow, Cornwall

A catalogue record for this book is available from the British Library

ISBN 978 1 78023 852 4

To Art in Russia,
an unforgettable presence

CONTENTS

AUTHOR'S NOTE

Imagine a character beginning: 'I'll tell you a story. The whole tragedy of our twentieth century in Russia began with a beautiful fantasy. Beauty was something in us, or outside us, or both, that made it possible for human beings everywhere to unite.'

In 1940 Edmund Wilson's magisterial *To the Finland Station*, 'A Study in the Writing and Acting of History', looked mainly to French historians and theorists of revolution for what had recently created Lenin's and Stalin's Russia. It was a sign of the times. The Soviet Union had emerged in that history as a powerful political rival to the West. By contrast, my story, written a quarter of a century after the Soviet Union's demise, reinterprets the Russian Revolution as rooted in a vision of moral beauty. It is not designed to overwrite political accounts of the 1917 upheaval, but the intention is to restore dignity to the utopian imagination that dared to wonder what might be 'the right way to live'.

It could also be called '127 Years of Yearning', a passion passed on to Russian artists and thinkers by German philosophers from a century earlier, on the matter of beauty.

Immanuel Kant published his *Critique of Judgement* in 1790. The Bolshevik Revolution happened in 1917. That's the timescale. Kant set down what he meant by human creativity in his Third Critique, which has generally been thought of as being 'about aesthetics'. In fact its almost inexhaustible topic was how the human imagination plays with ideas of wholeness and harmony. Not what we are but what we might be, if only we could become more creative, was the aesthetic task. Our very capacity for moral imagination showed what freedom meant to us. There was this desire in the late eighteenth century, around the time of the French Revolution, to create the beautiful state, and in Russia, in the early twentieth, the prospective overthrow of the 350-year-old tsarist regime sparked it anew.

Glossary of Names

IMMANUEL KANT (1724–1804), German philosopher who rewrote the theory of knowledge as what the human subject could know. His three 'Critiques', from 1781, 1788 and 1790, dealt in turn with reason applied to the natural world, morality and imagination. The effect of his Subjective Idealism was to define a moral imagination fit for utopian dreaming.

FRIEDRICH SCHILLER (1759–1805), primarily a dramatist, saw theatre as the source of *mass* national instruction of the future. Schiller turned Kant's philosophy of human moral progress into a journey also towards beauty.

FRIEDRICH SCHELLING (1775–1854), theology student at the Tübingen seminary and one of the authors of the fragmentary 'The Oldest Systematic Programme of German Idealism' drafted in 1796. His Romantic version of Subjective Idealism departed sharply from Kant's critical rigour and opened up utopian dreaming to poets and geniuses who could transform society with their insights.

FRIEDRICH HÖLDERLIN (1770–1843), poet, occasional philosopher and admirer of Schiller, co-seminarist with Schelling and Hegel, incorporated his deep love of ancient Greece into utopian sentiment brought on by German excitement at the French Revolution.

JOHANN GOTTLIEB FICHTE (1762–1914), post-Kantian philosopher who developed Idealism into a metaphysics of the German national spirit and introduced an element of spiritual self-sacrifice. His philosophy impressed Bakunin.

GEORG WILHELM FRIEDRICH HEGEL (1770–1831), the greatest German philosopher after Kant, turned Idealism into a description of the mind progressing in its rationality through history. The end result would be a society perfected by philosophy.

ALEXANDER HERZEN (1812–1870), an almost unique Russian liberal figure, who studied German Idealism alongside French political radicalism and utopianism, spent most of his life in European exile, agitating for an end to tsarism and to find a form of modern progress suitable to the unique conditions of Russia.

NIKOLAI STANKEVICH (1813–1840), organizer of Moscow's most famous philosophical circle in the 1830s and outstanding student of Hegel in Berlin.

KARL MARX (1818–1883), philosopher, economic theorist, belletrist, was responsible for the transformation of Hegel's Idealism into Marxism as a political programme, also in Russia. Marx sharply differentiated his practical thought from all forms of utopianism because he believed his programme was scientific, while utopianism was a fantasy. Marxism carried Hegel's philosophy of history forward as a plan of action in a country in search of self-definition.

HEINRICH HEINE (1797–1856), German poet and satirist, leading figure of the reform-minded decades between the French Revolution and the 1848 revolutions in Germany and Central Europe.

MIKHAIL BAKUNIN (1814–1876), thinker, political activist and journalist who gave his name to anarchism because of his relentless campaign to liberate Russia from tsarism and to use that model, while sharing ideas with Marx, to also disrupt power in other European countries. His early critiques of Hegel and Johann Gottlieb Fichte helped establish Russian revolutionary discourse.

RICHARD WAGNER (1813–1883), composer, dramatist, author and participant in the 1849 revolution in Dresden. In his music dramas which, in the tradition heralded by Schiller, were intended to revolutionize society in spirit, after the political groundwork was done, Wagner blended aspects of German Idealism with the pre-Marxist political radicalism of the German 1840s.

LUDWIG FEUERBACH (1804–1872), philosopher who transformed the German Idealist heritage when he argued for a materialist account of the world, with God as a projection of human qualities.

IVAN TURGENEV (1818–1883), Russia's third great novelist after Dostoevsky and Tolstoy, secular and poetic, after studying German philosophy in Berlin wrote stories reflecting his disillusion with the growing revolutionary tradition.

FYODOR DOSTOEVSKY (1821–1881), novelist, thinker, traveller in the West, combined a deep love of the moral and artistic messages he discovered in German Idealism with a hunger to see Russia spiritually transformed through a reinvention of Russian Orthodoxy.

VLADIMIR SOLOVIEV (1853–1900), religious philosopher and poet who transformed Schelling's Nature Philosophy into the foundation of a Russian ethical personalism.

GEORGY PLEKHANOV (1856–1918), political activist, journalist, the outstanding Russian Marxist of the late nineteenth century, who first became Lenin's inspiration for the revolution and then his opponent. Plekhanov, though he urged the time was not ripe for definitive upheaval and the transition to a proletarian state, thoroughly absorbed a German Idealist cum Marxist outlook on culture and society, and his thought patterns became embedded in Soviet practice.

ALEXANDER BLOK (1880–1921), Symbolist poet who used religious imagery to portray the revolution as the moment of Russia's spiritual transformation.

VYACHESLAV IVANOV (1866–1949), poet, dramatist, classicist, who studied in Berlin and was an admirer of Kant, Schiller and Hölderlin. Ivanov was a unique Russian early modernist, who helped bring elements of Symbolism, theatre and music on to the revolutionary streets.

ANDREI BELY (1880–1934), mystically inclined poet and novelist deeply involved in Russia's *fin de siècle* self-definition out of the spirit of German philosophy.

NIKOLAI BERDYAEV (1874–1948), major figure in Russian religious philosophy and acute critical commentator on the Russian intelligentsia and its political tendencies. Forcibly exiled to the West by Lenin in 1922.

KAZIMIR MALEVICH (1878–1935), greatest painter of the period and surely Russia's greatest painter of all time, combined inspiration from Western modernism with a love of Russian themes based on village life and collective salvation. His dedication to the revolutionary moment was also influenced by the new scientific climate of Einsteinian relativity.

NIKOLAI EVREINOV (1879–1953), dramatist and avant-garde theatre director who filmed *The Storming of the Winter Palace* before emigrating to the West in 1926.

VLADIMIR LENIN (1870–1924), journalist and political activist, founder of the Bolshevik Party that seized power in the October Revolution of 1917.

Introduction:
The Arc of Utopia

When the spark of the French Revolution arced over to Russia early in the nineteenth century it lit the lamp of philosophy. Not French philosophy – Rousseau and the French Enlightenment were not the immediate inspiration for how tsarism might be overthrown – but German Idealism. German Idealism was concerned with beauty; more exactly with creating a beautiful experience of life. The Russian autocracy was right instantly to view 'philosophy' with alarm, associating it with atheism and the free exchange of ideas. And yet German thought was, whatever the tsar's policemen opined, indirect in its approach to change, even inherently conservative. Nor was religious belief its enemy. What it did present was a complex new view of human rationality as morally inclined.

Its idea of reason was closely related to happiness, and since still mainly feudal society restricted the freedom of the majority, the idea that many more people might lead fulfilled lives under a better order of things was certainly a progressive political goal. But because German Idealism was also conservative, and anxious about change, it was interested in continuity with the past, including the Christian past, and out of that combination arose an extraordinary expansion of the idea of History, writ large, and how Reason drove it forwards, through faith and on to the kind of philosophy that could synthesize morality, rationality and poetry into a great new vision. History and Reason were the new twin engines of philosophy.

In the 1830s, when all but one of its original practitioners were dead, an emerging Russian intelligentsia immersed itself in German

Idealism. And so it was a complex – and, to some, impenetrable – German way of thinking that ignited the hopes of a tiny intellectual minority seeking the overthrow of tsarism in a still deeply feudal country, far more so than the German lands. How a theory of knowledge generous enough to include the beautiful and the good became a theory of history and a political programme in Russia is the essence of this utopian story.

Karl Marx once said that whenever Russians got hold of Western ideas they took them to extremes. *Arc of Utopia* lingers over some of those extreme moments on the way to 1917.

The aim is not to rehearse the relatively familiar story of Russian revolutionary thought, but to relive the utopian impulse as it unfolded in Russia; to remember how philosophical dreams were turned into social reality, in culturally astonishing ways, and eventually – outside the scope of this book – at huge human cost.

For the century and more that Marxism dominated the Western outlook, 'utopianism' was a phenomenon that Marxism had relegated to history as a device of the bourgeoisie to hang on to its own power and privileges. The French 'utopian Socialists' who preceded Marx by a generation were grudgingly acknowledged for their concern with working conditions in the new industrial age, and with new forms of communality as traditional forms disappeared. But Saint-Simon and Fourier, and Robert Owen in England, were held to be dreamers whose visions could never be realized because they were not founded in a scientific view of history as class warfare. Moreover, utopianism could be relegated to the dustbin of history because a new *science* of progress had been discovered. In our time *scientific* socialism has fallen like Icarus from the sky. We can see what happened. It too was never a science.

The principal illusion was the so-called science of historical materialism as the basis of universal progress. Engels felt that Marx had discovered 'the great law of motion of history'.[1] It was history arising out of class struggles. Historical materialism was no one's particular point of view, or dream. It was infallible like a law of the cosmos. One only had to understand it to encourage the way society was growing.

Russia acquired this way of thinking through the relatively late import of Marxism, in the last three decades of the nineteenth century. The Russian Revolution was the grandest of dreams of materialist perfection. But its ideas remained very close to the creative and the artistic, beneath the political surface, because Marxism didn't spring from nowhere, but out of Idealism. Russian revolutionary thought drew on a German Idealist critique of the human imagination. It sprang out of a moment when philosophy was interested in *how* we handle the ideas of wholeness and perfection we have, with what moral ambition and what desire for balance and harmony in our affairs.

One of the lessons of the history of ideas is that if you declare a certain phenomenon unreal you create a path by which others can present it as real. You create fine, telling distinctions and others reverse them. You set limits and others use those limits as a springboard. This is what happened to Kant's critical philosophy in the hands of the Romantic philosophers Schelling and Hegel. They trumped Kant just as Marx trumped Hegel. Lenin did it to Marx. In each case, restrictions and qualifications that were put in place around a new and perhaps dangerous idea were – gleefully, wilfully, optimistically, unwisely – removed by the next generation. Kant was critical, Hegel was dialectical; Hegel was a dialectical Idealist, Marx a dialectical materialist. These interlocking terms and the often ironic changes in their meaning from generation to generation powered a dominant strain in German/Russian thought from about the time of Hegel's death in 1831 to the time of the collapse of Soviet Communism in 1991.

Consider two scenes, the first in the eighteenth-century German principality of Württemberg and the other in twentieth-century Petrograd. In 1796, in a quiet, picturesque Protestant seminary in Tübingen, south Germany, Schelling and Hegel, apprentice theologians studying in the company of the poet Hölderlin, planted a tree to mark the French Revolution. In 1917, displacing the scene of Idealism more than 4,000 miles (6,000 km) to the northeast, from the centre to the edge of Europe, dissident Russian soldiers and sailors, demoralized by the course of the Great War, stormed the Winter Palace. As Lenin, waiting for his moment since the tsar's abdication in February, seized power on behalf of the people on 25 October 1917, the assailants of that night and the following day drove out the Provisional Government, whose principal actors had been hiding in the great granite-columned Baroque palace on the river Neva, and Russia began a new life. *Arc of Utopia* spans these two climactic moments in Western history, one intimate and the other epic, and both intensely poetic.

It is difficult fully to understand what was happening in that Tübingen circle of Romantic thinkers without examining Kant's revolution in philosophy, so the story begins with how the French Revolution affected Kant, and digresses to look at how Friedrich Schiller, who was a dramatist, a poet and a historian, as well as a philosopher, suggested how German Idealism might be carried forward in the revolutionary context as moral vision and as public art. The scene of poetry and Romantic yearning in Tübingen then becomes the background to Hegel's great systematic account of the historical development of the human mind.

Among the great Russian figures who read Hegel and searched their hearts and minds for clues to their country's future were the writer and activist Alexander Herzen, the novelist Ivan Turgenev and the political radical Mikhail Bakunin. Each of them created out of Hegel an oeuvre which included their own actions, as well as their writing, which helped them make sense of their dreams and disappointments.

Herzen, born in 1812, and Marx, born in 1818, were near-contemporaries who, although they once met in a mid-nineteenth-century London full of European political exiles, intellectually passed each other by. The patrician Herzen was not a class warrior, and the result of his philosophical education was to make him distrustful of theory. But he urgently wished upon the Russian common people their liberation from autocracy. Marx dismissed and even feared Herzen as a Russian nationalist. But both Herzen and Marx figure in our story for the way they carry forward the utopian dream, Herzen because, steeped in the world of those Tübingen seminarists, although critical, he inspired the next generation to go on looking to German philosophy for answers. Meanwhile Marx's relevance to this story hardly needs me to spell it out. Marx, with Engels, transformed Hegelian theory into a great engine to drive historical change in the world at large; and Russia, the first Marxist state in the world, installed that engine and let it run. Georgy Plekhanov was convinced Marx was right, and wrote essays on art, culture and economics that would advise the new country. But to talk about Plekhanov, whose direct influence was at its height in the 1890s, is to run ahead. Already, fifteen to twenty years before, Dostoevsky and his friend the priest Vladimir Soloviev had deep reservations about a materialist revolution but wanted world transformation. In fact Soloviev turned back to the Tübingen moment to rediscover the German utopian legacy in religious and mystical terms, while Dostoevsky reinvested German ways of thinking in a popular Russian religious actuality. In these unofficial spiritual leaders of nineteenth-century Russia a quite different programme for the future emerged; and perhaps Russia has never resolved, even today, the problem that its philosophical legacy began with, namely the Idealist versus the materialist explanation of life, and, in the always burning Russian context, the meaning of the nation, and the need for its transformation.

What was the outcome of this hectic exchange of theories and dreams, from late feudal Germany to pre-revolutionary Russia, over four generations? In one respect the result is evident: the Bolshevik Revolution was the attempt to run Russia for the next seventy years as a high-walled, brutally policed state, a desperately fallen Communist paradise. But the revolution wasn't only about the political future. The power of the German-Russian intellectual exchange that struck early twentieth-century Russia also fuelled some of the most extraordinary art in the history of the world, driven by a desire to capture what Bakunin called 'our beautiful Russian life'.[2] The ambition was to secure for Russia, and then for all mankind, a full, and fulfilled, and 'whole' life, and the political and the artistic dream were inseparable.

1

The Wisest Man

Immanuel Kant, the most significant German philosopher of the eighteenth century and perhaps of all time, was wise enough to understand that the rational and the non-rational live side by side. The irrational is normally outside the domain of philosophy, but the non-rational domain, of our artistic and moral strivings and our fears and delights, is very much with us when we think how we perceive the world depends on our own humanity. Whatever might or might not be the case out there, according to some unknowable objective state of affairs, it is what our collective human mind can construct that matters.

Kant lived through two world-changing upheavals which confirmed him in the view that humanity should sort out its own affairs, without reference to explanations delivered by the Church. The human agent mattered; the divine agent was a fiction. The Lisbon earthquake of 1755 almost annihilated a great European city, and Kant wrote about it as a young man; and then towards the end of the century the French people revolted against absolute monarchy, executing their king and passing through a year of Terror. Again Kant, having made his career as a university professor and now at the height of his powers, picked up his pen. The Lisbon earthquake and the French Revolution happened with such force that they demanded he interpret their meaning for contemporary European society: what these cataclysms meant for modern, not medieval, ideas of how to live, and, above all, their impact on morals.

The elemental disaster that consumed four-fifths of Lisbon left Europe aghast. At least 100,000 people died in a city ranked the fourth most populous on the continent. The shock was the equivalent of today's Rome being reduced to rubble. In a deeply Roman Catholic country, it seemed to the pious that God was furious with the citizens of Lisbon, while atheists were flattered when they noticed that while all the great churches in the Portuguese capital had crumbled, the brothel district had remained intact.[1] Traditional and modern views of the world were immediately in conflict. Although no spokesman for fornication, Kant was on the side of the atheists in the ensuing controversy.

It was not the punitive rumblings of a putative divinity that interested him, but rather the earth science behind the catastrophe of 1 November 1755. Within months of receiving the news the young university lecturer from Königsberg had published three essays, and scheduled a lecture course for the summer semester of 1756: 'On Physical Geography and On the Basic Aspects of Natural Science'. Königsberg was a great Baltic port, like Lisbon one of the finest in Europe, and, amongst its own pious or even faintly superstitious inhabitants, not quite convinced of the newly touted powers of reason, anything that could be done to avoid divine wrath was welcome news. Kant had read Georges-Louis Leclerc, Comte de Buffon, the French naturalist who had published an account of the earth that rendered it unlikely God was in charge. That in itself was surely the greatest revolution of modern times, a real incentive for atheism. Buffon himself had read Newton, whose mechanics guided him towards geology. Scientists would only start to understand a century later that earthquakes were not caused by an angry God but by tectonic shifts in volatile areas, but where Kant made a start was in considering the disaster from a purely human viewpoint. How might the city be rebuilt more safely? was the gist of his newspaper articles. If there was a moral lesson to be learnt, it was that humanity could manage its own well-being, through increased scientific understanding.[2]

And so, when he was 28, his future thinking began to emerge. Reason, not religion, would be his focus. Whatever nature inflicted, rational human beings had the capacity to stand back and consider their situation and how best to handle it.

Reason meant freedom: freedom from superstition, freedom to deliberate according to scientific evidence, and freedom to build a uniquely human world. Reason was confidence in the good society that humanity could achieve unaided. Reason promised to build a better future for the whole human species, if men and women would emancipate themselves from chasing shadows and work for self-improvement.

Kant was not a utopian philosopher in his own view. His work was not designed to sit alongside Plato's lost city of Atlantis in *Timaeus* and *Critias*, Thomas More's *Utopia* (1516), Harrington's *The Commonwealth of Oceana* (1656) and Denis Veiras' *L'Histoire des Sévarambes* (1677–9), he said.[3] He was, by contrast, always a practical philosopher, who began from what did happen before he pointed out what should.[4] But he was certainly a philosopher of progress, and it is with him that the story of a modern fancy-led, Romantic, political phenomenon, poetic, idealistic, extravagant and fantastical, poised between the imaginative and the imaginary, the creative and Quixotic, the fertile and absurd,[5] begins. It was the idea of a humanitarian Utopia, organized by scientific minds for the greatest human well-being.

Utopias were only ever as good as the people who inhabited them, so some attention had to be paid to human nature. For Kant the Lisbon earthquake was a good moment to see how untutored human emotions came into play in a crisis. Survivors everywhere gawped and gossiped and thanked their lucky stars. Many were awed by the power of nature, and some, perhaps many, were also afraid; not because they were sinful but because as mere flesh-and-blood creatures they felt powerless and humbled when the earth cracked and the sea rose. Many years later these thoughts about our capacity for fear and respect in the face of a mighty nature, alongside our reason, would find their way into Kant's 'analytic of the sublime', part of his work on aesthetics.

In fact he was writing on the sublime when he witnessed the French Revolution, and between one text and another, now in *The Critique of Judgement* (1790) and now in 'The Contest of the Faculties' (1798), he was fascinated by the reach of reason in coming to terms with dramatic upheaval. In France it was not nature but humanity that had smashed the existing order, but the awesome spectacle had a similar emotional effect. In fact, just as he had been curious and concerned on behalf of all Europeans in the wake of the Lisbon disaster, Kant was now fascinated by the Revolution taking its course and, above all, how Europe's spectators viewed it. Were they gawping, praying, rejoicing or what?

'We're not interested in the events in France because we want to witness acts of heroism and evil deeds,' he wrote.

A kind of magical transformation of the French state, and an upsurge of the new as if from the bowels of the earth, is not our concern. No, nothing of all this. It is the mindset of the spectators watching the play of these great transformative forces, and how that mindset reveals itself publicly. It is the participation of the players on one side against another, a participation at once general and unselfish, all the more given the danger that taking sides could turn out to be very detrimental, that interests us. It is how that mindset lets those sides speak, and loudly. It is how (because of the universal element) it characterizes the human race in general and at the same time (because of the selflessness) it proves at least in terms of aptitude that humanity has a moral character, and this in turn allows us not only to hope for progress towards a better world, but for it actually to be happening, based on present human capacity.

The Revolution of an intellectually cultured people, which we have seen happening in our times, may succeed or not; it may be so full of misery and of acts of abomination that no right-thinking person, hoping that with a second chance he might successfully carry it out, would ever risk an experiment at such a cost – this Revolution, I say, nevertheless, excites in the minds of all who have watched it (who are themselves not caught up in actual events) a willingness to participate that borders on enthusiasm, and the expression of which brings its own dangers, and which therefore can have no other cause than a moral aptitude in the human race.

This cause which affects us morally is two-fold: firstly it is the cause of Law, that a people has the right not to be prevented by other powers from giving itself a citizens' constitution, as it thinks to be good; and secondly it is the purpose at stake (which at the same time is a duty) wherein a people's constitution can in itself only be legally and morally good when by its nature it has been created to offer fundamental principles for not fighting wars of aggression, and this cannot be other than a republican constitution, at least in the idea, and further to commit to refraining from war (the source of all ill and of the decline of civilization), such that the progress of the human race, for all its frailty, is negatively guaranteed, at least not to be hindered along the forward path.[6]

Kant concluded that the French Revolution could also transform the German-speaking world; could send it too 'along the forward path'. It was a conclusion that historically bridged the two neighbouring cultures. The French were so much more advanced democratically than the Germans, but now perhaps there could also be change on the German side. In Prussia, where Friedrich Wilhelm III had just succeeded his father and grandfather, much of the press was reactionary and the country had a terrible history of war; on the other hand it did have a new sovereign in place. Less cautious as he grew older, Kant in 1798 dared to give reason a distinct content in favour of republican government, and expressly hoped for a transformed political landscape in which the German people, through philosophers teaching their leaders, would be educated to understand the scope of freedom.

Kant applied the word 'revolution' to himself. His was the Copernican Revolution in reason, he said. It was the moment when modern reason measured its own scope. Yet he was essentially, as the titles of his major works declared, a critical philosopher, keen to delineate those areas of experience reason couldn't reach. The Lisbon earthquake even became a metaphor for him, for, while science could probe and measure the earth's crust, he was sure the human mind could never understand its inner core. His philosophical measure therefore was that scientific reason, pure reason as he called it, had its limits. Not because some other, truer realm of being existed beyond the actual, but because the human mind could ultimately only have certain knowledge of itself; of *what it projected on to the world in order to understand it*. Things in themselves, free of human involvement, were unknowable.

There was this constant duelling between subject and object, reason and the ultimately unknowable, in Kant, which it's useful to understand in terms of where German philosophy had arrived back in the 1750s, when Kant began his career. Then German philosophy was an ongoing contest between the experimental science of Newton and the enduring theodicy of Leibniz. At the time of their deaths, Georg Wilhelm Leibniz in 1716 and Isaac Newton in 1727 had both established themselves as the inventors of calculus, but their positions couldn't have been more different. Calculus, as the mathematical study of change, gave way to two distinct philosophies of nature, in which Leibniz took the dynamic approach, and Newton the mechanistic. For Leibniz there were forces inherent in bodies, and in the universe, that made them behave as they did; whereas for Newton matter was dead in itself, but subject to laws according to its weight and mass. Newton, not Leibniz, helped Kant make sense of the Lisbon disaster. Yet Kant's approach to nature was never entirely mechanical. Indeed, that was why his philosophy consisted of three 'Critiques', or three simultaneous approaches to knowledge. Kant's genius was to show how each approach intersected with and affected the other two. As he might have said, the cosmos may or may not harbour the patterns of its own future growth. We can't actually know and I doubt it. But what we can know is the emotional dynamism in the human subject which is full of longing for such patterns to exist. We human beings really want the universe to cohere and have moral meaning for us. And so the task of philosophy is to understand the human subject, and the limited certain knowledge it has, along with the tendencies of its yearnings to go far beyond.

'The Contest of the Faculties' was at once Kant's most extended response to events in France and his final statement on progress before he died. It was a superb moment for European humanity, something like the philosophical equivalent of Beethoven's 'Ode to Joy'. Kant wrenched optimism out of the naive context in which he found it in Leibniz, where it functioned as a rather simple-minded 'everything is for the best the way it is', and re-installed it at the heart of a more sophisticated and self-critical modern outlook. Leibniz imagined a benign God setting the forces of the world in motion. He pictured God as an intelligent designer, we would say today, moreover one who wanted the best for us. But when the Lisbon earthquake happened, that idea looked ridiculous. The disaster was tragic and comic proof that the human order of things was no vast clockwork set in motion by a benign higher power, but a fragile construction likely to be overwhelmed. 'All this is for the very best end, for if there is a volcano at Lisbon it could be in no other spot,' laughed

Voltaire in *Candide* (1759). Yet Kant was not as sarcastic as Voltaire, the great publicist of the French Enlightenment, nor as saddened as Voltaire's fictional mouthpiece; and his own philosophy of reason always stood out from, and against, French rationalism, because of what it inherited from Leibniz, allowing for emotional longing.

That difference is commonly explained as stemming from German philosophy's relative lack of hostility to the Church.[7] Protestantism was more of an adjunct to the German scene of philosophy than the Roman Catholicism that the French philosophers commonly viewed as a corrupt accessory of the French state promoting social subordination through fear. Philosophers didn't have to protest against Protestantism. Protestantism did not deal in sin but in the qualities of individual consciousness, and that was territory philosophers could readily take over. Kant was heir not to the deism of the French Enlightenment therefore, a rather tricky truce in the three decades before the Revolution, but to the Enlightenment's humanitarian optimism, to which he brought a critical edge. As rational creatures we can formulate great goals for the future of humanity, but what nourishes our faith in them and keeps us going? Are they dreams or real goals? Kant found his answers in examining our moral and beautiful imagination.

To treat the human subject as an imaginative subject was Kant's greatest achievement, in my view, and, as so often with German Idealism, it did two seemingly contradictory things. It at once powered him on in a vision of modern rational progress and kept him close to Leibniz. Leibniz gifted him the idea that human beings both have a sense of 'purpose' and often discern it in objects around them. In fact what he took from Leibniz wasn't an easy borrowing for Kant, because Kant was vehemently opposed to the anti-Newtonian theory now spreading across the Continent, that matter was alive; that it had purpose. Kant was too much a man of the Enlightenment to accept what he saw as the new irrationality of Johann Gottfried Herder. But he did believe in the human capacity to *imagine* any inherent purpose in things, and thus to adopt a utopian outlook.

Kant ended up proposing two versions of natural philosophy. In the First Critique the human mind understood nature through patterns of causality which, while they didn't touch 'things in themselves', provided entirely workable explanations of the physical world. The Second Critique was then a kind of celebration, of the fact that, in answer to what was physically unknowable, there was no hindrance to the moral future of a self-determining mankind.

So then what of those *feelings*, such as might move a spectator of an earthquake or a revolution to rejoice, or despair? That became his third approach. Kant's *other* approach to nature, alongside the cognitive, was to remember in effect how much we love it. We take our measuring tools to nature, to understand how it works. But we also see it as the bearer of beautiful patterns to which our imaginations respond lovingly and which we long to reproduce in art. What Kant perceived was that there was a kind of shared pattern-making that situated men in the natural order. As rationalists alone they might well feel orphaned, because they could not know 'things in themselves'. But pattern-making was compensation for that.

In effect, Kant came back, in his Third Critique, to the view that Leibniz had taken before him. Imagination was an indispensable adjunct to the life of inquiry and the practical moral life. 'Nature must always be explained mathematically and mechanically, provided it is remembered that the principles themselves, or laws of mechanics or force, do not depend on mathematical extension alone, but on certain metaphysical reasons.'[8]

The metaphysics were evident in the human response to nature, still in Kant's memory from Lisbon. For those citizens of Lisbon, nature was beautiful and soothing. But then its seas and mountains dwarfed them and its storms highlighted their mortality. Kant then restated Leibniz's alternating view as his own aesthetic metaphysics. Nature's beauty encourages us to dream of creating harmony in the human world, but our projects will always have physical limits. We can't know or control those limits, but we can know what is morally the right thing to do. Our task is to live up, imaginatively, to our moral freedom.

But we should come back to politics, which is most people's idea of a revolution. The strangest thing for historians to wrestle with is that Kant disapproved of revolution in theory, because it hardly respected the strict moral law he taught, and yet he exulted in that moment in 1789 when it happened in practice. He delighted in the greatest example of progress in his lifetime. Indeed, it was the only time in his life when he was somewhat crazy, his friends said. Nothing would dissuade him from the view that Jacobin Paris was a step on humanity's road to freedom. When the Republic was declared he called out with excitement: '"Now let your servant go in peace to his grave, for I have seen the glory of the world."' He was, aged 65, and still ten years later, in the 1798 essay, 'openly a republican'.[9]

The reactionary view was that the mass of human beings were too violent to be self-governing, to which Kant retaliated robustly:

> But 'how they are' actually means what we have made them into with our unjust coercion and our seditious attacks delivering them into the hands of the authorities, that is, stubborn and inclined to rebellion; whereupon of course, when they relax the reins a bit, unhappy consequences ensue, which make the prophecies of those statesmen who quite wrongly think they are so clever come true.[10]

This was the true progressive teacher in Kant speaking who, far from finding the common people ignorant and stupid, would allow for their fundamental religious instincts of reverence and fear, and even for their violence, to be understood as part of the aesthetic realm as they struggled to realize their freedom. Obliquely, his Third Critique was written in their defence as sensual, bodied creatures. Kant loved humanity and the idea of its freedom, and he had a distinct picture of post-Christian progressive man to promote.

Still there were always limits. Enthusiasm was permissible, but not fanaticism. Enthusiasm (for which Kant borrowed the French *enthusiasme*, setting it against the German *Schwärmerei*) is

> the idea of the good joined to emotional excitement. This state of mind seems to be sublime to the extent that as people commonly say, nothing great can be achieved without it. On the other hand all emotional excitement is blind, either in the choice of its goal, or, in the case when the latter has been rationally determined, in the manner of going about its goal.

The idea of the good joined to emotional excitement could manifest itself as anger. Anger was the example Kant gave when he was talking about permissible political excitement, and it was different from hatred and the desire for revenge. Enthusiasm likewise differed from fanaticism because it was moved by rational ideas, and its effect on the mind was more powerful and longer-lasting.[11] By contrast,

'fanaticism is a madness, seeing something on the far side of the complete boundary of the moral life, i.e. it is wanting to dream according
to principles, to rage with reason.' Enthusiasm may well be a passing
madness, but fanaticism is evidence of a twisted mind. With enthusiasm the power of imagination is released, whereas fanaticism is
constrained by no rules. Enthusiasm grips the healthiest of minds,
whereas fanaticism is an appalling disease.[12]

And so to actual human players in any future revolution: how
could philosophy guide their virtue? Kant considered weak personalities with a nice side to them; shallow moralizers who would like to
be seen as noble but were in fact rather feeble-hearted with no idea of
what duty meant; and religious apologists whose aim was to destroy
any last vestige of human self-reliance in the face of evil. Then there
were religious folk who wanted to reduce us all to grovellers and
beggars for mercy. But consider also in moments of upheaval such
human faults as false modesty, hypocritical remorse and the poses
of self-contempt and total victimhood. It's right to enthuse, but as
philosophers ultimately we need reason as our orientation, and to
demand a very high standard of moral conduct from ourselves, as
our goal.[13]

The progressive cause involved Kant in a prolonged survey
of second-tier moral motivation, which became essential to his
understanding of the political. It took him on a journey through
aesthetics, that finally also touched on art appreciation and the
value of the critic, as the philosopher considered all the nuances
of response people were capable of, from weepy sentimentality to
hysterical overreaction, to painful self-immersion in unreal causes.
An aesthetic explaining how we appreciate art and nature also had
to include the range of our responses to political spectacle. Before
Kant died, in 1804, he was inclined to study not the individual moral
actor, caught in his private drama, but the common man, the man
of common sense, in the crowd. I'm inclined to think he laid down
the clear moral law in the first place because he couldn't abide the
way his British opponent David Hume fell back on foggy notions of
tradition and common decency. Kant wanted absolute rational clar-
ity. Yet Hume had talked of a common sense, leading to a common
purpose, as the normal social inheritance of all of us, and that was
just what the older Kant, confronted by revolution, now wanted to
understand with his second-tier investigations.[14]

He had thought about the role of the spectator, with regard to Lisbon and to Paris. When he devoted the gist of his 1798 essay to the role of the distant spectator, who couldn't be involved in events in revolutionary France because Prussia lay more than 100 miles (160 km) to the east, he focused on the crowd of spectators, who included himself. Repeatedly the *Critique of Judgement* interrupted thoughts on the reception of works of art with an implicit reflection on the enormous political potential of moving and rousing moments in real life. Clearly looking at art and looking on during political events had much in common. Art was presented to us as *Darstellung*, for which the Latin equivalent was *exhibitio*. *Darstellung* was the power of the artistic imagination to represent an idea in sensuous form. The idea itself, par excellence the idea of freedom, remained hidden.[15] In a fascinating passing comparison with Judaism's prohibition of the graven image, and implicitly with Islam's non-figurative tradition, Kant thought the lack of representation of the idea or the deity actually encouraged political fanaticism, because there was nothing in sensuous form to hold on to.[16] Here was a kind of first philosophy of the well-ordered Western political protest march, and its supportive audience.

As late Kant turns our attention to spectacle, to the popular parade that is also the drama of contemporary history, as he examines how a new self-critical secular humanity is internalizing the gamut of old religious feeling, we might even feel he has learnt from the street processions of the Catholic Church. For what else takes us on an Enlightenment path, from the *auto-da-fé*, the ritual profession of faith in which heretics were paraded before their final punishment, to the spectacle of the guillotine being rationally discussed in the coffee houses, and sympathizers with the revolutionary cause spilling out into the streets? Voltaire, ridiculing the yet to be enlightened university of Coimbra, imagined precisely the ritual response of the *auto-da-fé* to the Lisbon disaster, even as priests had roamed the ruins looking for unbelievers to hold to account.[17] But then as an old form of mass emotional-religious manipulation transitioned into the new demonstrativeness of the progressive masses, the possibility of a modern, secular, social and political will, and its dramatic expression, came into focus.[18] The idea of an aesthetic common sense, and the possibility of universal moral consent,[19] gave rational ground to new hopes. A politically progressive European public was born.

It was worth dwelling on the good man whose example could further the progressive cause, because long before 1917 finally brought the crowds out on to the Russian streets, it was the exemplary individual who helped build the revolutionary story. Kant's good man had a disinterested feeling for beauty.[20] The formal arrangement of form and intention, 'purposiveness without a purpose', characteristic of the beautiful work of art, was, as if humanity put its best aspirations on show in art, also a model for individual dedication to a cause. The encouragement and example of beauty mattered all the more as a cause's good outcome could often seem unreachable.

In other words it was beauty of character, and the capacity to respond to beauty in art, in the end, that prepared eighteenth-century man for the right kind of revolution, Kant believed. Such a man or woman could see beauty in art, nature and society with the same pleasure and the same acuity; and be fired by the one to love the other. When we look at a tulip, for instance, isn't it the case that its intricate form compels us to feel 'it must be like that'?[21] So why can't we live in a beautiful, honest, equal way? Is it just that we have not yet realized the 'inner necessity' guiding us to live beautifully? In future, as moral beings with an aesthetic capacity we will do more than dream.

My reading of Kant depends on the way the three critiques relate to each other. The First and Third Critiques, the rational and the aesthetic, are linked by analogy. There we discern cause and here inner purpose. Couldn't it be, then, that embedded in our existence are causal principles that we *cannot* grasp rationally, only imaginatively? Kant thought so, and that thought linked his Third Critique to his Second, on the freedom we have to make a world in which those imagined connections do become real because we *want* them to. In the Second Critique Kant established that we could have certain knowledge only of the moral law: in other words, of the will we have to do the right thing. Moreover, if it is the only thing we can know for certain about ourselves and our world, that we have this will to the good, isn't it enough to make us happy? Art reinforces that feeling of a great moral common project by leaving us shot through with shared delight. All the Critiques are joined by analogy, as Kant's work really does become an Ode to Joy.

My reading suggests that Kant resurrected as the modern political hope of liberty, equality and fraternity those metaphysical principles that Leibniz said just couldn't be omitted from the right picture of the human, albeit in a post-religious age. It's right that we should feel morally compelled by the pictures of harmonious all-round development that we conjure on behalf of a better society. It may well be that some hidden causal principle is actually moving the world in that progressive direction. We can't know of any such principle in nature, but we can know the scope of our own hearts and minds to tempt us to believe in beauty and goodness.

Kant explained the trail that had led him to his final position:

> To wonder at beauty and to be touched by the multiple pur-
> poses of nature, feelings to which a thoughtful mind is prone,
> before it has any clear idea of a reasonable Creator of the
> World, have something in them akin to religious feeling. In
> the first instance they appear to work on the mind through
> a form of judgement which is analogous to the moral and
> analogous to what moral feelings are effected in us (of grati-
> tude and respect in the face of a cause unknown to us). Thus
> they awaken moral ideas in the mind and when moral senti-
> ment influences the feeling of wonder it is invested with
> much more [emotional] interest than a purely theoretical
> wonderment can bring about.[22]

This wonderful footnote is part of a long final explanation of how religious feeling is incorporated in Kant's book of the imagination, his Third Critique, and it seems to link back to what he calls in his opening pages an 'exemplary necessity' to which there is, indeed, universal assent. This necessity can't be rationally deduced and can never become 'apodictic'. But moments of agreement over what is beautiful do suggest that we have, as human beings, a kind of common sense that guides us and these in turn inspire us, in unison, to create a world for ourselves that would be equally per-fect.[23] Consider again the perfection of the tulip. Every part exists in its own right and contributes to the whole flower. Every aspect of the tulip is not just a means to the end of being a tulip but also an end in itself. Isn't that how society should be organized? Isn't that just what the French Revolution hopes to achieve?[24]

Kant was a philosopher of progress, not a utopian philoso-pher. But the arc of Utopia starts from his celebration of moral and artistic imagination. His was a world of dignity and dreaming, of right-thinking, of progress, of principles, of philosophers advising monarchs, and of the mass of people as potential true republicans, self-critical and self-restraining. It pointed forwards to a society in which a new kind of man, free in his heart and progressive in his mind, guided by beautiful works of art, would campaign for a new harmony and freedom in society, with that society itself to be built like a work of art.

2

Good Men, Drama and Dialectic

Not only German writers and thinkers had become moral spectators of the French Revolution. The creators of the utopian spectacle were just as keen to identify progressive supporters in other countries. In August 1792, the Revolutionary Assembly made 'sieur Gille' an honorary citizen of the republic, naming him on 26 August among eighteen foreign 'friends of humanity and of society'. 'A great People in the enthusiasm of the first days of its freedom' reached out to 'the German publicist', whose name was actually Friedrich Schiller.[1]

He came from the duchy of Württemberg, and a passion against injustice burned in his heart. His engagement was personal and passionate, not unlike Kant's with the Revolution but expressed artistically, and with the fervour more of a rebel than a political progressive. Schiller was known across Europe for the fiercely libertarian and egalitarian drama he wrote while still a schoolboy, *The Robbers*. The French citation perhaps reflected the unauthorized motto 'Against Tyrants!' that had appeared over the first German printed edition of the play. Moroever in 1792 *Die Räuber* had recently premiered in Paris as *Robert, chef des brigands.*[2]

To be hailed a Jacobin hero, having been seen to anticipate the revolutionary spirit in the 'brigand' character of Karl Moor, sealed Schiller's political reputation for the next century. Scholars would ever after face the task of disentangling the real Schiller from the revolutionary story that grew up around his name.[3] Part of the Schiller legend is how closely, in pre-revolutionary Russia, he was associated with a commitment, as the men of 1792 had it, 'to defend the cause of peoples against the despotism of kings, banish prejudice from the earth and roll back the limits of human knowledge . . . to hope that one day men will form a single family before the law, as they do before nature: a single association . . .' The arc of Utopia was launched by 'a nation that has declared its renunciation of all conquest and its desire to fraternize with all peoples . . .'[4] Schiller passed into Russian literature as this noble and freedom-seeking hero.

In some ways not at all unjustly. He was the greatest rebel of the German literary age: a kind of Byron who had read Rousseau as a schoolboy, Jean-Jacques Rousseau being the republican-minded commoner who had swept literary Europe with his pre-revolutionary passion for equality. The young Schiller scandalized both the literary and the political establishment with the degree to which he could set direct feeling down on the page. He had an impassioned and deeply personal sympathy for liberty. At the German premiere of his great, flawed 'robber' drama about the warring brothers Karl and Franz Moor, in 1782,

The theatre was like a madhouse, with eyes rolling and clenched fists, and hoarse shouting in the auditorium! People who were strangers to each other fell weeping into each other's arms, women staggered to the door, close to fainting. It was a general undoing of things, like those scenes of misty chaos out of which a new creation springs.[5]

Schiller was 23 that year, and a regimental medical officer in Stuttgart. He went absent without leave to attend the performance, was then arrested, escaped and fled 'abroad' to Mannheim in search of a job in the theatre. This particular story of personal rebellion happened after *The Robbers* was written, but tensions had arisen much earlier. Schiller's father had himself had been forced to take a post as military surgeon to avoid ruin, and his employer Karl Eugen, the Duke of Württemberg, had constrained the son to enter his military academy. The young Friedrich, with a religious upbringing that made him proud, and a delicate poetic inwardness that caused him to be hurt, strained against deeply repressive army discipline for years. Meanwhile he came across earlier dramatic material featuring a young man who had turned to crime out of lost honour. Before he studied medicine at the academy Schiller had embarked on law, only to find in it the epitome of the injustices and the repressions against honest feeling that the Stuttgart school practised. And so his play was made.

In fact the play about a good and a bad brother, moral decency against moral hypocrisy, was as much existential as it was political, just as it struck Dostoevsky when he read it years later, but what it had was the emotional power to rage against despotism and cry out for individual justice. Schiller never disowned it, but since he was neither an anarchist nor a revolutionary, he spent the rest of his career, artistic and philosophical, showing how rebellion fitted into a greater, calmer scheme of things.

His enthusiasm for the French upheaval, or what the National Assembly picked up of it in the summer of 1792, was in truth just a brief feeling of kinship. No sooner had he received his French citizenship than he was on the verge of intervening on behalf of the imprisoned Louis XVI.[6] Then came news of the king's execution, an act of unacceptable violence. Schiller stayed with his great theme of liberation from tyranny. His last play, *Wilhelm Tell*, in 1804, was a stirring masterpiece that would be lionized across Europe by a century of freedom-seekers for their nations. But amongst other things that The Terror left Schiller, just like Kant, wanting to solve, was the problem of fanaticism. Schiller had watched it play out miserably in the beheading, not only of the French king, but also of the very men who had signed his citation, themselves executed by the time the paper documents reached him in 1798.[7]

Not all Schiller's admirers were pleased with his turn to philosophy meanwhile. But after a bout of severe illness, philosophy became the chief outlet for his dramatic talent, and here we pick up the trail of his other impact on the revolutionary story, as a disciple of Kant and a pioneering dialectical thinker.

In the period 1793–5 Schiller decided that if a utopian future awaited a liberated humanity, fundamental conflicts in human nature had to be resolved. The project would have to include the search for the exemplary man, who would be steadfast but not immovable, principled but flexible, dignified but not stiff, generous but not careless, in his adherence to the cause. In pursuit of the right balance of qualities apt to secure movement forwards without totally removing the brake, Schiller's list of binary choices was potentially endless. One source of inspiration for his pursuit of the golden mean was

Aristotle, but as a student of Kant he had also noticed that distinction between *enthusiasme* and *Schwärmerei*. Now his contribution to philosophy as a dramatist was to explain that these descriptions were not static; they were states of being that came and went. The life in each of us alternated between potential extremes, he felt, as we tried to steer a wise course. That process which could be called dialectical was, psychologically, 'Life Itself', our emotional life as such and surely we could come to understand it better.

Schiller had the same problem as Kant with fanaticism, and rejection of revolutionary violence became the driving force of his greatest philosophical work, *On the Aesthetic Education of Man in a Series of Letters* (1795). In that intricate blend of poetry and rhetoric, autobiography and abstraction, Schiller announced his modification of the revolutionary programme. Real human beings would have to be aesthetically educated first before humanity could be reborn. They would have to take a step seemingly back, before the revolution could march on. The great human limitation was that people's moral, spiritual and intellectual enthusiasms were beset by self-deception and excess.[8] Let some process of personal refinement, then, run its course, deepening the typical man's responses to the world, and his self-understanding, so that he can better serve the cause through what he is as much as what he does. An aesthetically educated person, in Schiller's sense, would never betray the progressive cause by resorting to violence. Karl Moor's protest against an unjust order had led him to plunder and murder. The Terror in France had unfolded similarly. But the older Schiller rejected the temptation to break the law. The *Aesthetic Education* of 1795 came close to a symbolic repudiation of his French honour three years earlier.

He would keep the humanitarian goals of 1789 but change the means by which to pursue them. The Aesthetic State for instance would banish all forms of coercion, privilege, selfishness and barbarism, but it would do so with a particular picture of humanity re-educated by beauty in mind:

Beauty alone makes the whole world happy, and each and every being forgets his limitations while under its spell. No privilege, not autocracy of any kind, is tolerated where taste rules, and the realm of aesthetic semblance extends its sway.[9]

Of the many goods the Aesthetic State looked forward to, the hope shared with the Enlightenment generally was to deliver knowledge 'into the common possession of Human Society as a whole'. But otherwise Schiller's argument was with very German forms of repression that were preventing the French vision from transplanting itself to German soil. He attacked a fiercely enforced official morality in the duchies where he had lived, Stuttgart and now Weimar, and an unwillingness to trust 'nature'. But then it was his great originality to see these problems also at the heart of Kant's philosophy. Wrestling with the strict formal morality that was what we would call today Kant's official position, before he made 'aesthetic' concessions to the life of spontaneous good feeling, Schiller looked for a philosophy of change married to a philosophy of play.

All the while his deepest wish was for individual freedom:

> In the Aesthetic State – even the tool which serves – is a free citizen, having equal rights with the noblest; and the mind, which would force the patient mass beneath the yoke of its purposes, must here first obtain its assent.

'Like the pure Church and the pure Republic', the Aesthetic State was presently not a reality. But to aspire to it was the most profound need of a humanity becoming ever more aware of its capacity for beauty and goodness.[10] It was an unusual definition of freedom to stress that individuals, whatever their class and status, even when they were presently engaged in public service, should be allowed to come into their own, unfettered. The Aesthetic State launched a way of thinking about creativity and human character that took a distinctly different path from the Anglo-Saxon emphasis on freedom as the right to non-interference. Schiller believed in what political science would much later call 'positive freedom'.[11] He felt that human beings were capable of a developed inner life, of a personal roundedness and a social fulfilment, but that the political order had to make that development possible and even actively encourage it. The target was an extraordinary inflection of liberated impulses and voluntary restraints. 'Human nature', he famously wrote in the essay 'On Grace and Dignity', *Aesthetic Education*'s precursor, 'is a more coherent whole in reality than a philosopher, who can only achieve results through separation, is permitted to reveal.'[12]

It took everything Schiller had as a philosopher to preserve the democratic aims and vision of the French Revolution but to modify the means of their achievement, such that progress became a personal goal as much as a political dream. His aesthetic idealism was never going to be easy to summarize, not least because its deepest effects depended on how his Miltonian poetry worked on the page. But it was just this aesthetic vision at the heart of German Idealism that would one day articulate and justify the Russian Revolution; indirectly, through its very grasp of reality, and personality, as dialectical; casuistically, through its stress on the need to pass through contradictions, through moments of one-sidedness and hence untruth, on the way to living the whole truth; and rhetorically, by declaring the revolutionary goal 'real, whole, reality' and 'Life Itself'. Schiller meant 'aesthetic' in multiple senses. One concerned the ordinary man of feeling who yearned to live the full life that only the entire range of Kant's three Critiques, of reason, morality and imagination, could encompass. But Schiller was also demanding the highest role for beauty in civic life, because only beauty's capacity to relay harmony and inspire conciliation could keep, without repression, a great mass of feeling in balance with moral goodness, and not make the revolutionary, as a person, one-sided. With Schiller the arc of Utopia soars up. His dialectical thinking, a pitching against each other of diverging human impulses and ideas in the interests of building a more comprehensive, more harmonious and more united kind of society, built and staffed by compatible 'whole' personalities, would become, transformed, the engine of the Hegelian and Marxist Utopias.

The autobiographical element was evident. As he matured, Schiller needed to tame his own extraordinary forcefulness as a thinker and his emotional intensity. The true meaning of the end of *The Robbers*, when Karl Moor gives himself up to the authorities, is that the gesture is voluntary. The aesthetically educated man can restrain himself. He is capable of self-sacrifice which balances his enthusiasm and his longing. Neither his reason nor his heart carries him away because beauty has taught him that all excess is wrong. He keeps himself steady, focused on beauty: beauty as harmony, reconciliation and grace. There is a secondary meaning, to be sure, in Karl Moor's end: the way he contrives for a poor man to receive the reward for his capture. But already in this moment the social campaigner in Schiller, who would right the wrongs of an unjust society, was dwarfed by Schiller, the new philosopher of a free humanity. Or rather, it was of greater concern to him, in the end, that Moor as an individual should save his soul. Otherwise the sentiments expressed, and the balance of the words used to express them, pulled in two directions.

Schiller wanted freedom for individuals fully to realize themselves. He insisted that society should not inhibit the full flowering of the personality. Feudal society was repressive. In Schiller's own case it had threatened to block his talent by forcing him to conform to narrow strictures. But it wasn't so much a breaking-out Schiller envisaged as this *becoming* of one's full self. The idea he incorporated in the *Aesthetic Letters* was of Aristotle's *enteleche*, the notion that everything, and therefore every human being, is imbued with its own inner purpose. He borrowed from Aristotle's biology and set in a political context that purposive future notion of 'positive freedom' with which the whole Communist ethos would be associated.

The most striking feature of Schiller's way with philosophy was that it lent itself to dialectical expression because it was, itself, intensely dramatic. The many social, political and psychological factors capable of thwarting the full flowering of the individual were conjured up as moments of essential human conflict, such as befell Karl Moor and Wilhelm Tell. Kant was at fault because at the high point of his career, which defined his 'official' position for philosophers of his day, he accepted a fundamental conflict between the sensuous man and the moral law. Life Itself was not paramount; the moral law was. Schiller the creator of gripping characters for the stage, wanted something subtler; something that recognized necessary conflict and learned from it. Aesthetic humanity was destined to become ever more inwardly complex, as it sorted its instincts and urges.

But there was also a second sense in which Schiller's philosophy was dramatic. There was that sphere in which Kant didn't close down the dialogue between the warring faculties but did permit the search for shared ground between the moral and the fond, and that reminded Schiller of classical tragedy. First the strategy of the *Critique of Judgement* reminded him of Aristotle on tragedy, and then it suggested how art as such could become the ultimate mediator, drawing out those conflicting impulses and reconciling them in a higher state of being.

Schiller tells us, poetically, more poetically than Kant, that we must balance our natures. His prose shuttles back and forth like a slow-moving piston, subliminally persuading us of his dialectical arguments. 'Melting beauty' softens us. Energizing beauty has an astringent effect. We encounter beauty in art often, we live with it daily, and in its presence opposites dissolve and contradictions vanish. Melting beauty undoes harshness. Energizing beauty prods us out of torpor. Energizing beauty counteracts the soft culture of the self-indulgent age we live in, while melting beauty undoes a culture too dominated by rules. And so humanity progresses. Over the century in which Communism seemed a real option for the Western future, as well as for Russia, much ink was spilled over what the dialectic meant. But the heart of any explanation was missing if it didn't refer back to Schiller as the dialectic's dramatic, poetic and moral precursor.[13]

Schiller's 'aesthetic idealism', though not irrational, was, just like Kant's accommodation of the non-rational, an anti-Cartesian enterprise. It worked with conflicting tendencies in human nature, in the belief that a superior kind of humanity could emerge and no longer go to war. No more war was above all the German hope. Schiller had written a history of the Thirty Years War, still etched in the memory of a continent. One of Kant's most famous essays was 'On Eternal Peace'.

Aesthetic idealism, while it looked forward to a peaceful future among nations and peoples, pitted against each other, symbolically, the ruling class and the mass of common humanity. The first wielded the authority of 'reason' in accordance with the divine right of kings. The second were trapped in the needy material life. In anachronistic terms, Schiller sided neither with the bourgeoisie nor the working class, but at the outset of that monumental nineteenth-century conflict, was looking for a way to solve it; to soften the aggression on both sides without relinquishing the utopian vision of a better humanity all round. In future terms the strategy was indeed bourgeois. But the *Aesthetic Education*, with its famous claim that 'man is at his most human when he plays', wasn't only playing for time. It was expressing the tensions of the epoch by other means, in times of censorship. With his key aesthetic terms Schiller *seemed* to be talking about works of art, but the work of society was equally salient. Abstract form and material life, the yoke of the tyrant versus

Life Itself, pulled in opposite directions. *Form* represented the traditional form of the state, while *Stoff* symbolized the bare existence of millions. Lurking in *Form* was the overextension of Enlightenment reason at the cost of ignoring ever more pressing demands for better mass welfare. Writers who experienced the *Form/Stoff* tension in the creation of their work on the page, or the stage, might have an answer, as might haptic artists trying to create art out of physical materials. Writers and artists might give advice to philosophy, on how to resolve the great problem of artistic creativity, namely how to retain the Life in the form. The goal in both art and politics had always to be, fully, Life.

In yet another extension of the argument, the individual dominated by the *Stofftrieb* (material drive) would struggle inwardly to contain physical greed and anger, whereas the empowered man might, by imposing order on others, sacrifice his humanity to the *Formtrieb* (form drive). Revolutionary theory, even and perhaps all the more at this early stage, was always mindful of how to secure good men, rounded and self-aware, moderate and not cruel, for the cause.

It's not clear that Schiller's noble campaign to have the *Spieltrieb* (aesthetic sense) prevail over all these lower-order conflicts of interest in human nature could ever correspond to a political state. But what matters, again and again, is the dialectical shape of the argument, which, whether it is applied to individual or social progress towards freedom and justice, seeks out that advance in terms of a new synthesis, and projects progress towards Utopia as an upward spiral.

The utopian project of German Idealism was striking in carrying over old religious attitudes, instead of following the French Enlightenment model and going to war with a politically dominant Church. The French Church was Catholic and an accessory to monarchy, whereas the Lutheran Church was itself born of protest. That's why Schiller asked for our *voluntary* self-limitation in the interests of a better world. Lessing before him, in *The Education of the Human Race* (1780), had discoursed on how loving virtue for its own sake was what the reason in us absolutely wanted.[14] That voluntarism was also Kant's moral law. We don't have to obey the moral law. We are creatures with free will. But we are better human beings if we choose to commit ourselves to the good, and, indeed, our reason inclines us that way.

It was as a 'beautiful soul', almost a secularized Jesus figure, that Schiller's exemplary aesthetic man became best known in Russia early in the nineteenth century. A generation and a half of aristocratic Russian intellectuals, from the 1820s on, would own to that ideal of the beautiful soul, hoping against hope for freedom in a repressed country. If it was hardly in the beautiful soul's delicately individualized marriage of grace and dignity, of tenderness and resolve, nor in the socially acceptable perfect playfulness of the aesthetic man, that revolution in Russia was likely to be born, Schiller's aesthetic idealism was still one of the first bridges, because it introduced a moral idea of freedom, guided by a philosophical view of what would constitute a better society.

The role of art was always a curious one in what Marx would see as Schiller's German bourgeois idea of Utopia, not least because everything fitted together so well: the classical work of art, the humanist vision, the well-tempered exemplary personality and the ways of history. But the fact is that, just as with the dialectic, the importance of art in transforming Russia into a revolutionary society, and sustaining it over seventy years, can't be understood without a return to the Idealist view planted by Schiller. Schiller's philosophy originated in contemplation of how a classical work of art was made: how form and content combined. His definition of the work of art as 'freedom in [the] appearance' meant that although freedom was a metaphysical idea it could manifest itself in the perfect work of art. Perfection depended on how exactly form corresponded to content. The created object worked as art when artists found the 'inner necessity' binding their inspiration and their material. As the work of art became the metaphysical equal of a natural artefact – Kant's tulip – it became itself a symbol of and a reminder for the kind of modern society in which part and whole, actual bodily life and overarching political idea, would be perfectly bonded. Individuals would both play their part in the whole and be free.

Much of Schiller's thinking about art was worked out in discussion with Goethe, the other great genius of the age, who was his contemporary, his opposite and his complement. Their relationship became another foundation for the dialectic, as Schiller wrote in the *Aesthetic Education* of how beauty in art, to which both had dedicated their talents, overcame division: 'both these conditions disappear in a third without leaving any trace of a division behind in the new whole that has been made.' Hegel seems to have developed his own use of dialectical argument after reading this letter.[15]

Schiller and Goethe discussed at great length the making of their poems and plays, the choice of symbols, and, from Goethe's side, how poetry and natural science interacted and mirrored each other. Schiller felt that beauty or the right choice of symbol had a power to convey metaphysical truth, or they were a reflection of such an insight into 'inner necessity' on the part of their creator.[16] Goethe practised a non-Newtonian science always with the symbol in mind that would show how 'real reality' entailed the constant living inter-action of the natural world and human consciousness. Real reality was neither static nor dead, but as if dynamized from within, in a way only this actual and ongoing relationship between object and subject could disclose. Of the two men Goethe was the more out-going, Schiller the more inward; Goethe physically the more at ease, Schiller somewhat sickly and troubled. Out of the sublimation of even that difference, between the 'naive' and the 'sentimental', which he recast as a theory of poetry, and out of the basic difference between ancient Greek spontaneity and modern hesitation, Schiller imagined yet another version of the aesthetically reconciled future in which we might all be at one with ourselves and with the society around us, like reborn Greeks for the modern European age.

The encounter with Goethe only added to the enormous challenge Schiller set himself, to hold on to harmony in a dying aristocratic era challenged by democratic forces. Goethe had had his own struggles, symbolized in the mythical figures of Prometheus and Ganymed. The younger Goethe wavered between summoning human beings to be 'noble, good and ready to help' and hailing a generation of contemptuous Prometheans quite justified in their violence against outdated strictures on the part of rulers who didn't care for them. One Goethe poem was sweet in the face of what humanity could achieve alone and the other fierce. One was har-monious and humanitarian, the other was crude and angry. When a decade on an older and decidedly conservative Goethe rejected the French Revolution, he and Schiller became themselves symbols of political attitudes that would be discussed for the next fifty years in Russia: whether the good man should be politically committed or whether, increasingly unimaginably, indifference and selfishness were permissible.

German Idealist philosophy became so complex, and, indeed, dialectical, with Schiller because it was trying to preserve a rich and soulful idea of human nature. It looked forward to a struggle with a narrow concept of positivistic science and the hope that any real revolution must mean so much more than just a transfer of political power.

But I want finally to touch on what the young Schiller hoped for theatre in a revolutionary context because it seems to restore to a simple vision, in the end, the great discussions of the German Idealist epoch as to what progressive humanity could do to help itself.

In *The Stage as a Moral Institution* (1784), Schiller stressed the moral potential of the stage to complicate human nature in the right kind of modern way, and to use that difference to open up more social and political freedom. In 1847 Dostoevsky's brother Mikhail translated and published this essay in the influential journal *Notes of the Fatherland*:

Humanity and tolerance have begun to prevail in our time at courts of princes and in courts of law. A large share of this may be due to the influence of the stage in showing man and his secret motives. The great of the world ought to be especially grateful to the stage, for it is here alone that they hear the truth. Not only man's mind, but also his intellectual culture, has been promoted by the higher drama. The lofty mind and the ardent patriot have often used the stage to spread enlightenment.

The autocrat should allow the theatre a free hand in the interests of justice and progress:

Considering nations and ages, the thinker sees the masses enchained by opinion and cut off by adversity from happiness; truth only lights up a few minds, who perhaps have to acquire it by the trials of a lifetime. How can the wise ruler put these within the reach of his nation? The thoughtful and the worthier section of the people diffuse the light of wisdom over the masses through the stage. Purer and better principles and motives issue from the stage and circulate through society: the night of barbarism and superstition vanishes.

Theatre combated mistaken systems of education:

> This is a subject of the first political importance, and yet none is so left to private whims and caprice. The stage might give stirring examples of mistaken education, and lead parents to juster, better views of the subject. Many teachers are led astray by false views, and methods are often artificial and fatal.

Theatre was nation-building and democratic:

> Now, if poets would be patriotic they could do much on the stage to forward invention and industry. A standing theatre would be a material advantage to a nation. It would have a great influence on the national temper and mind by helping the nation to agree in opinions and inclinations. The stage alone can do this, because it commands all human knowledge, exhausts all positions, illumines all hearts, unites all classes, and makes its way to the heart and understanding by the most popular channels.

Finally Schiller suggested a new understanding of the usefulness of the artist, the potential whole man, trying to work out his own psychology before a public at large:

> The stage is an institution combining amusement with instruction, rest with exertion, where no faculty of the mind is overstrained, no pleasure enjoyed at the cost of the whole. When melancholy gnaws the heart, when trouble poisons our solitude, when we are disgusted with the world, and a thousand worries oppress us, or when our energies are destroyed by over-exercise, the stage revives us, we dream of another sphere, we recover ourselves, our torpid nature is roused by noble passions, our blood circulates more healthily.

The healed man was the happy man, capable of a utopian universality of outlook. Utopia was therefore the stuff of Schiller's peroration:

The unhappy man forgets his tears in weeping for another. The happy man is calmed, the secure made provident. Effeminate natures are steeled, savages made man, and, as the supreme triumph of nature, men of all clans, zones, and conditions, emancipated from the chains of conventionality and fashion, fraternize here in a universal sympathy, forget the world, and come nearer to their heavenly destination. The individual shares in the general ecstasy, and his breast has now only space for an emotion: he is a man.[17]

Schiller's founding contributions to a vision of Utopia, as drama and as dialectic, as the free choice of the good man, and the 'inner necessity' of an improving world, would one day find their Russian embodiment.

3

Excitement in the Seminary

To follow Kant and idolize Schiller was to imagine life changing dramatically. The transformation would start from the top down with intellectually and emotionally highly developed individuals ridding Europe of its feudal remnants. These advanced and exemplary citizens would challenge the institutional Church and refresh society. The promise held out by beautiful souls was not political revolution but a refinement of spirit ushering in a richer individual experience in a more liberal world. The suggestion was that previous centuries of despotism had stunted individual imagination. To mobilize imagination to an unprecedented degree was to render a *violent* transition to a new society unnecessary.

Individuals would have minds in love with virtue and hearts aware of the need for restraint. Marx would one day declare all this hedging and hesitation the strategy of the bourgeoisie to hold on to its privileges. But if today we want to understand how Idealism metamorphosed into Marxism, and an eighteenth-century vision became a twentieth-century revolution, this partisan explanation is not helpful. What matters is that the German Idealist plan depended on Kant's metaphysical view of the glories of the human imagination as such, that it could reconcile the actual and the possible by considering our greatest ambitions in aesthetic terms.

The leading German theology students of their day were still mastering their Kant and Schiller when the First Republic guillotined Louis XVI. Some of the greatest names in German culture, Hegel, Schelling and Hölderlin, were apprentice theologians at the Tübinger seminary, at a time that almost exactly paralleled the hope and The Terror, and the incipient expansion of a new world power, in the neighbouring land. They were fiercely excited.

Hegel, the great future philosopher of the nineteenth-century condition, and Hölderlin, an exquisitely unworldly poet, arrived at the picturesque old-world seminary in 1788. Schelling joined them there in 1790, soon after the symbolic storming of the Bastille. Tübingen had flourished on the banks of the river Neckar for six centuries, a centre of ecclesiastical literacy in the conservative Württemberg duchy. As it had with the young Schiller, wanting to write plays in the name of freedom, not perpetuate an unjust order by serving in the military, Württemberg's very conservatism threw down a challenge to the young men watching events in France: where was freedom in the German lands? How could they understand the French Revolution positively, while matching it to the religious beliefs they already found precious?

They differed radically in character. Aged only fifteen, an arrogant and visionary young genius, Schelling considered those who didn't agree with him were fools.[1] Hegel, born in 1770, was, said Schiller, a calmer, wiser, rather ascetic figure, albeit one who could be 'sullen and somewhat sickly'.[2] Hölderlin was intensely emotional, and struggled to keep himself under control. Institutions always upset him, and a tangle of deep personal longings bound him to the transformational spirit of 1789. He was not a rebel but a natural outsider.

This is what Hölderlin had to say about the distant experience of revolution:

> To be honest, this lovely period is almost over for me. I no longer attach myself so fondly to *individuals*. My love is for humankind, though not of course in the corrupt, slavish, torpid form which, however restricted our experience, we only too often find it in. But I love the great and beautiful potential even corrupt people have. I love the generations of the centuries to come. For this is my keenest hope, the belief that keeps me strong and active: our grandchildren will be better than we are, freedom will come one day, and virtue will thrive better in the holy warming light of freedom than in the icy zone of despotism. These seeds of enlightenment, these quiet aspirations and efforts of individuals trying to shape the human race, will spread and gain strength and

bear splendid fruit . . . That's what my heart yearns for . . . Oh, and if I find a soul who like me strives for that goal, there is nothing more sacred or dearer to me in the world. And that is the goal, Brother of mine, the shaping, the improvement of the human race.[3]

Hölderlin expressed these sentiments in 1793, just as he left Tübingen for a series of unsatisfactory private tutoring jobs. His personal life would always be tortured, but glory lay ahead for him as a German poet. His fusion of classical limpidity and Romantic yearning would leap so heart-wrenchingly off the page no reader would want to live other than in a resurrected ancient Greece. In his handful of published poems he had not yet arrived at that distilled vision, but it was as clear for him as for Hegel that a new age waited to be defined. It would be a German reinvention of the harmony and beauty, and emotional robustness, of ancient Greece, but with the dawning Romantic age it would entail an idea of citizenship unknown to the more straightforward Greeks because it had to be understood in terms of imaginative inwardness. The Tübingen men conjured with a modernity in which an imagination nurtured by Protestant mysticism and the Lutheran Bible was pressing to realize its ideas in society. There would be no more debilitating and blocked self-consciousness, with these visions confined to inwardness and silence, because dreams of a better society could be realized. It was all rather complicated and indeed philosophical, but a new kind of German society, however potentially fragmented, would now strive for perfection – and, uniquely in Europe, through a theory of knowledge. Every individual would *understand* himself, herself, as a whole and in the sociopolitical whole, because of what Kant had made plain.

Hölderlin, like Schiller, loved the prospect of unfettered individual development as the prelude to an expanded civil society. He too hedged it around with a vision of eternal beauty, just in case it got out of control. But then civil society meant to him Socrates and Alcibiades. Unlike Schiller's philosophy and his poetry, constrained by its sober forms, Hölderlin's beautiful vision was so immediate and ecstatic it was as if he were drunk on it. With France transformed, Hölderlin's dithyrambs sang of a new German nation, its people reborn in grace and dignity. Less of an Idealist philosopher, more of a Romantic poet, Hölderlin wrote for the heart and the soul of that almost too refined German individual who for the next century and a half would both ennoble and wrestle with the democratic future, because of his too vivid 'memory' of Greece:

> Dear brothers, perhaps our art will ripen soon,
> Since, like a youth, it has been long fermenting,
> to stillness of beauty: only be pious as the Greek!

And,

> Germans ... you are poor in actions and full of thought
> or does the deed issue forth from thought, as
> Lightning issues from the clouds? Will books soon live?
> O beloved ones, then you may take me,
> And make me suffer for my blasphemy![4]

When the extraordinary Hölderlin raised his eyes to the ancient gods and inscribed himself in their myths he was in danger of losing his grip on the present, and the practical, entirely. Yet, rationally reworked, his ur-story of an ideal land sustained an idea for a modern Utopia that was exactly what Schiller began and Hegel would carry forwards.

In Hölderlin's contribution to German Idealism, there was much that would one day inspire the Symbolist movement in Russian poetry,[5] and, if there was nothing that politics could get hold of in a later Russia, still Hölderlin sets down for us a marker for understanding the mystical German beginnings of the Russian revolutionary story. Spiritual transformation would mingle with national revival and political rebirth.

A few poems Hölderlin wrote while at the seminary fused feats of Greek heroism with the courage of poet-artists for all time. The undertone was sympathy with contemporary French radicals. One day his fellow Protestant seminarists gathered to listen to him read 'Dem Genius der Kühnheit' (To the Genius of the Bold). The epic verses were steeped in imagery from Luther's Bible. At their heart were verses from the Book of Isaiah, blazing with the icon of the 'cup of trembling ... the cup of my fury'. Isaiah told the story of how when God saw his chosen people persecuted he was enraged. When the people drained the cup of *his* fury, they lay about drunk, and helpless, they had no moral backbone, and God was just as furious as before. But then God rescued his people by passing the cup to their enemy, so now the enemy were powerless, and the downtrodden would find their strength, and rise up and resist. The word Hölderlin took from Luther's version of Christian insurrection was 'der Taumelkelch', *Taumel* meaning frenzy or fever. It signified the terrible excess of the French Directory contained momentarily and symbolically in a German *Kelch*, a ceremonial goblet.

The downtrodden people should rise up. Tyrants should be murdered. Harmodius and Aristogiton, heroes of Greek liberty, had shown the way. Hegel echoed Hölderlin's exact words in one of his Tübingen notebooks, when he observed that someone must slaughter the tyrants and establish equal rights for the citizens.[6] The new Romantic generation, summoning boldness, was departing from Schiller's conciliatory impulse. Hölderlin's poem said Truth was the only monarch and that only boldness – *Kühnheit* – would secure its reign, after which a beautiful innocence and peace would follow the years of necessary violence. Beauty would make the difficult process of 'life emerging from infinity', into History, bearable. It would justify the upheaval.

Hölderlin explained in a rare philosophical fragment:

All cognition should begin with the study of beauty. For he has gained much who can understand life without mourning. Incidentally, enthusiasm and passion are also good, [as is] religious reverence, that does not wish to touch, to understand life, and then despair, when life itself emerges from its infinity. The deep feeling of mortality, of change, of one's temporal limitations inflames a person, so that he attempts much, it takes all his strength, and does not let him succumb to laziness, and there is a long struggle after chimeras until finally something true and real, to understand and with which to occupy oneself, can be found again.[7]

A new kind of knowledge was needed to understand a suddenly much more complex world, with feudal and faith-based simplicity left behind, and the unknown consequences of liberty ahead. Modernity was a moral strain and a personal challenge.

Hegel felt the same strain as he tried to balance liberty with alienation, or the private sense that the world had changed so fast it had lost its meaning. Those Lutheran ideals just couldn't ground themselves. Hegel wondered what equality could mean, honestly, in a world dominated by the power relations of master and slave, now that there was no countermanding sense of equality before God, and the slave was emerging as his own person. Just as Kant presented as a theory of knowledge his 'Copernican Revolution', of a new humanity intrinsically limited but through politics newly enabled, so for Hegel the individual in a post-feudal society struggled to sustain self-respect because he no longer found himself at the centre of a wholeness or a collective to which he could belong with pride. How should he 'know' his world? Who was this individual that the French Revolution had liberated? How could he live? How, inwardly, as well as outwardly, could he be happy and free?

In fact Hegel was slow to emerge as the great philosopher the world would come to recognize thirty years later, and only an essay on love, from which these themes are taken, gave a sign.[8] When he worried about that wholeness and belonging, Hegel couldn't help turning back to the Gospels. Why not let the reconciled dual personality of Christ inspire a new social psychology? Christ was never isolated. Christ was love. He was the way to being at one with oneself.

The modern problem, and Hegel was quick to see it in an atomized society, was that isolated human subjects sought a bond with the people around them, to feel complete, but couldn't necessarily find it. Society risked becoming incoherent. Without love

> there is no living union between the individual and his world; the object, severed from the subject, is dead; and the only love possible is a sort of relationship between the living subject and the dead objects by which he is surrounded.[9]

Without love there was no meaning. Hegel's first philosophizing was therefore to try to imagine the opposite; to imagine true fraternity in a material world, while accepting the absence of Christian consolation in its traditional form. Hegel's fear was that without the Christian interpretation the world of matter was simply dead and our own flesh-and-blood existence of no consequence, unless the new egalitarianism could make up for that loss:

> True union, or love proper, exists only between living beings
> who are alike in power and thus in one another's eyes living
> beings from every point of view; in no respect is either dead
> for the other.

The love bond should be perfectly reciprocal, he insisted, quoting Shakespeare's Juliet: 'the more I give to thee the more I have.' Moreover it would 'exclude all oppositions'.

Hegel's view of love showed his dialectic in embryo. Here was that system of mutual interchange and reciprocity, eventually absorbing all contradictions, that he would propose as the engine of happiness and, projected into the temporal dimension, the engine of progressive History. The young theologian had some difficulty expressing himself, Goethe thought, but clearly he was working out his ideal of love in terms of the three secular French revolutionary ideals.

Schelling, five years Hegel's junior, was quite unlike him. He was explosive in temperament and prodigious in expression. Two philosophical essays published in 1795, his last year in Tübingen, revelled in the *boldness* of the age which implicitly associated the poet with the celebrated warrior heroes of the ancient world. The stars of Schelling's early essays were poet-philosophers like himself, consummate modern heroes. *Philosophical Letters on Dogmatism and Criticism* hailed the *genius* – another contemporary keyword – of the man who knew how to live in freedom. After Kant's critical philosophy what else but freedom? But Schelling reoriented 'critical' philosophy until it stated something quite different from what Kant had intended. For Schelling it was not now imagination as an aspect of reason but imagination unfettered and autonomous, with the unique power of 'insight', that would save the world. What was stopping the human race coming into its own? Only this lack of insight. The tyrant of recent history had been reason. But now reason was overthrown.

Schelling's was a story of how a maximalist poetic philosophy would reinscribe humanity in the meaningful cosmos. Its reach would be broader than the reason that for so long was harnessed to enlightened despotism. Unlike with Kant, it would not be limited to moderate Enlightenment ends.

Like revolutionaries from Descartes to Voltaire, Schelling agreed that in *dogmatic* theology (and philosophy for centuries had indeed shadowed theology like a humble courtier) the existence of God required the individual's self-surrender. Dogmatic rulers, the implication went, had found that surrender very useful in retaining their power. But now individuals were free. With their vast imaginative resources they were answerable to no worldly authority.

It was a moment of existential choice for Schelling, that summer of 1795, with every man in his inner life bound to choose between feudal 'worship' and Idealist 'wit'. Schelling told his peers their philosophical minds were free to roam where they pleased in search of truth. The developed ego could rise free and triumphant over the mere physical and contingent world and, from that vantage point, convey a higher wisdom:

> We don't want to complain, but to be glad, that we are standing finally at an inevitable parting of the ways, that we have looked into the mystery of our spirit, on the strength of which the virtuous man becomes free by his own efforts, while the unvirtuous of himself trembles before a legislative power he can't find in himself and for that very reason is bound to hand over to another world, to place himself in the hands of a punitive judge. Never again in the future will the wise man seek refuge in mysteries, in order to conceal his principles from profane eyes. It is a crime against humanity to conceal principles that can be universally communicated. Yet nature itself has set limits to this communicability; for those who are worthy of it she has preserved a philosophy which of itself becomes esoteric, because it can't be learnt, can't be preached, can't be hypocritically imitated, nor yet be mouthed by its secret enemies and spies – [a philosophy which is] a symbol for the union of free spirits, by which each recognizes the other, which they don't need to hide, and which, intelligible of course only to them, will be an eternal puzzle to the others.[10]

The young Schelling made of post-Kantian philosophy a revolutionary conspiracy with personal freedom as its content and individual brilliance as the price of entry to the band of brothers. There were even in the seminary 'secret enemies', 'overseers' or 'spies' making a last-ditch attempt to contain secular philosophy within the Church's conventions by paying lip service to it. But they wouldn't prevail.

Later, in his Identity Philosophy, Schelling would enlist nature on the side of explosive individualism. His teaching was that nature and insight, the external and the internal truth of human existence, were perfectly related. Nature and man were made identical, both of them subject to the same 'inner necessity'. Inner necessity related to the lawfulness of the whole universe. Goethe and Schiller, and Kant, had all been interested in that idea, but Schelling gave it a new militancy by attributing insight into it to the special few who could lead the world to a new place. The imaginative elite could point out the potentially perfect way of things to those who couldn't see it. Soon, as Schelling continued to work on his ideas, the elite could also see into the ways of History.

The temperaments of Hölderlin, Hegel and Schelling were different, but they shared enough jointly to plant that liberty tree to mark their moment in post-1789 Tübingen.[11] All of them wanted to find the key to the modern soul born of the French upheaval, and the kind of society to which highly developed individuals would belong. They were German thinkers and turned to the myth of the ancient Greek polis as their main guide to democracy. But otherwise the freedom of the creative artist, and a Christian sense of a purposeful universe, inspired them.

In 1796 they got together again to draft 'The Oldest Systematic Programme of German Idealism'.[12] The eight-paragraph fragment in Hegel's handwriting began by asking: 'How must the world be constituted for a moral being?' They stated that they wanted to write a history of how 'this whole miserable human making of state, constitution, government and legislation' came about. 'Miserable' referred to the history of the autocratic German states to date. Their story, they declared, their German story, would relate *true* reason's recent defeat of 'all superstition, and its persecution of a priesthood which these days fakes a belief in reason'. It would show 'the absolute freedom of all minds or spirits who bear the intellectual world within them, and have no need to seek either God or immortality outside themselves'.

'The Oldest Systematic Programme' showed how difficult it was for the Idealists to escape from theology, and how, thinking they had replaced it with philosophy, they were ready to build a Utopia in philosophy's name. Their programme, short on detail, was to build a Romantic Aesthetic State.

Schelling would give 'the philosopher . . . just as much aesthetic power as the poet' in his ideal world. Hegel felt that too. Aesthetic power was the mission Hegel would take on himself to imagine a new world from scratch, whereby he would give History a meaning. There can only be talk in History of peoples who build a state, he famously said, and that too was a kind of aesthetic activity inherent in human presence in the world. For Hegel, History was crafting itself. It was like a cosmic force; like God the Creator. In partnership with philosophy, History was 'a self-correcting process which does lead to truth in the present, or, at the very least, to enhanced self-knowledge'.[13] It was the new German religion to be creative, and to imagine states built out of the creative process, and all that belonged to the new theory of knowledge, pioneered by Kant in sympathy with the Enlightenment and carried forward unbounded by the Romantics.

Schelling and Hegel came to represent, by the end of their careers, two great systematic answers to the place of the individual in the modern world: the subjective answer and the objective answer. Schelling interpreted the role of the individual in terms of his capacity to see his way through to Oneness with the world around him; to invent it if necessary; to imagine it metaphorically; all of which was like a displaced reaching out for God. Hegel, by contrast, considered how actual individual lives could become emancipated in the collective as part of an inevitable objective process called the progress of reason.

In fact Hegel changed radically through the 1790s, coming to believe that the French Revolution failed because it didn't grasp the interdependence of the individual and social.[14] He associated The Terror with all that was negative and fragmented and frenzied about the modern mind, later writing correctively in his *Philosophy of History*: 'Crude desire, a savage and rough exertion of will, falls outside the theatre and the sphere of World History.'[15] If a new vision for mankind was to be realized, then all the violence that sudden change sparked had to be absorbed into the onward march of a decent and civilized Humanity, regulated by reason. The individual and the personal had to be balanced with engagement in community. The name of that capacity was *Sittlichkeit* and it was a web of social practices and institutions beyond the natural and beyond the individual. As if it were the Christian Holy Spirit in a new guise, *Sittlichkeit* was objective spirit, and it answered that 1796 question raised by all the friends: namely, how should the world be made for a moral being? There had to be this ethical polity, combating authoritarianism from above and individual estrangement from below.[16] Rules were only *sittlich* when they were elastic and alive, vital and responsive, but at the same time individuals had to be prepared to conform to the true demands of reason, which set a limit.

Hegel's solution to the challenge of 1789 involved him in a complex vocabulary that constantly examined the relations between the individual and the whole. He worried far ahead of his time about anomie, and his *Phenomenology of Spirit* (1807) was a masterwork showing how society might hold on to an idea of wholeness and coherence. The individual soul should not fall into emptiness as the price of progress. Hegel considered any style of psychology which did not keep wholeness in mind decadent.[17] *Phenomenology of Spirit* together with *Philosophy of Right* (1820) delivered a lesson in social and political harmony. Individualism could be disruptive, but, managed and steered, it didn't need to be. Hegel's oeuvre is so vast, and his thinking so intricate, that it seems to me no contemporary reader can dismiss it without a degree of personal delving, prior to understanding what, for better or worse, it inspired in Marx, and what of it lodged in the Soviet Russian version of Utopia. No country in the modern world, surely, was so powerfully steered by philosophy as was twentieth-century Russia, just as Schelling and Hegel would have wished it; only under Communism the vitality died.

Competition with theology drove the German Idealists to *systematize* their vision. Because they were so steeped in a tradition in which philosophy and theology had cooperated with and embellished each other, so now they rivalled Leibniz and Spinoza in the completeness of their systems. The seventeenth-century impulse had been to establish a gorgeous fretwork of how mind and nature were bonded, as decorative as the leafwork on a church pew. Voltaire laughed at Leibniz's theological optimism in the wake of the Lisbon earthquake, but Leibniz had comforted many German readers by infusing the cosmos with a constant, synchronized artistic practice on the parts of God and man. Everything cohered in his world. Leibniz's individualism was not disruptive, nor atheist. It did not dismiss 'higher authority'. Moreover the orderly system of the 'inner necessity' of nature, as perceived by a philosopher who was at once a mathematician, the discoverer of calculus, and a theologian, appealed because his conclusions did indeed seem scientific.

Whether this science including metaphysical principles really could continue as science, in defiance of Anglo-Saxon empiricism and French rationalism, was a moot point. But for almost the next two centuries it constituted a separate and unique tradition with a powerful hidden influence on world politics. Hegel became the Leibniz of the nineteenth century, as he took over the idea of the ultimate spiritual calculus: the notion of a 'higher' law governing the way things turned out to be good and true in the march of History as we live it.

The vision was always spiritually ambitious, not wanting to separate the scientific from the artistic, the poetic, the imaginative and the worshipful. For Schelling that was the point of science, to tell us about the Oneness of everything. The 'bold' Tübingen Schelling thought Oneness itself, by that very name, would become a 'constitutive law of history':

It's hard to resist enthusiasm, when one has the grand thought that just as all the sciences, the empirical not excluded, are hastening towards the point of perfect oneness, so humanity itself will finally realize as a constitutive law of that history the principle of oneness, which from the beginning has underlaid human history as regulative. It's hard to resist enthusiasm when one has the grand thought that all the rays of human knowledge and experience of many centuries will finally come together in one burning moment of truth, and make real the idea that already several great minds have imagined, namely that out of all the different sciences in the end there must be only one – just as all the different paths and wrong turnings that the human race has taken until now will finally converge in one point, around which humanity will gather once more and as one perfect person answer to the same law of freedom. This moment in time may be far removed, and may for the time being only stimulate polite laughter at bold [*kühn*] hopes for the progress of humanity, but for those for whom these hopes are not madness it holds out the great task of at least preparing through common effort that great period of humanity through the perfection of the sciences. For all ideas must have realized themselves in the sphere of knowledge before they can realize themselves in history; and humanity will never become one before its knowledge arrives at oneness.[18]

That the human mind could even envisage One True Science of the right way to live was moral proof enough that every effort must be made to bring that perfection about through common effort. The effort should be scientific. Here was another profoundly German Idealist answer to how the world should be made for a moral being. At the same time, always, it turned on that 'other' notion of science.

Wissenschaft, the German for science, featured in Nietzsche's title *Die fröhliche Wissenschaft* three-quarters of a century later, and it seems to me a good illustration of what science could mean when Idealism still held sway (despite Nietzsche's fierce anti-Idealism). When Nietzsche claimed *Wissenschaft* as the basis for understanding joy, he never intended to submit joy to laboratory testing. It was rather a way of committing philosophy to the complexity of the human make-up, body and soul, and especially to those aspects of humanity that had once been absorbed by religious faith and were now in want of a name, and in want of students to take them seriously. Science, *Wissenschaft* in the sense in which German humanism – and Nietzschean anti-humanism – inherited it from Goethe and Hegel, took seriously all the opposing and complementary forces within the human soul that vied with each other to speak 'the truth'. It was this process of vying, moreover, this competitive interplay of vital forces, not any specific object of knowledge, that was the dialectical 'truth' of the human sciences.

Schelling wrote that the One True Science could be achieved *durch gemeinschaftliches Arbeiten*: 'through common effort', or 'through communal work'. For Hegel science was after the roundest and fullest of lives for all humanity. 'Now I am convinced that the highest act of reason is an aesthetic act in the way it embraces all ideas, and that truth and goodness are only sisters in Beauty,' the Tübingen authors wrote in their 'Systematic Programme'.

The Tübingen seminarists agreed that philosophy in its new role would transform the life of the common man through what a later age would call propaganda, not least because the common people were used to the familiar images of 'sensuous religion', of God the

Father and Jesus the Son, and the Trinity completed by the Holy Spirit. The philosopher had work to do on his propaganda output, but with an artistic gift he could work up his alternative picture book to create 'a new mythology . . . in the service of the Ideas [of freedom] . . . a mythology of Reason'. If he could bridge the gap between the sensuality of popular understanding and a minority intellectuality, a particular Schellingian preoccupation, 'then everlasting unity will reign among us.' The humble people will never again tremble before priests and wise men. Superstition out of the way, the time will be ripe for the 'equal development of all strengths, in each and every individual . . . then general freedom and equality of minds will prevail! [It will be] the last and the greatest work of humanity.'

German Idealism is often interpreted as conservative at heart. But to insist on the conservative/revolutionary distinction is to look past that unique and peculiar point of departure in which it responded to the French Revolution by invoking beauty and dialectic. Beauty was a potential revolutionary resource because after all it was something that *all* men could feel. Kant was the first philosopher to isolate as a fundamental human drive *the capacity* to dream of harmony and wholeness and therefore to put up men as candidates for an aesthetically led revolution. In a time of violent change, it was as if Kant had discovered in human nature a very real capacity to want a better world but not to want conflict. The Idealists took that beautiful double idea and ran with it. They relabelled it so that it immediately acquired political significance. Where Kant called the aesthetic imagination 'regulative', the Idealists called it 'constitutive', and you can feel in those very terms the political shift from the 'regulative' ways of enlightened absolutism in continental Europe towards a new constitutionalism in which the people themselves would make majoritarian societies fit to live in. What Kant restricted to a kind of dreaming beside other more certain forms of human knowledge the Romantic Idealists turned into a moral force to better the world.

They believed in the future working-out of a new, dialectical, self-questioning, philosophy of knowledge and all of them saw in that philosophy answers to the contemporary problems of mankind, because dialectic was a conciliatory force that could overcome contradictions. Its power was conducive to a wholeness of society and a rounded experience of human existence.

The German Romantic Idealists foresaw the not yet quite named idea of the New Man, and toyed with Our Moral Future, along with History and Truth. All of them admired the polymathic achievement of Goethe, scientist and poet, playwright and statesman, a living Oneness in himself and not least mascot of their highly poetic and dialectical idea of *Wissenschaft*. Hegel said he learnt everything from Goethe. All of the Tübingen seminarists also admired Napoleon, from which one might infer that they all had a place in their understanding for the Great Leader who would lead the New Men forward. The initial capitals of their enthusiasms are mine, to make plain their status as ghostly heralds of a Communist future. But I won't give up the idea that they were also connoisseurs of moral vision and maturity.

They explored the friction between naivety and worldliness; between child and adult; between spontaneity and experience – and these psychological tensions at the heart of the modern created an idea of progress which could embrace them *both*, in each instance without loss. So painful it was, they intimated, to discard long centuries of theological security. But it could be done. So painful it would be, to lose the initiative of secular freedom, but freedom needn't be forfeited in a reinvention of the World Spirit, and individualism could be accommodated in a new set of worldly-spiritual values. If the question those values raised was how to be fully human in a brimmingly modern but alarmingly unanchored age, Hegel's abstractions brought the emotional contradictions to the page and pointed the way *dialectically* forward.

4

Reason, Fashion and Romance among the Russians

The enthusiasm for German philosophy that gripped the nineteenth-century Russian intellectual scene was a first echo from the east of the Germans' own *Begeisterung* for the democratization of France. It was fashion. The writer and thinker Alexander Herzen said his countrymen worshipped the great and the obscure German names equally and without discrimination.[1] But it created a pattern for the future, and habits that have lasted to the present day.

Specifically, from around the mid-1830s a generation of cosmopolitan Russian noblemen, a scant and privileged few, visited Germany to bring Western civilization to Russia, or they studied the new German culture at home. What drew them was the greatest flowering of literature and thought known to the contemporary West, as Madame de Staël evoked it in the record of her own discovery of Germany, *De l'Allemagne* (1812). What they found was a standard of humanity sorely lacking in a Russia still reeling from the brutal punishment of the Decembrist Uprising of 1825. That occasion had been a bloody response to a grand moment of intellectual and moral courage. Demonstrations and attempts to seize power in St Petersburg and the south of Russia by plucky souls in the military, calling for a constitution and the rule of law, had been quickly suppressed, with five leaders hanged and the remainder of the activists sent to Siberia. Herzen, born in 1812, and whose generation the Decembrist Uprising deeply touched, wrote of the 1830s and early 1840s as a moral revolution among the few:

What was it touched these men? Whose inspiration re-
created them? They had no thought, no care for their social
position, for their personal advantage or for security; their
whole life, all their efforts were bent on the public good,
regardless of all personal profit; some forgot their wealth,
others their poverty, and went forward, without looking
back, to the solution of theoretical questions. The interests of truth, the interests of learning, the interests of art,
humanitas, swallowed up everything.[2]

It was the courage, and the quality of heart, that Herzen saluted. In
the end he thought German philosophy led at least some Russians
astray, but what they experienced was so important it helped bring
about a new era in Russia.

At first, German philosophy was 'grafted on to Moscow University'
in lectures disguised as covering the politically acceptable subjects
of physics and agriculture. Mikhail Grigorievich Pavlov, who was
the professor there, also of mineralogy, from 1820 until his death in
1840, would stop students with the question: 'You want to acquire
a knowledge of nature? But what is nature? What is knowledge?'[3]
Schelling's philosophy of nature led the more ambitious students
to start on Hegel:

They discussed these subjects incessantly. There was not a
paragraph in the three parts of the *Logic*; in the two of the
Aesthetic, the *Encyclopedia* and so on, which had not been
the subject of desperate disputes for several nights together.
People who loved each other avoided each other for weeks
at a time because they disagreed about the definition of
'all embracing spirit', or had taken as a personal insult an
opinion on 'the absolute personality and its existence in
itself.' Every insignificant pamphlet published in Berlin or
other provincial or district towns of German philosophy was
ordered and read to tatters and smudges, and the leaves fell
out in a few days, if only there was a mention of Hegel in it.[4]

A kind of compacted intellectual crust, a 'Russo-German regime',
formed over thoughtful Russian life, with 'strange underground currents silently undermining it'.[5] By those currents Herzen meant at

once the personalities involved, and the actual condition of Russia, both of which he thought would eventually incline truer Russians – like himself – away from abstractions. Both for and against Herzen's view of the natural Russian way, this was the era in which emerged a passion among his countrymen to *solve* the problems of life, not merely contemplate them.

And so from their first contact with German Idealism, Russians argued, and split into factions, and tussled over the right vision of the future. Russia's future in respect of the German Golden Age was their topic. A new Russia would build on that German kingdom of the mind, and of the poetic language, that had flourished in the era of Goethe and Schiller, and Schelling and Hegel. In 1840, though already politically contested in Germany itself, this era had only recently passed. Hegel had died in 1831, prematurely, and Goethe completed a fine old age the following year. The main players were gone, but in Russia Idealism, with its celebration of Art and Humanity, was essentially a new discovery.

The few Russian intellectuals who could afford to travel wanted the pleasure of 'abroad'. They were immensely curious about the West. Italy, which would soon have its own nascent revolutionary nationalist movement, attracted them. But it was the quality of a German education the Russians pursued above all. Frustrated revolutionary energy, just as it had opened up a whole era in philosophy, had helped stimulate an ideal of education that transformed the German universities. The Prussian educationist Wilhelm von Humboldt's notion of *Bildung* corresponded to Schiller's poetic vision of 'aesthetic education'. *Bildung* was education based on a curriculum broad enough to encompass an ideally rounded human nature. *Bildung* therefore drew the Russians to Berlin.

A rare Russian writer and thinker two generations earlier, Alexander Radischev had gone to study law in Leipzig in 1766. He read the English and French empiricists there, and Herder and Locke. Immediately after the Napoleonic Wars a privileged few Russians studied in Göttingen. But now it had to be Berlin, whose university founded in 1810 had as its very ethos universal education for its own sake.[6] The red-brick, very un-Russian city on the Spree attracted the top German academics. Hegel had held the philosophy chair in the Prussian capital until his death, and in 1840 Schelling had recently returned there. The young Russian *barins* listened in and socialized, mingling with the big names and their followers. Herzen, who had been exiled in the northeast of Russia until very recently, may have been a little jealous when he returned to Moscow and heard what was happening.[7]

Nikolai Stankevich and Mikhail Bakunin registered to read philosophy at the same time as did the future novelist Ivan Turgenev. For them philosophy was the science of the sciences and the key to modern humanity's self-understanding. Turgenev even wrote a thesis inspired by an Idealist view of nature, though he was happier delving into literature and revelling in German music. Bakunin meanwhile philosophized his way into politics with such power he would challenge Marx. In their midst lived and worked Stankevich, an angelic figure and philosophically the most gifted of all. These sensitive, multilingual talents relayed what they learnt back to Moscow.

How hungry Moscow was to hear from them! The great critic Vissarion Belinsky had declared in 1837 that Germany was not only the new Jerusalem, but ideally suited to become the cultural benefactor of a new Russia:

> Germany is the Jerusalem of modern humanity, it's where it should turn its gaze, with hope and trust; it's where Christ is coming again, only this time not persecuted, not covered in the sores of torture, not wearing his crown of torment, but in rays of glory. Until now Christianity has been truth in contemplation, in a word, faith; now it has to be truth in consciousness – philosophy. Yes, German philosophy is clear and distinct, like mathematics, a development and explanation of Christian teaching as a teaching based on the idea of love and the idea of raising up humanity to divinity, by means of consciousness. I think that Germany must bequeath to young and virginal Russia both its family life and its social virtues and its world-embracing philosophy.[8]

Too poor to travel, but still avid for German books and German views three years later, Belinsky, as busy as a publicist and a publisher as he was as a critic, begged his friends abroad:

> Isn't Bakunin thinking of translating . . . the correspondence between Goethe and Schiller? They would be articles for

scholars and journalism at the same time. You can rummage through the whole of [E.T.A.] Hoffmann . . . Nothing's been translated. Anything you find let [us] know . . . In general send me as many German stories as possible . . . Make an effort, boys! Send answers to all of this as soon as possible![9]

Belinsky, Stankevich and even Herzen himself went through decided 'Hegelian' stages in their thinking. The effect their reading left on them changed their lives dramatically from day to day, hurling them from one new commitment to the next. His relatively few Hegel years led Belinsky to huge outpourings of regret and painful recantation. 'I too was carried away by the current of the time,' noted a dour-sounding Herzen in retrospect.[10] The vast new order of Hegel's system appealed to a generation hungry for a different form of Russian life. His 'world-embracing' combination of unlimited knowledge and absolute order was a promise and a challenge. Like the great Russian ideology of the future, to which it would lead, Hegelianism had an appeal somewhere between calculus and magic.

It promised change without demanding revolution. It embodied what Russia most needed, namely a philosophy that held off dwelling on religious eternity and focused on finding new universal principles in history. Herzen learnt a lesson of scientific methodology from Hegel, but, in Russia generally, to the few others who read him, or read about him, Hegel conveyed the message of distinct national paths in cultural development. It was just one step on for Russian readers of the historicizing and nationalist aspects of Idealism, as Hegel after Tübingen developed them, to speculate how philosophy could be applied to the Russian political situation to find a way out of it.

Of course this potential is why the tsarist authorities were hostile to philosophy as such. The Russian autocracy, its power shored up in popular perception by the Orthodox Church, banned the teaching of German Idealism in Russian universities from 1826. But then that immediately magnified its power to attract young freethinkers.[11] They experienced Schelling's *Naturphilosophie* as a hymn to blissful personal inner freedom; a first step to bypassing existing worldly authority and changing the world. As Schelling expounded on freedom and genius, and Hegel on the development of individual consciousness in a more complex society, Herzen's generation grew up to think and feel differently, with a more humane Russia in mind.

The feeling was focused in the strong friendships they enjoyed as a privileged few. The young Herzen and his friend Ogarev and their wives had famously enacted a scene from a Schiller play in a homage to the revolutionary potential of love and friendship.[12] Schiller had theorized friendship – comradeliness, one might even say – as an essential feature of a new political world. Friendship, and therefore the capacity to act idealistically on the world, in concert, was the fruit of what a shared education and shared ideals could produce. It was personified by Herzen and Ogarev in Moscow, and by the circle of friends around Stankevich, now in Moscow, now in Berlin; and again these Russian friendships seemed to answer the enthusiasm that had lifted German revolutionary sentiment off the ground.

Herzen was modest, attributing to Stankevich the first real Russian scholarship on Hegel.[13] He himself was the greater writer for a wide readership:

> The philosophy of Hegel is the algebra of revolution; it emancipates a man in an unusual way and leaves not one stone upon another of the Christian world, [leaves nothing] of a tradition that has outlived itself.[14]

Hegel had left behind the philosophy of eternity, on which political despots had leaned for centuries. Hegel was an abstract thinker, but also a great psychologist who mapped the path to intellectual independence, hence that 'unusual emancipation' Herzen singled out. In sum, to study Hegel was a vital step to imagining a secular, republican Russia capable of leaving serfdom behind.

As the 22-year-old Stankevich wrote, even before he left for Berlin:

> I don't think that philosophy can definitively solve all our most important problems, but it can bring [us] closer to their resolution; it can act as the foundation of great knowledge, it can show a person the goal of his life, and the way to that goal, by broadening his mind. I want to know to what degree man has developed his reasoning, then, knowing that, I want to show people their achievements and their calling, I want to summon them to the good, I want to inspire all the other sciences with a unifying thought . . . I have faith, but

I want always to limit and consolidate faith with intellect. I was delighted to find in Hegel some of my favourite ideas. This was not the joy of vanity, no, I was happy that a man with a great mind, who had proceeded through the whole ordeal of thought, was not alien to these beliefs.[15]

Once on German soil, Stankevich felt overwhelmed and uplifted. 'Berlin is this German city on which each of us has pinned his hope.'[16] 'He was', wrote Turgenev, 'preparing to devote himself to work indispensable to Russia' when he succumbed to consumption in 1840.[17]

Still, it would be hard to claim, as a result of these Russians' Berlin studies, or the studies of their friends in Moscow, that one particular philosophy was adopted as the clue to Russia's future. Rather it was a mixture of historicism and organicism which made its impact. The most exciting idea was that of Russia entering History as a bona fide player. As humanity had entered a new stage of flourishing, premised on its awareness of freedom, Russia too would have its time; would, following Hegel's requirement of any people worth noticing, build a state. Organicism was a view of culture imported from biology, and it allowed inferences from patterns in nature to patterns in the life of the mind. J. G. Herder, in his *Ideas towards a Philosophy of the History of Man* (1784–91), had encouraged the view of 'the rise of man' out of nature. 'We see the form of organization ascend, and with it the powers and propensities of the creatures become more various until, finally, they all, so far as possible, unite in the form of man.'[18] When Goethe and Schiller discussed the idea of 'inner necessity' they similarly bridged the story of nature and the story of the human, as two aspects of things becoming what they ideally are. Mankind as a species was at last coming into its own, capable, in Schiller's view, of an exceptional non-violent communal existence.

That the coming-of-age of humanity also applied, variously, to individual nations, Herzen picked out as the most important idea to arrive from German thought. The conflation of the historical with the organic encouraged Russians to think about their national distinctiveness and how it might emerge.[19] The science of becoming could be taught as biology, or agriculture, or physics. Lorenz Oken, 'the most imaginative but also the most fantastic representative of idealistic morphology', was well known in Russia, thanks to frequent mention of him in the so-called 'fat' journals of the intelligentsia.[20]

Or Russia's future could be taught as literary criticism. Belinsky thus imagined the national culture he was encouraging to grow, and in a series of brilliant essays put it on the historical map.

The search for the essence of the nation wasn't necessarily revolutionary. What it reinforced was the power of the people, as it had been demonstrated in revolutionary France. When German Romantic philosophy reworked the national idea and passed it to Russia, it served both the progressive Westernizing and the conservative Slavophile causes. One might think of the utopian arc, leading from German philosophy to Russia's rebirth, as having from the outset a fissure in its fabric, straining it and sometimes tearing it into two strands.

The Westernizing cause, that of Belinsky and Herzen, and of Bakunin to come, grew out of an Enlightenment faith in science. The natural sciences had moved into a new prominence through the scientific revolutions of the seventeenth and eighteenth centuries, and experimental truths had forced a decline in biblical and despotic authority. But the German way with science, as we have seen, was poetic and imaginative and passionate in its search for the bond between nature and the human, and less concerned with undoing worldly powers than with guaranteeing a certain holistic quality to individual experience. The dynamism of Leibniz and Spinoza had informed it, rather than Newton. Spinoza understood nature as the mind of God in action. By the time Herder thought he saw nations emerging according to the same innate laws by which organic nature unfolded, the authority of science in German discourse had been both deeply romanticized and politicized.[21] So when the Russian Westernizers encountered reason in Hegel, they admired what they found in accordance with the status of science; but they were carried away by historicism because it hooked up an engine to everything they wanted for their emerging nation. Something Hegel called the *Weltgeist*, the World Mind, was constantly and creatively unfolding, and the Russian people were part of it.

The Westernizers' Slavophile opponents used Idealism rather to resist progress. Their aim became to define the nation by preserving the original wholeness of feudal society, not risking the path of modern individualism, which might nor might not lead to renewed and enhanced social unity. They learnt their Hegel in order to reject his idea of progress. Where the Westernizers wrestled with their own alienation from Russian society, because as modern progressives they had put themselves out on a limb, the Slavophiles felt there was a One Russia experience to be had through holding on to peasant and religious traditions.

And so, if it had originally been the French Revolution that the Russian autocracy feared, in truth the German intellectual revolution was a far more powerful opponent because generally it gave the power to think politically. Suddenly it was an organic view of the growth of nations, and of the making of works of art reflecting and helping to discern the ways of those nations, and a new metaphysics of nature, that promised to unite the human and the physical sciences, and in turn demanded a contribution to *Wissenschaft* from every viable people; only nothing necessarily to do with their rulers. Hegel welcomed into History peoples who built a state. But in Russia the Westernizers felt Russia's very entry into History was blocked by rulers who were the people's undoing, prior to any statebuilding. Russia had first to develop the literature and philosophy on which some *better* state could rest, once the people had found themselves there.

Alexander Herzen was like a one-man utopian experiment. His German surname, meaning 'of the heart', was invented by his Russian nobleman father to reflect the boy's status as a love child, and indeed his mother was German, assuring his fluent reading of those philosophical texts others struggled with. But in all other respects Alexander Ivanovich was Russian. He had a private Russian education in a semi-European household that spoke Russian and lived in Russia. Russian servants and Russian schoolfriends shaped his early life. He always thought of himself as Russian. And yet he grew up to be that rarest of Russian intellectual phenomena, a genuine player on the European political left. In fact it was the long solitary hours when he read books in his father's library that probably freed him from narrow patriotism. The reading continued through his five years of internal exile, from the age of 23, and in European exile for the rest of his life. Herzen, a man built by a culture of reason, occupied a position, in European history, somewhere between Kant's World Citizen and a Marxist internationalist of the later nineteenth century.

In his memoir *My Past and Thoughts*, from which I've already been quoting, he identified with a generation characterized by 'a profound feeling of alienation from official Russia, for their environment, and at the same time an impulse to get out of it – and in sum a vehement desire to get rid of it'.[22] This was the generation that met in the famous *kruzhki*, the philosophical circles that they formed in St Petersburg and Moscow in the late 1830s. Herzen defended their centrality to the modern Russian story:

> The objection that these circles . . . form an exceptional, an extraneous, an unconnected phenomenon, that the education of the majority of these young people was exotic, strange and that they sooner express a translation into Russian of French and German ideas than anything of their own, seems to us quite groundless.

He pressed the point:

> Possibly at the end of the [eighteenth] century and the beginning of [the nineteenth] there was in the aristocracy a fringe of Russian foreigners who had sundered all ties with the national life; but they had neither living interest, nor coteries based on convictions, nor a literature of their own. They were sterile and became extinct. Victims of Peter's break with the people, they remained eccentric and whimsical, they were not merely superfluous but undeserving of pity . . . [But] protest, rejection, hatred of one's country, if you will, has a completely different significance from indifferent aloofness . . .

And so he defined the best of his generation's rebellion against autocracy, encouraged by its German self-education.

In fact what happened to Herzen is that he became a case study, in advance, of what would actually happen when Russia forged its utopian experiment. He was already encouraging that experiment when in Europe he became an apologist for a better Russia. Russia, that is, the home of the Russians, not the ways of their rulers, is a place of newness and experiment, and is where progressive Europeans should look, he told the French historian Jules Michelet.[23] Herzen's judgement, made in the wake of Europe's failed democratic revolutions in 1848, that the Russian people were now the greatest candidates for revolution, was striking. He tried hard to win Michelet over. The future lay with a 'Slav federalism ... in line with revolutionary ideas in Europe'. For there is an 'intimate bond between social revolution and the fate of the Slav world'.[24]

For historians Herzen has the distinction of having fathered Russian peasant socialism. In the end he tried to keep Russia independent of the German and French ideas that laid siege to its backward society and tempted its expectant intelligentsia with easy formulae. He drew a line under that extraordinary first contact with German Idealism we've been reviewing in this story so far. Meanwhile he had this view of the Russian people, that it *was* capable of what was new and experimental, if only it could be freed from the autocratic rulers who cared nothing for it. 'Russia is a building that still has about it the smell of fresh plaster, where everything is experimental and in a state of transition, where nothing is final, where people are always making changes ...'[25] Born in 1812, he shared in the political tragedy of his liberal European generation: the failure of all the successive revolutions after 1789. He was a student in Moscow when the July 1830 revolutions in France and Poland failed; a writer in Paris when the bourgeois revolution of 1848 collapsed. He died a year and a few months before the defeat of the first genuine workers' uprising, the Paris Commune, in 1871.

It wouldn't be right to call Herzen a utopian generally, but his autobiography provides a unique testament to that in-between Russophone realm in which Western-minded Russian intellectuals tried to do good by their stultified country. Herzen virtually invented the publicistic tradition by which Russian writers debunked and criticized the autocracy, indirectly at home, directly from abroad. Most of his career was forged in exile, where at least he could avoid the pressure of Russian censorship.

But if Herzen was the rational strand of the utopian arc slowly gathering height in Russia, we still have to take account of the nationalist contribution, remembering how both fed off the German philosophy that was the treasure trove of that generation, and both anticipated the culture of Russia's transformed twentieth century.

In Russian literary criticism of the 1830s it was not only a German philosophical content but the distinct shape of dialectical argument that began to emerge. Dialectic now structured views of the unique nature of Russian progress in the context of the history of the West. The idea was that French literature had reigned supreme in Europe for two centuries. But then in the mid-eighteenth century German genius emerged. If that was so, why should not the next flowering in the cultural history of the West be Russian, with characteristics drawn from and exceeding both these past stages in the history of mankind? Also in the conservative nationalist mind, in other words, Russia was destined to offer the West new leadership through cultural renewal.

The Russian question, as of the late 1820s already, was why should not the age of Pushkin, of a new Russia already aware of itself through art, herald the arrival of Russian greatness? The *Moscow Telegraph* was one of those nascent fat journals where the national future was the leading topic.[26] As one writer put it in 1829:

> Every people has its age, just like every person, taken individually. According to the blessed chain of being of Providence, which imprints the beauty of creation on everything that exists in nature, every age has its partialities which express themselves through physiognomy, feelings and tongue.[27]

The reviewer of the first translation into Russian of Schiller's *Wilhelm Tell* continued: 'In Russia only a hero and a giant [*bogatyr*] could overcome all the difficulties and transplant on to our native soil the bold creations, so full of life, of the immortal Schiller.'[28] The very theme of this deeply Romantic drama about a hero of the people was popular, patriotic and freedom-seeking, as imperceptibly the reviewer seemed to merge the theme of translating Schiller with liberating Russia. The need was for 'a hero and a giant' who was also an artist: a Napoleon of the poetic page. Belinsky, the critic searching year by year the output of contemporary writers for that hero, would be trumped in the next generation by Fyodor Dostoevsky, a real, if dangerous, candidate for the role of cultural *bogatyr*.

The greatest generation in Russian cultural history was this post-Decembrist generation that, suitably chastened by the executions and banishments that followed the 1825 debacle, eschewed the direct political approach under the tyrannical Nicholas I, while promoting ever greater contacts with 'the new direction of the human mind'. In that mind they hoped to find, hidden but discoverable, 'true laws'. They wanted to see, disclosed to Russia by German philosophy, 'that new direction [of the human mind], in which are hidden the true laws of the Beautiful'.[29]

Beauty was as important a stand-in for political change as it had been in Schiller's German Württemberg and Weimar. It has been said that only a tiny minority of the upper class was interested in German aesthetics early in the Russian nineteenth century, as if that rendered it an irrelevant fact. The truth was that an intellectual-artistic Germany of the mind, through a unique combination of the aesthetic, the moral and the scientific, was handing over to Russia the hope that there was that inner necessity governing that country's future development, and that some inherent laws essential to the future might carry the imprint of beauty, in which case they would be irresistible.

In the *Moscow Telegraph* reviewer's encomium of Schiller we get an advance insight, indeed, into how tightly the Russian revolutionary story will be interwoven with the power of art, and the effect on the public of 'the true laws of the Beautiful'. The cosmic pattern was everything. The same beautiful pattern was to be found in nature and in history, and in the optimum human personality, because of those beautiful laws.

The German-minded young Russians of Herzen's generation came of age imagining a post-Christian humanism of freedom and love, which Schiller underpinned with his idea of the beautiful soul. Stankevich had already come among them as one such soul. He was, uniquely, a new good Russia's first home-grown legend.

Was there one great Idea, like Love, or Truth, or Reason, or Spirit, that could hold together the diversity of Russia? Stankevich seemed to believe that, and, albeit with the meekness of an angel, to flesh out the possibility. Such an Idea was just what Russia needed, and such a man. Furthermore, as a revolution in philosophical understanding, the outcome of the Idealist encounter would be beautiful, because it would manifest itself as poetry. So Russia, united by an Idea, might become beautiful.[30]

Herzen, in the years immediately after Stankevich's death, was already troubled by the academic annexing of the new wisdom in Russia and wrenched it back into immediate political relevance. Since the present age in Russia demanded that something be done, he felt Hegel must continue to matter. He saw in Hegel a kind of poetic vision of fully rounded personalities suited to right action, a theory particularly relevant in Russia where change was overdue. In a world where History was reasonable and a better life lay ahead for whole peoples, the real goal of Hegelian reason was to guide the action of leading personalities.[31] Progress in History didn't happen in straight lines, Hegel taught, but it followed a pattern, exemplified by philosophy itself, in which contradictions and anomalies were gradually integrated into a growing and living whole. Once again the vision was of 'artistic completion and vital plentitude' as Hegel brought even Herzen, in his younger incarnation at least, to imagine the future divine city on earth.[32]

The Russians who turned to German Idealism wanted a programme. They wanted to make Russian life meaningful, and to give themselves courage, while not succumbing to fantasy.[33] They derived moral feeling from their German reading. It persuaded them that individuals had a duty to refine themselves to fit a more open and less coercive society. Schiller had envisaged the Aesthetic State, in which they would exercise self-control over their raw human impulses, and neither abuse freedom when they had it, nor, fearing it, seek an excess of regulation from an external lawgiver. At the urging of Professor Karl Werder, the dramatist and Hegelian who was a friend to all the Russian circle in Berlin, one of Stankevich's last tasks in Berlin was to read Schiller's great work of 1795 and thus to grasp the Idealist project in its ultimate aesthetic and personal, character-building and state-building, perspective.[34]

As the greatest literary chronicler of the age, Pavel Annenkov, put it:

> All took the moral factor as the starting point for any activity, whether in life or literature, all acknowledged the importance of aesthetic demands on themselves and on works of the intelligence and the imagination, and not a single member of the circle held any such notion that one could do without, for instance, art, poetry and creative work generally in the political education of people any more than life.[35]

From this time on, pressure for change in Russia would often entail the ideal or model personality, not now drawn on the Napoleonic model which had impressed the Tübingen seminarists, but reverting to Schiller's modified Kantian idea of the good man. A Russian writer expressing his 'view of life' should himself be 'worthy', said Annenkov. In a socially needy world it was important whether a man showed himself to be 'selfish' or not. Progressive politics did not tolerate 'egoism'. So it was fashionable to prefer Schiller, honorary citizen of revolutionary France, to Goethe, the lofty and disinterested individualist.

German Idealism undoubtedly excited 'metaphysical pathos' in post-Decembrist Russia:

> Any description of the nature of things, any characterisation of the world to which one belongs, in terms which, like the words of a poem, awaken through their associations and through a sort of empathy which they engender, a congenial mood or tone of feeling on the part of the philosopher or his readers.[36]

Arthur Lovejoy's definition might have been invented to describe what Annenkov called Russia's 'Marvellous Decade'. Precisely because it was a matter of aesthetics and empathy it wasn't obvious *how* the Romantic could become the political.

Herzen also blamed an emergent sense of national identity that, the more it was craved, the more it seemed elusive:

> Such a halt at the beginning, such a failure to top out one's building, these houses without roofs, foundations without houses, and ostentatious front halls leading to a modest dwelling, are quite in the spirit of the Russian people. Are we not perhaps satisfied with front halls because our history is still knocking at the gate?[37]

5

Philosophy as Dream-history

B y the time the Russian students arrived in Berlin the scene of German philosophy had already changed. Its eminence was no longer Hegel, who had died in 1831. The next focus of their interest, Ludwig Feuerbach, never reached Hegel's popularity or stature. But the scrutiny he turned on Idealism made him the man of the moment. Turgenev recorded reading *The Essence of Christianity* in 1841, just as it was published. Its common-sense element delighted Herzen and he and Bakunin read it about the same time as it was on Marx's desk. As the new wave of German ideas travelled back to Russia, it was Feuerbach who taught atheism and socialism to Dostoevsky's generation, the set that might be called 'Young Russia'.[1]

Feuerbach's message was all too simple. Christianity expressed human striving. The personality of God was the personality of Man, and all the rest was fantasy. The new anthropology was immensely attractive, as a demystification of hitherto untouchable power. Right up to the Revolution, Russian writers and thinkers would be tempted to exalt the Feuerbachian Man-God. They celebrated a humanity that had broken free from the religion of the God-Man, as if in a prelude to breaking free from autocracy. 'God was my first thought; Reason my second; Man my third and last thought,' Feuerbach wrote.[2] Man's new relationship to the world was that of the conductor at last able to conduct his own orchestra. Seventy years later Lenin would use the same Feuerbachian metaphor as once escaped the lips of the composer Richard Wagner.[3]

Despite the simplification, there was something essentially decent about Feuerbach's new faith in Humanity and his contempt for the Hegelian World Spirit. It was socialist in temperament, and if a German socialism was to get underway, philosophy, or its successor, had to divorce metaphysics. And it did. Feuerbach stunningly downgraded philosophy, which German culture had held in such high esteem for a century, from the position it claimed to hold as universal science. All that delving into abstractions was the cause of alienation from a meaningful life, said Feuerbach. The new humanism, which was a materialism, had to encourage a belief not in individuals through their 'inner' power to divine truth, but in their 'natural' feeling for their collective interests. For Feuerbach, man was at his best as an unselfish 'species-being' with a gift for solidarity.

The period in their history that the Germans call the *Vormärz* discovered this power of solidarity, which carried with it the great men and women of the age, including Wagner and the future Marxian dragooned into becoming a Marxist, Karl Marx himself. The name of the age meant the 'Lead-up-to-March' and it summed up two decades of social and political agitation. From the promising July Revolution in Paris of 1830 through the 1841 publication of *The Essence of Christianity* to the scattering of local revolutions in the German lands from March 1848, what defined the era was the failed bourgeois experiment in shifting power, from which Marxism would then depart radically.

Feuerbach injected into German philosophy an antidote to the metaphysics of Kant and the Romantic Idealists by accenting the natural and the material life. He called for 'the fusion of philosophy with the positive science of man as a concrete, natural and historical being, shaped in intercourse with others and with the natural world around him'.[4] This seemed to mean at the time that politics would no longer be born from pure reason, or from theology, or from beauty, but from the science of man; also that a politics informed by that concern for human beings as natural creatures, not creations of God, would take the place of philosophy as a guide to the moral life. But there were many remnants, and 'contradictory, scattered pieces of an anti-liberal counterculture', that complicated the picture.[5]

The poet Heinrich Heine, born in December 1797, the very year when Kant and Schiller had felt the political pressure lessening with a change of monarch, was another characteristic figure of the political *Vormärz* and, in parallel developments in literature, the most brilliant. He wanted to write for the masses, in a way the Romantic generation never did; and he brilliantly debunked the Romantic and self-protective fictions that had held the high culture of the Idealist age together. Of the pantheism, for instance, most recently preached by the Nature Philosophy of Goethe and Schelling he wrote in his essay 'The Romantic School' that it tended to make people politically indifferent. A scholar and poet of the 1790s like Schiller may have had a sense of freedom, but 'the great active mass' did not. 'There's growing now a new race with ... free thoughts and free pleasures, these are the people I write for.'[6] These new men were not metaphysical poseurs. They were 'entirely without cosmetics and sins'. In spirited prose and amusing verse Heine satirized the German Wilhelmines of the early nineteenth century, the so-called Biedermeier age, with as much vigour as Mayakovsky would attack the tsarist Russian *burzhui* eighty years later. Against the static political situation of the German lands after Napoleon's final defeat in 1815 and Europe's lapse into conservativism, 'Young Germans' like Heine, and the publicists Karl Gutzkow and Ludwig Börne, Ludolf Wienbarg and Adolf Glassbrenner, hammered away at the old idols as the last obstacle to an emergent German revolutionary consciousness. Nietzsche paid tribute to this era almost half a century later when he called one of his last works *The Twilight of the Idols*.

Essentially Heine was emotionally deflationary in accordance with the age: a destroyer of a stupid society hiding behind foggy ideals, and a campaigner for a more intelligent one to replace it. During the Cold War, Western scholars convinced themselves of there being no overlap between Marx and Heine because Heine was for the good whereas Marx was the cause of a divided Europe. But Eastern bloc critics were more astute when they wrote that 'Germany's past and future, which Marx summarized philosophically with his genius for generalization, appeared in the verse of ... *Germany: A Winter Fairy Tale*.' Heine's epic was, they said, 'a sort of poetic counterpart to the young Marx's *Critique of Hegel's Philosophy of Right*'.[7]

Both Heine and Marx were born on the very edge of the German Confederation close to the French border: Heine in Düsseldorf and Marx in Trier, with the smoke of the still not extinguished French revolutionary fire on the horizon. The edginess of their existential situation as German Jews helped them brilliantly assess the German situation under a police state, and both conditions goaded them into political radicalism.

For Heine in 1843, in that 'Winter Fairy Tale' that so closely shadowed the young Marx's critique, the Germans were as wooden and pedantic as Heine remembered them before he went into Paris exile. They were by temperament subservient and subordinate, 'having swallowed the rod inside themselves' that was used to keep them under control. The poet blamed the Church: 'It sang the old song of resignation/ heaven's lullaby/ Hush hush unwashed people/Yours is not to cry.'[8] Marx put it in strikingly similar terms in his 'Contribution to a Critique of Hegel's *Philosophy of Right*: Introduction', published in March 1844. Germans had to get over their 'inner priest' and their timidity and pettiness. Revolutionary virtues like consistency, penetration, courage, ruthlessness and breadth of soul were lacking.[9]

And so, where Schiller would have preferred grace and dignity, and moderation all round, a new political idea surfaced, in which ruthlessness and penetration and consistency and courage would be seen as activist virtues. As a nineteen-year-old schoolboy Marx scribbled:

Kant and Fichte soar to heavens blue
Seeking for some distant land,
I but seek to grasp profound and true
That which – in the street I find.[10]

The street would come to mean the factory gate. But immediately in what had now become philosophy it meant the place where people traded the means to stay alive. It was the material lives of people that mattered, not the state of their soul. The ideals of ancient philosophy and the Christian gospel had continued to inform Kant and his successors. But in Marx everything was about what Schiller called *Stoff*.

Schiller had wanted a balance between *Form* and *Stoff*, not for the sheer indigent materiality of the mass of lives to overwhelm existing social structures. But why now should the political be no more than the art of good behaviour? No change was going to come from that view which played directly into the hands of the complacent bourgeoisie.

But it also wasn't going to come from Feuerbach's anthropology alone. Marx's Hegel essay of 1844 threw down the gauntlet. Beside any real longing for revolution Feuerbach looked feeble. Why weren't the Germans more like the revolutionary French? Comparing the German and French situations led Marx to analyse why Germany lacked a revolutionary *engine*, and, subsequently, what could be done about it. The answer was to stop attacking Idealism and instead create a class enemy:

> For the revolution of a nation, and the emancipation of a particular class of civil society to coincide, for one estate to be acknowledged as the estate of the whole society, all the defects of society must conversely be concentrated in another class, a particular estate must be the estate of the general stumbling-block, the incorporation of the general limitation, a particular social sphere must be recognized as the notorious crime of the whole of society, so that liberation from that sphere appears as general self-liberation. For one estate to be par excellence the estate of liberation, another estate must conversely be the obvious estate of oppression. The negative general significance of the French nobility and the French clergy determined the positive general significance of the nearest neighbouring and opposed class of the bourgeoisie.

Heine had ventured, on occasion, in his patriotic way, that actually the Germans were not that bad, just a bit too comfortable in their nice lives on the Rhine.[11] Love, Faith and Hope had become mere red-nosed quaffers of wine. Freedom had twisted its ankle. But German greyness and lethargy irked Marx. No contrast meant no drama. No ambition meant no political energy:

> But no particular class in Germany has the constituency, the penetration, the courage, or the ruthlessness that could mark it out as the negative representative of society. No more has any estate the breadth of soul that identifies itself, even for a moment, with the soul of the nation, the genius that inspires material might to political violence, or that revolutionary daring which flings at the adversary the defiant words: I am nothing but I must be everything.

It was the moment of collective sentiment that Feuerbach had picked out as the key characteristic of a newly liberated political humanity. Marx shared it, but insisted it had to have a class origin, and not one rooted in the *middle* classes:

> The main stem of German morals and honesty, of the classes as well as of individuals, is rather that modest egoism which asserts its limitedness and allows it to be asserted against itself. The relation of the various sections of German society is therefore not dramatic but epic . . . thus the very opportunity of a great role has passed away before it is to hand, and every class, once it begins the struggle against the class opposed to it, is involved in the struggle against the class below it.

In these early passages Marx was longing for German society, presently 'philistine' and 'mediocre', to engage not in petty-bourgeois squabbling but in some real, binary class antagonism a future Marxist could get his teeth into. But it couldn't happen before class conflict was simplified and radicalized, as it had been in revolutionary France:

> In the German lands for the time being, the higher nobility is struggling against the monarchy, the bureaucrat against the nobility, and the bourgeois against them all, while the proletariat is already beginning to find itself struggling against the bourgeoisie. The middle class hardly dares to grasp the thought of emancipation from its own standpoint when the development of the social conditions and the progress of political theory already declare that standpoint antiquated or at least problematic.

For Marx, a right-wing interpretation of Hegel, a kind of neo-Leibnizian all-was-for-the-best, had drenched the age in quiescence. And so his own agenda became to overturn Hegel; to substitute a materialism for his Idealism, while quietly holding on to what was good in Hegel: the idea of the progressive universal cause driven by a dynamic view of History. Feuerbach's materialism didn't claim to be philosophy, because philosophy itself was alienating to the common man. But, against that, it was a materialism without an engine. And so Marx insisted that materialism and philosophy could combine as a transformational social force, and in so doing he planted the seeds of an ideal society created entirely by philosophy, Soviet Russia. The well-known moment is worth revisiting particularly in the light of that outcome. Against Feuerbach Marx wanted philosophy to be an immediate, first-order, driving force, just as the Idealists had imagined it; only philosophy 'turned the right way up'. Philosophy, materialist in character and with a political class origin, would build, and represent, a new universal humanity, and then its goal would be achieved and it could fade away.

> In France, it is enough for somebody to be something for him to want to be everything; in Germany, nobody can be anything if he is not prepared to renounce everything. In France, partial emancipation is the basis of universal emancipation; in Germany, universal emancipation is the conditio sine qua non of any partial emancipation.

It had to be philosophy, with its claims to universal truth, to convince every German. Only the absolute in a new form, one might say, would overcome the hesitations of a rather inward and individualistic people formed by Luther's doctrine of 'faith alone'. Marx was strongly aware of Luther's Protestantism as being the foundation stone of the modern German mind and, indeed, of its revolutionary potential. And so he imagined a different process of revolution from what had happened in France in 1789.[12]

The story of the future that Marx began to map out in the 1844 essay was so extraordinary that it is no wonder that Friedrich Engels, his future ideological and political partner in the forging of international Communism, would say that 1848 was the year from which all their aspirations dated, and to which they constantly returned, as to unfinished business.[13] What Marx wanted in 1848 didn't happen. The revolutions across Germany and Central Europe were defeated. But *The Communist Manifesto* appeared, and the Communist cause went forward as philosophy – the active, world-changing philosophy in which Marx placed his hope.

But we haven't quite finished with Marx's analysis of the German situation in 1844:

In France, every class of the nation is a political idealist and becomes aware of itself at first not as a particular class but as a representative of social requirements generally. The role of emancipator therefore passes in dramatic motion to the various classes of the French nation one after the other until it finally comes to the class which implements social freedom no longer with the provision of certain conditions lying outside man and yet created by human society, but rather organizes all conditions of human existence on the premises of social freedom.

The problem in Germany is that 'no class in civil society has any need or capacity for general emancipation until it is forced by its immediate condition, by material necessity, by its very chains.' Partial change leaves a dominant bourgeoisie still to pursue its own interests:

It is not the radical revolution, not the general human eman-cipation which is a utopian dream for Germany, but rather the partial, the merely political revolution, the revolution which leaves the pillars of the house standing. On what is a partial, a merely political revolution based? On part of civil society emancipating itself and attaining general domi-nation; on a definite class, proceeding from its particular situation; undertaking the general emancipation of society. This class emancipates the whole of society, but only pro-vided the whole of society is in the same situation as this class – e.g., possesses money and education or can acquire them at will.

On this very point Marx had quarrelled with his co-editor Arnold Ruge, who turned out to be far too much the bourgeois intellectual in Marx's eyes. 'Let us not say to [the world] "cease your nonsensical struggles, we will give you something real to fight for." Let us simply show the world what it is really fighting for and thus something the world *must* come to know.'[14]

The democratic political process Ruge held out for would, alone, never get there. A reform of consciousness was needed, evidently the task of a philosophy, that, as both theory and propaganda, would emancipate the proletariat, the universal class in embryo.

Where, then, is the positive possibility of a German emancipation?

Answer: In the formulation of a class with radical chains, a class of civil society which is not a class of civil society, an estate which is the dissolution of all estates, a sphere which has a universal character by its universal suffering and claims no particular right because no particular wrong, but wrong generally, is perpetuated against it; which can invoke no historical, but only human, title; which does not stand in any one-sided antithesis to the consequences but in all-round antithesis to the premises of German state-hood; a sphere, finally, which cannot emancipate itself without emancipating itself from all other spheres of society and thereby emancipating all other spheres of society, which, in a word, is the complete loss of man and hence can win itself only through the complete re-winning of man. This dissolution of society as a particular estate is the proletariat.[15]

And so the proletariat as a revolutionary force was born. The Russians around Marx, even as he wrote this essay, could have no idea; nor did Marx have any inclination to apply his theory to Russia, where there was no capitalism to speak of, minimal industrialization and no working class. And yet wrong, 'no particular wrong, but wrong generally', perpetuated against Russia's people abounded and out of that would come the greatest insurrection of all.

Marx was 26 when he imagined the German proletariat becoming so aware of its own interests that 'the complete loss of man . . . and the complete re-winning of man' might happen. It was the Old Testament absolutism of the vision that made it seem something more than politics, and more than philosophy, and surely Marx would not have denied that. He wanted to change human will, like a man purging his individual will in order to receive God's will, and he imagined it happening collectively to a whole socio-economic class. Kenosis, for centuries a ferocious instrument of Christian self-improvement, would now in its collective form empty out the bourgeois world and create a proletarian paradise to replace it.

He would stir up conflict so it could be resolved. What mattered was first to generate the energy of conflict and then to use it to bring about that all-surpassing transformation of consciousness. When he wrote about conflict Marx, with his classical education, often used that figure of speech that Schiller and Hegel loved too, the chiasmus. Chiasmus criss-crossed opposing principles and set them in creative tension with each other. It was from Schiller that Hegel learned to argue dialectically and Hegel presented the method to Marx. If you pit against each other opposing forces in the human personality, and in culture at large, and follow how they work in ongoing and shifting tension with one another, you can also see how tensions can be resolved, and the world move on.[16]

That was a dialectical way of thinking about the two polities side by side, the French and the German. Even as they appeared to be distinct and antagonistic forces, the best hope for humanity was that they would merge their strengths while cancelling out each other's weaknesses. The French strength was solidarity. The German strength was philosophy. The French-German hope was expressed in the very name of the *Deutsch-Französischer Jahrbücher* where Marx's Hegel essay appeared, and to it corresponded a further particular wish to unite the spiritual life with the material in a new kind of practicality. Add a third set of principles in conflict, the abstract versus the concrete, and you could imagine the final making real of ideas that for centuries had only hovered in the ether. To get out of the Hegelian trap of quiescence, 'in Germany, where practical life is as spiritless as spiritual life is unpractical',[17] you could not settle for a Utopia that was *only*, as Hegel devised it, an endless process of becoming, with tensions but no timetable short of eternity behind it. A political force had to be created that had nothing to do with the failings of abstract universalism, but retained the necessary aspect of the universal and now endeavoured to make it concrete. Revolutionary France had to become something new again through a marriage with German potential, and 'Germany' likewise come into its own by absorbing the French passion for political emancipation. The thinking life should join itself to life in the street, and thus the dichotomy between spiritual and material would simply be transcended, in some third revolutionary condition.

In sum, and at last, concrete, what philosophy could call a practical universality was to be the outcome of a Franco-German determination to make the human species fully self-aware as to the detriments of exploitation. The hitherto downtrodden of the world, the victims of endless and indefinite 'wrong generally', were entitled to escape real and bodily misery and lead a higher kind of life.

Still what had any of this to do with Russia, where national self-awareness was in the hands of the tiny few? Marx's struggle was not against serfdom, at the time still the dominant problem in Russia, but exploitation undermining universal brotherhood.

Marx actually met a few Russians in Berlin the winter he was writing his Hegel essay, and wasn't impressed.[18] The message the young students had been sending home was, whatever it was, hopeless. One Scythian in the Greek Army didn't mean that Scythia would become culturally Greek.[19] Belinsky, as it happened, had read the same bestseller as Marx, Jean-Jacques Barthélemy's *The Travels of Anacharsis the Younger in Scythia*, and, without either man being aware of the overlap, wholeheartedly concurred. 'We unhappy Anacharsises of the new Scythia!' he had complained to a friend in 1841. Marx in 1844, no doubt from his reading of the newspapers, had a sense of a Russian inertia even worse than the German, and the handful of politically progressive Russians in Berlin struck him as irrelevant, piggybacking on Western situations and Western thinking. Moreover, if the Germans of the *Vormärz* and the Russians under Nicholas I were both living in pre-capitalist police states, *at least the Germans had philosophy*.[20] How fortunate, relative to Russia, Marx decided the Germans were!

> Whereas the problem in France and England is: political economy, or the rule of society over wealth; in Germany, it is: national economy, or the mastery of private property over nationality. In France and England, then, it is a case of abolishing monopoly that has proceeded to its last consequences; in Germany, it is a case of proceeding to the last consequences of monopoly . . . An adequate example of the *German* form of modern problems, an example [is] how our history, like a clumsy recruit, still has to do extra drill on things that are old and hackneyed in history.
>
> If, therefore, the whole German development did not exceed the German political development, a German could at the most have the share in the problems-of-the-present that a Russian has. But, when the separate individual is not bound by the limitations of the nation, the nation as a whole is still

less liberated by the liberation of one individual. The fact that Greece had a Scythian among its philosophers did not help the Scythians to make a single step towards Greek culture.

Luckily, we Germans are not Scythians.

These unexplored passages from the early Marx are crucial to understanding what happened to the utopian idea in Russia – the idea whose realization Marx would gift to Russia – because they seem to say, long before Marx gave Russia more serious thought, by learning the language and reading the economic literature, that Russia would have to become, philosophically, more like the German, it would have to become philosophical as such, to stand a chance of political revolution. And of course that is exactly what would happen, with the culture that Herzen and Bakunin, amongst others, would help to build:

> As the ancient peoples went through their pre-history in imagination, in mythology, so we Germans have gone through our post-history in thought, in philosophy. We are philosophical contemporaries of the present without being its historical contemporaries. German philosophy is the ideal prolongation of German history. If therefore, instead of the *oeuvres incomplètes* of our real history, we criticize the *oeuvres posthumes* of our ideal history, philosophy, our criticism is in the midst of the questions of which the present says: *that is the question*. What, in progressive nations, is a practical break with modern state conditions, is, in Germany, where even those conditions do not yet exist, at first a critical break with the philosophical reflexion of those conditions.

On the German *Vormärz* model, Marx's analysis of the Hamlet-like nation that has *only* philosophy is negative. But then the analysis becomes dazzlingly prophetic for Russia's revolutionary future, because Marx says philosophy is a nation's prior *Traumgeschichte*, its anticipatory 'dream-history':

> The German nation must therefore join this, its dream-history, to its present conditions and subject to criticism

not only these existing conditions, but at the same time their abstract continuation. Its future cannot be limited either to the immediate negation of its real conditions of state and right, or to the immediate implementation of its ideal state and right conditions, for it has the immediate negation of its real conditions in its ideal conditions, and it has almost out-lived the immediate implementation of its ideal conditions in the contemplation of neighboring nations.

In other words, look at what you want in philosophy, but don't rest content with contemplation. Look to 'the immediate implementa-tion of [your] ideal state and right conditions' before the impetus is lost. Even had he paid attention to Russia in the 1840s Marx couldn't have applied this thesis to a country without philosophy at all, but he might have wished German philosophy upon it, eventually to build a better future.

Marx had a Westerner's distrust of Russia. It was only late in his career when, flattered by the apparent power of his vision, he was prepared to waive his principal doctrinal requirement for revolu-tion, that capitalism should be sufficiently advanced for its collapse to be likely. Perhaps Russia could prove to be the exception. There might yet be a direct shift from a barely initiated capitalism to a worker-controlled economy. And yet all the time what he gave no further thought to was happening there: the creation of the people's ultimate 'dream-history', first of all as philosophy. As his philoso-phy, not least. What Marx would have needed to experience was his own input into Russia *as a philosopher*, far more than as an econo-mist. He would have needed to see into the future: how little over a quarter of a century after his death Marxist-Leninism, painfully encumbered as philosophy, would *force* into reality the dream of a universal proletariat on Russian soil.

With regard to what Marx would lend Russia, at once to over-come and transcend its Scythian isolation, perhaps the dialectical engine felt real to him and his contemporaries because of its affinity with the piston engine. The piston engine really was transform-ing the socio-economic relations of the world. No historian can prove that the industrial revolution, which fired Marx's compas-sion, in the actual technical nitty-gritty at its heart also fired his dialectical imagination, and therefore the philosophy he offered to the world in response. But the dialectic toing and froing back and forth between forces in conflict clearly resembled a scientifically demonstrable process to generate heat and fire and energy and motion, and Marx himself saw the connection. When James Watt built the first locomotive the pistons were powered by steam. As they agitated back and forth the train moved forward along the rails. Watt's double-acting steam engine was 'a prime mover that begot its own force', said Marx, adding that its power was entirely under man's control.[21] Add to that the spectacle of the only real danger to piston engines – that they might overheat and 'blow' if they didn't have a safety valve – and it wasn't difficult to imagine that capitalism might implode in the same way, if it didn't cease its relentless expansion. But then its breakdown would offer the ultimate political opportunity to establish a new way of dominating nature through technology, in favour of the workers.

This was thinking in images, creatively, to balance the abstractions, which Marx often did; then he harnessed it to factual findings, which is why it was both actually and subliminally so compelling. In his actual researches on the factory floor Marx found that the faster and more efficient the machines became, the more labour was extracted from the workers. Hours were reduced but the effort required to do the work was disproportionately intensified, with those working in the spinning industry doing the equivalent of walking 20 miles (32 km) in 1832, where 8 miles (13 km) had been the case in 1815.[22] He had the right cause. Only how could he philosophize about it? Well, he could abstract from the very engine that was driving industrial plant the dynamic idea that would bring together his material and moral concerns in a new theory of the industrial future. Hegel had already pioneered it as dialectic.

Marx's creative-philosophical development was fascinating from the moment he structured two chiasmic utterances on the last page of that crucial 1844 essay. The underscorings (signified here by italics) were his own to make the dialectical points. The first was that

As philosophy finds its *material* weapons in the proletariat, so the proletariat finds its *spiritual* weapons in philosophy, and as soon as this lightning flash of thought hits the earth in this naive local land, the emancipation of *the Germans to human beings* will be complete.

The second was that

> The *head* of this emancipation is *philosophy*, its *heart* the
> *proletariat*. Philosophy can't realize itself without the
> *Aufhebung* of the proletariat, and the proletariat can't
> achieve *Aufhebung* without the becoming real of philosophy.

No reader will thank me for talking about the 'sublation of
the proletariat'. *Aufhebung* is one of those words impossible to
translate so I have left it in the original German. But it means the
moment when something that has been a force in the world, and
thus engaged in conflict, loses its force because the conflict has
been resolved. Since the proletariat's existence in conflict was an
expression of unhappiness and incompleteness, the overcoming of
that conflict must be a great moment. Indeed, it marks the end of
an old world and the beginning of one that is new. In that conflict,
philosophy fulfilled its ultimate purpose, to achieve harmony. Now
there is no unjustly treated proletariat in the world, there is also
no more need for philosophy. Of course that was a theory like the
withering away of the state, with the proletariat finally in charge
of its own destiny. Neither withering would happen in the only
real political system to put it to the test, as the officially proletarian Soviet Russian state shored itself up with dead theory. But
there was this great symmetry to Marx's vision, of which Russia
was destined to fall foul.

Ten years later, in the mid-1850s, when Marx was himself leaving philosophy behind; when he felt he was caring at once for the
body of every last worker and 'the body of the factory, i.e. machinery
organised into a system'; when every day he had to contemplate a
devilish combination of ironwork and human sinew, he found himself nevertheless turning back again and again to Idealism to give his
thinking moral alongside political content, through the dialectical
structuring of his arguments. We can see how much of Idealism Marx
carried over, not least the lingering Christian myth, in the minds of
the Tübingen seminarists, that humanity might transcend its earthly
condition because God had a Son who suffered bodily too.

And so the story of the Utopia that Marx would help to inspire in
Russia was a barely imaginable conjunction of Christian metaphysics married to the potentially liberating power of heavy industry to

transform the quality of ordinary lives; if only the workers could own the means of production; if only there could be a new Feuerbachian teleology of humanity based on an idea of honest work, not exploitation.

It was a right and even biblical cause for those who had always suffered 'wrong, in general' to face a better future. But for that future to be inevitable? Marx designed History so that the proletariat had to win. And how could he believe his argument was rational? Because always essentially it was Hegelian: a question of matter, the proletarian human body, in dialectical engagement with the one-sided philosophy of spirit of the bourgeoisie, and finally transcending the conflict in a new unity of body and mind on a higher plane. Has not the whole history of Western philosophy been a misunderstanding of the body, cried Nietzsche, somewhere in the hinterland of this great event when Marx transformed Hegel's *Phenomenology of Spirit* into *Capital*, by imagining an engine for bare humanity to become happier?

One irony, one gain for philosophy, was the way Marx recovered the Idealist preoccupation with artistic creation in a new idealization of labour. For Marx now not the rare Romantic genius of a Schelling, not the refined Schillerian architect of his own balanced life, but every worker, combining in himself the Greek functions of *poesis* and *techne*, was an artist. *Techne* governed his relationship with nature and *poesis* the artistic shaping of his own life. Industrialization had taken these functions away from him. It had 'reduced to a mere fragment of a man . . . the fully developed individual, fit for a variety of labours, ready to face any change of production, and to whom the different social functions he performs are but so many modes of giving free scope to his own natural and acquired powers'.[23]

To give the masses a more satisfying life and a more comfortable material base; to give them a home in the world; to end their role as producers of other people's wealth; to wish them all that fullness and satisfaction and harmony and vitality that Schiller and Herzen and Nietzsche hymned: it was here, in this aspect of his utopian vision, a classical Western vision of creativity and the creative self-made life, that Marx seems to have come out of a different stable from the belligerent and obsessive world ideology he engendered. Marx dreamt of unfreezing the concepts he adapted from Hegel, not of rigidifying them.[24]

But then came the Russian Marxist-Leninists who stepped out to greet the locomotive of history, the historical materialism of Karl Marx and Friedrich Engels, that would speed up their country's modernization. What they wanted, now that Marx had given them philosophy, or theory, was to marry it to a new Russian practice.

6

Bakunin on Fire

W hen Herzen recalled how 1830s Moscow was gripped by German philosophy he pictured two of its leading figures 'each with a volume of Hegel's philosophy in hand, and each filled with the youthful intolerance inseparable from vital, passionate conviction'.[1] One was the critic Belinsky who, in those letters to friends in Berlin, hungered for all things German. The other was Mikhail Bakunin, a man Herzen would one day call 'a Columbus without an America'.[2]

Bakunin, by the time of his death in 1876, was poised to have a profound effect on the climate surrounding the Russian Revolution. Gaze into novels by Turgenev and Dostoevsky and this massive, shaggy, bearded figure steps forward out of the fictionalizing shadows as a harbinger of utopian fantasy and self-destruction. He wanted political transformation for a world mind and a world soul but not at all by political means. He longed for 'democracy . . . [not yet] in its affirmative abundance . . . and therefore in [an] evil state . . . [to] be destroyed . . . so that from its free ground it may spring forth again in a newborn state, as its own living fullness'.[3] That pursuit of 'living fullness' has been seen as his supreme delusion and tragedy.[4]

Born in 1814, he was by social origin a dissident aristocrat, who from his late teens upset his father's class expectations. German Idealism seized him when, retiring from the military service which he detested, still aged only 22, Bakunin 'strayed without map or compass into a world of fantastic projects and efforts at self-education',[5] said Herzen. The first object of his reading was Johann Gottlieb Fichte.

Fichte came from a family of poor and pious ribbon weavers in rural Saxony. He was a gifted boy and received, courtesy of the local priest, a favoured education that took him to the universities at Leipzig and Jena. Kant was impressed when Fichte came to meet him in Königsberg, but Fichte immediately took the older man to task for limiting the scope of human knowledge. At the same time he worried about the individualism of the age, which conflicted with his residual piety. Out of that conflict of a maximalist head and a submissive heart came a vision of 'inner' and 'outer' worlds in harmony, if only they could be correctly perceived. The effect was to make reality a figment of the self-perfecting human mind, a project for the moral control of knowledge. Fichte, born in 1762, was intensely subjective and ideologically ambitious. Karl Jaspers would write of him, in the light of Germany's own twentieth-century political tragedy, that he was 'a constructor who drilled his message home, fanatical and dogmatic, nationalistic and moralistic, activistic as a rhetorician, inclined to sensationalism in making his points, a barbarian, of questionable decency, not infrequently untruthful'.[6]

The German influence on Bakunin and his generation was set to be philosophically profound. All the German Idealists were pursuing a post-Enlightenment theory of knowledge that would balance 'inner' and 'outer', subjective and objective, in pursuit of truth. What developed – and the prototypes for this dialectical understanding were already there in Goethe and in Kant – was for 'inner' and 'outer' to relate to each other reciprocally; now to provide a vantage point to see the other, and now to merge. But there was this potential for Romantic and political excess, and that is what seems to have affected Bakunin. Digesting German Idealism, he left aside the nature philosophy and the aesthetic fine-tuning of the human sensibility, and went for the absolute vision.

Fichte's 1794 *Wissenschaftslehre* ('Doctrine of Science' or 'Theory of Scientific Knowledge') historicized that vision. It described how a new all-embracing knowledge, a magnificent merging of nature and mind, was gradually becoming a reality in some societies. The *Wissenschaftslehre* showed how a theory of knowledge could become a theory of history: of History writ large. That in turn could readily be translated into a social and national political programme to forge unity out of conflict. The 'Theory of Scientific Knowledge' brought Fichte such tremendous popular success as professor of critical philosophy at the University of Jena that his name reached Moscow.

Almost Bakunin's first philosophical act was to translate into Russian Fichte's essay of 1794 on 'The Vocation of the Scholar', in which Fichte demanded from his contemporaries an awareness of History. History writ large exulted in a humanity that was inherently progressive. It enshrined Humanity as a secular religion and it was a product of the belief of the age that reason was the supreme and totally fulfilling human quality. In the wake of the Enlightenment all educated men understood the way the world was moving, Fichte said, towards 'the development and satisfaction of *all* the wants of man, and indeed the harmonious development and satisfaction of them all'.

The problem was, no thinking person could fail to notice how 'by some unlucky occurrence [some societies, some countries] had been carried in an opposite direction'. Such people would need to enquire, by looking around and considering their contemporaries, 'in what particular degree of cultivation [does] the society to which we belong stand'. These were Fichte's words, now courtesy of Bakunin, translated to address young Russians. 'The uniform but constantly progressive development of all the faculties of man' must mean that they themselves, as educated Russians, should promote 'the actual advancement of the human race'. Bakunin's translation of Fichte, appearing in the avant-garde journal *Telescope* in March 1836, was a ringing call to the Russian intelligentsia to look at their country's history and to use German Idealism to solve its problems, even while under the knout of Nicholas I.

Fichte wanted to see a German equivalent emerge to the French Enlightenment *philosophe*. This would be a philosopher with so much more religious intensity and aggression. Fichte thought of this German as tasked with a quasi-religious mission to convey Truth to the uneducated. The educated man, *der Gelehrte*, 'must rouse men to the feeling of their true wants . . . there is in all men a feeling of truth, which . . . must be developed, proved and purified'. His task was to teach

> the wants arising out of the special condition in which
> [men] stand . . . [the educated man] sees not merely the
> present – he sees also the future; he sees not merely the
> point which humanity now occupies but also that to which

it must advance if it is to remain true to its final end, and not to wander or turn back from its legitimate path.

There was a zeal in Fichte, the equivalent of the *Schwärmerei* to which Kant and Schiller preferred a more moderate enthusiasm. As Christ appealed to the Apostles to go forth and spread the Word, as the salt of the earth, so, thought Fichte, could the educated man declare: 'I am a Priest of Truth; I am in her pay; I have bound myself to do all things, to venture all things, to suffer all things for her.'
Schiller cautioned, in a counter-essay:

The presumptions of the strength of imagination, in spheres where it only possesses the executive power, to seize for itself the legislative power too, have caused so much damage, in life as in philosophy [*Wissenschaft*], that it is of no little importance to determine exactly the limits set for the use of beautiful forms. These limits lie in the nature of the beautiful . . .[7]

All the German philosophers who rooted themselves deep in the Russian mind were maximalists who pushed for absolute change. The Fichte–Bakunin connection would run in parallel with the Hegel–Marx connection, both preaching revolution. For Marx the undoing of philosophy's constraints so far as the real world was concerned came through its thoroughgoing transformation into a body of theory that upheld the material interests of the proletariat. For Bakunin the new universal vision came from removing all constraints to Kantian aesthetic dreaming. On the more moderate German side, right from the outset, Schiller saw Fichte as seizing power for philosophy illegitimately, much as the Jacobins had done in France. His *Wissenschaftslehre* was a presumptive seizing of legislative power.

Transfusing Fichte's sentimental-revolutionary rectitude into his own blood turned Bakunin into such a bully that he almost ruined the lives of his two sisters, who were admirable intellectual partners but without the educational advantages their brother had. He seems to have been a dictatorial man given to quarrelling, and nearly all his St Petersburg contemporaries found him unbearable, 'a reptile' and 'weird'.[8] When in 1840 he moved to Berlin, the reason may not only have been intellectual. He had recently insulted a colleague in the literary-philosophical circles he frequented and had narrowly avoided a duel over the man's marital honour.

Bakunin's Berlin days however were amongst his best. He enjoyed Russian company, advanced his education by reading Hegel, and discovered his potential as a revolutionary without yet paying the price for defying all authority. One of his friends was the young Ivan Turgenev, not yet embarked on a life in fiction, and the sisters even came to visit. 'Michel' had many friends and admirers.

When he first read Hegel moreover something clicked that earned him the esteem of his critics back home. Writing an article called 'On Philosophy,' Bakunin saw the light shining beyond the 'dark night of the soul' that Hegel had elaborated in the *Phenomenology of Spirit*. It made him see, imposing Hegel on the already established Fichtean categories in his mind, how Russian intellectuals were so desperately alienated from the culture they longed to play a full part in. In a better world that need not be. There could be unity, not schism, harmony not discord.[9]

Already on record, before he left for abroad, as always wanting to further, and to belong to, 'our beautiful Russian life',[10] Bakunin seemed to accept Hegel's argument for the modalities of change. He accepted the sadness, as the necessary prelude to the eventual satisfaction that followed. Like Marx he saw religion giving way to politics. Yet by the time of his second Hegelian phase just a few years later, Bakunin had decided not to play the waiting game. The only way to move forward was to destroy all obstacles to freedom, before building society anew. Religion had passed through philosophy and become radical politics, or, as Marx would view Bakunin's enterprise, an extreme combativeness all of its own.

There are several magnificent passages in Bakunin's 1842 essay on 'The Reaction in Germany', which followed close on the heels of his 'religion is politics' statement of the previous autumn.[11] They show what talent he had, and what feeling for the energetic and outspoken times of the German *Vormärz*, with its contempt for traditional authority and its outspoken concern with ordinary people, and for the plight of the poor. Since Hegel had died in 1831 the intellectual climate had been transformed, and the Russians arriving towards the end of the decade had to play catch-up. That's why his position changed so fast. Bakunin, barely out of his Christian and metaphysical moments, found himself in the midst of a young, self-politicizing secular Germany. And now this was what he hoped a Young Russia could become. 'Gentlemen, you must confess that our times are dismal times and that we are all its still more dismal children!'[12]

The writing was grand, like a *Communist Manifesto* six years before Marx and Engels. Bakunin went on:

> Visible appearances are stirring around us, indicating that the Spirit, this old mole, has brought its underground work to completion and that it will soon come again to pass judgment. Everywhere, especially in France and England, social and religious societies are being formed, wholly alien to the present political world, societies which derive their life from new sources quite unknown to us and develop and diffuse themselves in silence. The people, the poor class, which without doubt constitutes the greatest part of humanity; the class whose rights have already been recognized in theory; which, however, up to now is still condemned by its birth, by its ties with poverty and ignorance, as well, indeed, as with actual slavery – this class, which constitutes the true people, is everywhere assuming a threatening attitude and is beginning to count the ranks of its enemy, weak as compared to it, and to demand the actualization of the rights already conceded to it by everyone. All peoples and all men are filled with a kind of premonition, and everyone whose vital organs are not paralysed faces with shuddering expectation the approaching future which will speak out the redeeming word. Even in Russia, in this endless and snow-covered kingdom which we know so little and which perhaps a great future awaits, even in Russia dark clouds are gathering, heralding storm. Oh, the air is sultry and filled with lightning.[13]

Bakunin's 1842 essay, ostensibly on the German situation, was a first, marvellous evocation of a revolutionary Russia. It highlighted its place, both promising and menacing, on the edge of Europe and its hopes and its philosophy. It was also the place where Bakunin first set down, aged 28, that 'democracy . . . [not yet] in its affirmative abundance . . . and therefore in [an] evil state . . . [has to] be destroyed . . . so that from its free ground it may spring forth again in a newborn state, as its own living fullness.' Wrenched out of its context here was 'the destructive urge' that was also 'creative', a total formula that would become terrifyingly simple. But it's important to know that it was born of a longing to apply German progressive thought to 'our beautiful Russian life' and rid it of centuries of enslavement. On the other hand Bakunin swept aside the complexity of Hegel's dialectic and substituted direct conflict as the only way to bring about that change.

As a Russian he was impatient. The time lag between intellectual developments in the German lands and in Russia was desperately frustrating. The first potentially political generation of the Russian intelligentsia were now moving in a German environment that equally said reform couldn't wait. And so of the 'Reaction in Germany' that might hold up the democratization of the remnants of feudalism in those principalities and duchies Bakunin wrote that there could be no compromise. The old had to be destroyed now. *All* its protagonists, activist and conservative alike, had to go under, for the new full life to body forth. Even his own revolutionary role would be swallowed up in the convulsion. What Marx prophesied for philosophy in bringing about a proletarian state, that it would disappear once that goal was achieved, Bakunin felt about his own role, already, as a philosopher-activist. He was ready to obey, and be destroyed by, the magic of *Aufhebung*. He invited the dialectical process, which gave negative phenomena a critical one-time use, to swallow him up, if only the good end could be brought about.

As Hegel was reinterpreted to advance the progressive cause, Bakunin's immersion in the plotting and propagandizing leading up to the European revolutions of 1848 had a profound impact on his role as an activist messenger to Russia. At no time did the history of Russian revolutionary feeling, except for the late impact of Marx, witness such a rapid turning-point. From 1839 to 1842, as the Russians caught up with the latest intellectual trends in Germany, suddenly the view prevailed that if there was to be Hegel at all then it must be a Hegel of the left, promoting the cause of universal emancipation. Only Bakunin, with his concluding words to the 1842 essay, 'that the destructive urge is also a creative urge', was, to repeat, not interested in the subtle tactics of dialectic to get the world to move forward. For him, as a Russian, any means to remove the tsar was acceptable.

That extremism so inflected Bakunin's views and actions also as a *German* revolutionary that Marx grew worried. He wanted to remind Bakunin of the words of Falstaff, that discretion was the better part of valour.[14] Two decades later Dostoevsky would mine the real Bakunin for his all-destructive character Pyotr Verkhovensky. Peter Supreme was a principal player in the aptly named novel *The Devils*.[15] The most indiscreet of Bakunin's revolutionary actions had been by that time to befriend and openly admire the murderer Sergei Nechaev.

It became a life of violent political dreaming. Fired by a sense of the monumental injustice of the Russian state, Bakunin couldn't avoid making the wholesale destruction of any political status quo his priority. If one wanted to find a psychological explanation for the violence, estrangement from country and family hugely affected him. His relationships with women didn't succeed and there was no prospect of a family. For many years the rumour went about, long enough to impress serious historians, that Bakunin was sexually impotent and that *that* made a difference to his painful life and fed the ferocity of his non-negotiating outlook. Meanwhile he was never reconciled to his father. In a dark private hour he may have conceded that he was weak, and that weakness was inverted into violence.[16] For whatever reason, very early Bakunin's aim became to break and enter by force the 'full life' that was denied him. He hungered after that 'living fullness' which had animated the heart of German Idealism since Leibniz and had inveterate mystical origins. But force enacted in real, material life meant destroying any state that came his way, while force in the mind meant destroying philosophy itself. So Bakunin ended up combining a remnant of metaphysics, that desire for 'living fullness', with a crude physical offensive against the enemy. He had to detonate the gap between mind and world, idea and reality. All the great metaphysical problems out of whose delicate reworking Kant had created German Idealism were to be blown up, to create the space for true liberty. For a time German philosophy had helped him prepare his powder, but then, blaming his studies for only adding to his world estrangement, Bakunin turned on philosophy and determined to destroy that too. *Pereat philosophia, fiat mundus.* Philosophy would give way to the art of building a perfect world and Bakunin would dramatize that story with his own life.

As the whole era in Europe struggled to make sense of new political impulses and social needs, Bakunin wasn't alone in dramatizing in his own person the power and limitations of German Idealism. Belinsky was another. Bakunin was doing for Russian philosophy in fact what Belinsky was doing for Russian literature. He was creating a map to help the country understand itself, a process tinged with terroristic violence and fierce hope and residual mysticism. Belinsky too went through his Fichte, and Schiller, and Hegel phases, struggling to find a Russian cultural originality and future mission. Both he and Bakunin saw Pushkin ranking with Goethe, doing for the unity of Russian culture what Goethe had done for the German, which is to say peacefully embodying it in one man of genius. But Belinsky's tool was and remained literature.

Herzen meanwhile also lived the drama of the era, mostly from beyond Russia's borders, and it's another comparison that can help us understand Bakunin. Herzen's great readings of Hegel, written in the bookish no man's land of Russian exile, stressed the courage and personal application needed to pursue knowledge, and self-knowledge. 'Dilettantism in Science' and 'Letters on the Study of Nature' were written just at the time Bakunin was in Berlin, when Russian readiness to learn directly from Hegel was at its height. Yet at the same time Herzen set himself up as a benchmark of wisdom and moderation in how to read the Germans safely, as a guide to Russian progress, and move on. It's a curious fact that almost all the Russian thinkers who came into contact with German Idealism in the nineteenth century felt on behalf of their country at once an attraction to, and an almost immediate revulsion from, abstraction. But again Bakunin seemed to want to blast his way out of that limitation.

Bakunin first met Marx in 1844 in Berlin when they were contributors to those short-lived political journals, the *Deutsche Jahrbücher* and the *Deutsch-Französische Jahrbücher*, edited by Arnold Ruge. Both Marx and Bakunin had received their education in German Idealism and seen the authority of Hegelian metaphysics collapse. Both were now aware of 'the poor class' and were filled with 'shuddering expectation'. Bakunin's most critical biographer wrote during the Cold War that,

> The pursuit of wholeness . . . is the pursuit not of the natural and immediate, but of the idea of a philosophical chimera as far removed from recorded human experience, past or present, as the Kingdom of God on earth. Bakunin's vision

of the unified human personality of the distant future may differ from the Marxist one in its rhetoric and the immediacy of its appeal, but it comes from the same philosophical stable and imposes the same constraints on the choice of means.[17]

Feuerbach, who saw himself living up to the literal meaning of his own surname, 'fiery brook', had a touch of this impatience, infectious in the very way he turned philosophy into an instrument of practical change. The temptation to reach for a hammer, in place of all this talk, came from the realization of how much Idealism and God had been instrumentalized by the undemocratic power structures of the past. Four decades before Nietzsche's philosophizing with a hammer, Feuerbach availed himself of the same blunt and heavy tool. Idealism and the Church were for the rich to maintain their positions in society. Religion was just a chimera, maintained to keep the people in their uncomplaining place.

Bakunin's version of change tomorrow was to be dynamite himself today. Through the 1840s he quickly became known as a political conspirator across Europe, and when he adopted the alias 'Dr Schwarz', it was as a mark of respect for dynamite's inventor.[18] With Bakunin, the Idealist vision of utopian wholeness turned, not into a vision of unalienated existence through meaningful labour, but a terrifying need to remove all constraints to subjective freedom. A self-willed historical actor, he was never far from the hero of Schiller's play *The Robbers* who had been part of every young Russian's education in the 1830s. He was half Schiller's Karl Moor in his eventual willingness to step over the line into criminality, half Fichte's idea of a Christ-like leader of the people. By the mid-1840s he was ready to follow and join rebellions wherever they broke out across Europe. Kraków 1846, when the Poles rebelled against their Russian occupier, was his first opportunity. He was now an international activist, slipping from one European country to the next, seeing what of the old order he could raze. 'I await my . . . fiancée, revolution. We will be really happy – that is we will become ourselves, only when the whole world is engulfed in fire.'[19]

The scattered outbreaks of dissent that counted as the 1848 revolutions were not successful. After the Russian authorities moved into Kraków and sequestered the city that had been under Austrian rule, the better to keep their own part of Poland under control, Bakunin returned to Paris for yet another defeated revolution in February 1848. He was in Prague in early 1849, scene of more nationalist unrest, and finally, when he became a wanted man in Bohemia, he slipped into Dresden over the border, carrying papers in the name of the dynamite man. There in pretty little Baroque Dresden in the spring of 1849 Bakunin was 'drinking in with every fibre of my body the intoxicating atmosphere of revolution'.[20]

The once very reluctant trainee Russian Imperial military officer in his teens now lent his remembered martial skills to the people of Dresden. He directed the erection of barricades from his headquarters at the town hall. He ordered the felling of Dresden's beautiful trees, to protect the rebels from the Saxon army, prompting the locals to cry out in dialect, 'Oh, our poor trees!'[21] He 'wandered among the barricades in a black frock coat ... smoking his cigar and making fun of the naivety of the Dresden revolution'. Finally he watched the city burn. This at least is how Richard Wagner remembered him. When Wagner recalled those heady days with twenty years' hindsight he used the activist Bakunin as an alter ego. In fame and maturity he wanted to suggest that he the great composer had only ever been an onlooker when in fact he too had been a consummate facilitator. Still, from the devastatingly cruel pipe bombs he ordered built and fired on the Saxon army, to the match that was struck at dead of night to burn down the old opera house, Bakunin far outdid Wagner in terms of violent action.[22]

Meanwhile, what of the remnants of Art and Idealism in that unprecedented political moment? The moment the professional revolutionary collaborated with the most revolutionary composer of the nineteenth century is usually quickly passed over in the telling of Bakunin's life and career. But it tells us so much about the way German Idealism was still going about its utopian work. Marx had retained Hegel's dialectic and his sense of the value of work as a form of self-knowledge embedded in the social world; he was also concerned with the unalienated life; and versions of all of this would arrive in Russia with Marxist theory. Bakunin meanwhile was a poetic and even hysterical kind of German Idealist, who never lost Schiller's faith in the poetic transformation of the world according to the aesthetic instinct. Whatever violence Fichte encouraged in him, he still believed in the revolutionary role of art. He made a note in 1843, after he had been reading the socialist and feminist George

Sand: 'To the thinker and poet is granted to anticipate the future and build a new world.' In the 1842 Hegel essay, meanwhile, Bakunin had quoted the third chapter of Revelation verses fifteen to seventeen, to say he did not wish to be 'a dry arranger' of a new order of things, but to go forth – and this we can infer from the rest of his life, and from other scattered utterances – in the name of poetry, of Art and of personality, because all of these, but especially the single human personality, transcended the contradictions of actual life. Escaping from 'the lukewarm' castigated in Apocalypse, he wanted to go forth in love, as Feuerbach and Wagner preached, and love must save him from abstractions. Love, in fact, a 'weird', 'reptilian' concept of it, some might say, was Bakunin's key to the fullness of life.

At a time when Wagner was filled with thoughts of how fast socialism and Communism were advancing, and how when that political process was complete would be the time for the transform-ation of art to begin, he and Bakunin met through a mutual Dresden friend and fellow conspirator. Wagner, who directed the orchestra at the city's Royal Court Theatre, convened revolutionary meetings in his garden.[23] Through *Gesamtkunst*, 'Total Art', he hoped to bring a new heroic sensibility alive that would also help to defeat capitalism, because capitalism created the wrong audience for art and hence the wrong kind of art, pandering to bourgeois tastes. Much of the political inspiration came from the Young Hegelians of the *Vormärz*.[24] Bakunin may have told him what he felt at the time: 'Even the best constitutions will not satisfy me. We need something else: spirit and vitality, a new world without laws and thus free.'[25] In Wagner the spirit and the vitality were of course on the stage and in the music, a safer place for them. Bakunin by contrast was dangerous.

Wagner remembered he 'had a singular and altogether imposing personality . . . anywhere between thirty and forty years of age . . . everything about him was colossal, and he was full of a primitive exu-berance and strength.' Wagner himself was hardly less of an imposing personality. They took frequent walks together.

Bakunin, temporarily freed in the countryside from the fear that the police would suddenly spring from round a corner and take him, talked of the Rousseauan idea of freedom that had first inspired him. He pictured himself as if in the same line of inheritance from France as the German thinkers of fifty years earlier. Later, catching up, he worked through Hegel until he knew enough to defeat Hegel in his own terms. The effect was to enable him to 'get philosophy off his chest' and take up the life of an activist.

And Russia, where did Russia fit? Wagner asked.

[Bakunin] looked to the Slav world for the regeneration of humanity, because the Slavs had been less enervated by civilization. His hopes . . . were centred . . . in the Russian peasant class. In the natural detestation of the Russian serf for his cruel oppressor the nobleman, [Bakunin] believed he could trace a substratum of simple-minded brotherly love, and that instinct which leads animals to hate the men who hunt them. In support of this idea he cited the childish, almost demoniac delight of the Russian people in fire, a quality on which Rostopchin calculated in his strategic burning of Moscow. He argued that all that was necessary to set in motion a world-wide movement was to convince the Russian peasant, in whom the natural goodness of oppressed human nature had preserved its most childlike characteristics, that it was perfectly right and well pleasing to God for them to burn their lords' castles, with everything in and about them. The least that could result from such a movement would be the destruction of all those things which, rightly considered, must appear, even to Europe's most philosophical thinkers, the real source of all the misery in the modern world. To set these destructive forces in action appeared to him the only object worthy of a sensible man's activity . . . The annihilation of all civilization was the goal upon which his heart was set. It amused him to utilize every level of political agitation he could lay hands on for the advancement of this aim.

Wagner's autobiography can't be regarded as totally reliable, but it seems to me his portrait of Bakunin is in many ways more interesting and more flattering than versions of him that only concentrate on his political anarchism. Throughout his life Bakunin felt that Russia was a peculiar source of cultural energy, compared with the West. Many times he paid tribute to Russia's fresh creative energy and originality. Perhaps one day Russia, through art, through revolution, in the same breath, would achieve its own total freedom and home.

There was the almost legendary occasion when Bakunin came up to Wagner after a rehearsal of Beethoven's Ninth Symphony, on Palm Sunday, 1 April 1849, and saluted the enduring power of that music to sustain Humanity. Wagner remembered the moment: '[Bakunin] walked unhesitatingly up to me in the orchestra and said in a loud voice that if all the music that had ever been written were lost in the expected world-wide conflagration, we must pledge ourselves to rescue this symphony, even at the peril of our lives.'[26]

Bakunin, for all his love of Beethoven, could be artistically astonishingly crude, as Wagner found when the subject of his projected opera about the life of Jesus came up. It was of course another revolutionary topic. 'I was inspired by a study of the Gospels to conceive the plan of a tragedy for the ideal stage of the future', Wagner began. Bakunin interrupted on the subject of the libretto:

> amid all the variations he [Bakunin] advised me to use only one set of phrases, namely, for the tenor, 'Off with his head!' and, for the soprano, 'Hang him!' and for the basso continuo, 'Fire! Fire!'. He had another strange instruction: 'You must make Jesus weak!'

On another occasion Bakunin announced he found *Tannhäuser* 'stupendously fine'. Wagner was alternately disconcerted and flattered.

Wagner took the imposing Russian home to eat at the family table, where Bakunin threw back his schnapps in a single gulp and scorned moderation. His wife Minna shrank back. 'These and other similar little characteristics showed that in this remarkable man the purest impulses of an ideal humanity conflicted strangely with a savagery entirely inimical to all civilization.' Wagner didn't say it, because he wouldn't meet Nietzsche for another twenty or so years; but there was something proto-Nietzschean about Bakunin's longing for a transvaluation of all values.

Espousing a world-changing materialism, the revolutionary composer and the sometimes art-minded revolutionary had a great deal in common because of their Idealist beginnings. Beauty *could* change the world, they believed, through drama and poetry, and aesthetic sensitivity could prepare humanity for a finer politics. Beauty *will* change the world through the power of my music-dramas, Wagner declared. Wagner drew inspiration from Shakespeare and Schiller and Beethoven, while Bakunin, cruder, somehow dragged with him a vision of art complementing liberty.[27] Perhaps he was affected by Hegel's view that art, having succeeded religion, was dying as the most prominent manifestation of the World Spirit, and was being replaced by philosophy, or total human self-awareness; but hadn't yet vanished. Whatever the theoretical case, if it is true that it was Bakunin's match that set fire to the Dresden opera house, the very place where he had heard the Beethoven a month before, then in that story we have exactly that strange conjunction of forces Wagner detected in the Russian, at once visionary and 'inimical to all civilization'; and a dramatic picture-book illustration of what speeding up the philosophy of History might mean.

The impact of their meeting and sharing the Dresden events seems to have been extraordinary, as if Bakunin were setting the scene for the cycle *Der Ring des Nibelungen* (The Ring Cycle) on which Wagner had recently started working; and setting the scene, not quite seventy years in advance, for the Russian Revolution to happen also as an event on the artistic stage, as the crowd converged on the Winter Palace once in real time and once again, three years later, for the sake of artistic recollection. On the stage as in the streets of Dresden, and as would one day happen in Petrograd, the old authorities no longer held sway over human life. As they retreated, new heroes stepped forward to lead the people. *The Birth of Tragedy Out of the Spirit of Music* – Nietzsche's 1872 title – would be another way of expressing the surge of utopian, transformative and transfigurative feeling that marked the moment when Wagner read Feuerbach and Nietzsche heard Wagner, and German Romanticism shaded into early modernism and looked forward to Russia 1917. Bakunin pursued and enacted that feeling on the barricades and in the streets.

Wagner eventually rejected Feuerbach's optimistic vision of humanity reborn without the gods, and concluded *The Ring Cycle* in a Christian spirit of self-sacrifice. Yet he retained, some say, at the heart of that great work, the memory of Bakunin as a self-abnegating hero, half-mythical, bearing the Feuerbachian vision, at once forceful and weak, visionary and savage, transformed into the character of Siegfried. On this interpretation Wagner's *Ring Cycle* might itself be seen as a proleptic allegory of the Russian Revolution.

And that would be fitting, because it would remind us of how the spirit of utopianism, 'materialist' on behalf of the real lives of toil of the common people, social democratic and Communist in politics as the century wore on, was still irrevocably shaped by the underlying metaphysics and morals of Idealism, by which I mean worries about what was subjective and what objective, and what was real and full of 'spirit', or could be made so, and what was empty of truth and deceptive. As a result, when it came to the new kind of society that should be built in place of the old, it was only natural to worry about subjective and objective forces in collision and to care about what constituted reality – some of the more abstruse aspects of Soviet culture. It would be totally appropriate to be concerned with what a good man should do, guided by what moral imperative, under a new political arrangement. As for the nature of that good man, mystical themes woven through Bakunin the man and through Wagner's culminating achievement included the kenotic notion of self-emptying and the biblical idea of 'losing life to gain it';[28] and of the Absolute as the Divine, summoning our total love, just as Schelling and Fichte had seen it. The German Idealist sang his way to Absolute Self-delivery in Wagner's twilit farewell to the Romantic *Weltanschauung*, and it would be this goal of glory and this vision of delivery that Russia would transpose into relations between the intellectual and the people, when Elysium became Red Russia. Then at last the estranged, useless Russian intellectual would be reunited with the eternally useful working people. 'In the 1840s Bakunin's attempts to realize millenarian ambitions had dictated political stratagems which, though grossly contradictory if interpreted as ways of ordering the real world, were consistent with the subjective needs of an alienated intellectual.'[29] All the while, beneath the move to secure the triumph of the proletariat for a newly united world culture lay a Romantic ache to recover man's lost unity with God. And to that, one day, tens of thousands, perhaps millions, would sacrifice themselves, and be compelled to sacrifice themselves, in a 'desperate simulation' of paradise.[30]

Was it Bakunin's love of playing with matches, or the actual fire that burned down the opera house, that helped inspire the fiery end to Wagner's *Ring Cycle*? And was that not already a short cut and a defeat? Nietzsche in his future quarrel with Wagner would see it that way, for how to live after the end of religion, after the departure of the gods, required unremitting courage, not a regress to the mystical creative-destructive myth of eternally vexed human being.

Meanwhile, as Siegfried waited to die in Wagner's imagination, and Brünnhilde who loved him immolated herself in fire, Bakunin was arrested for his Dresden doings, while Wagner managed to slip away. The Saxon authorities bowed to Russian pressure and returned Bakunin, the prototype international terrorist, to Russia, where he was thrown into the Peter and Paul Fortress in St Petersburg.

The next eight years almost broke the flesh-and-blood Bakunin as he was forced to confront Russian reality. Russian rebels against the autocrat had experienced it before: what always did and would and still does stand in the way of the dream. Catherine the Great had destroyed the printing press of that admirer of the American Revolution Alexander Radishchev and imprisoned him, while she annotated his complaints against her empire. The Decembrists were either hanged or marched in ball and chain to Siberia. In Soviet times almost a new human category, the alleged Party traitor, would experience the same torments as his tsarist predecessors. Like Bakunin, many incarcerated Russians would find, or be invited to find, a patriotic conscience and pour their hearts out in confession, to gain some relief.

In 1851 Bakunin wrote in his 95-page letter to Tsar Nicholas I, about his recent years of activism, that,

> In Bohemia I wanted a decisive radical revolution which would overthrow everything and turn everything upside down . . . Such a revolution, not limited to one nationality, would by its example and its fiery propaganda, attract not only Moravia, but . . . in general all adjacent German territory. In Russia I wanted a republic, but what kind of republic? Not a parliamentary one!! I believe that in Russia, more than anywhere else, a strong dictatorial power will be indispensable, but one which would concern itself solely with raising the standard of living and education of the peasant masses; a power free in direction and spirit but without parliamentary privileges; free to print books expressing the ideas of the people, hallowed by their Soviets, strengthened by their free activity, and unconstricted by anything or anyone.[31]

Bakunin's anarchist sympathizers in the twentieth century, in the anglophone world, found it acceptable to print that very short, confected selection from the *Confession*. But they omitted the painful tributes to the autocrat that went on for pages, the grovelling admission that the punitive father had always been right.

When, with his mother taking advantage of the death of Nicholas I to petition for her son, Bakunin was offered exile in Siberia in exchange for his cell walls, he took it; and another embarrassment for certain historians, and a late fillip to those with a fondness for a Freudian account of his personality, was the lavish praise Bakunin heaped on the governor there, a distant relative named Nikolai Muravyov, as a Russian hero. Muravyov was a high-ranking tsarist official, but apparently his leadership qualities would change the world. Bakunin deep in his Russian heart craved absolute liberty and an absolute leader and a father in equal measure. Still, once again, he slipped away when he could, out of his second cousin's jurisdiction and back to the European fray.

Politically at his height after the escape from Siberia, reasserting his freedom and still, almost alone among his generation, confident of his goals despite the collapse of the 1848 revolutions, Bakunin left a testament to that moment in the *Revolutionary Catechism* of 1866, of which points two to five read:

> II. Replacing the cult of God by respect and love of humanity, we proclaim human reason as the only criterion of truth; human conscience as the basis of justice, individual and collective freedom as the only source of order in society.
> III. Freedom is the absolute right of every adult man and woman to seek no other sanction for their acts than their own conscience and their own reason, being responsible first to themselves and then to the society which they have voluntarily accepted.
> IV. It is not true that the freedom of one man is limited by that of other men. Man is really free to the extent that his freedom, fully acknowledged and mirrored by the free consent of his fellow men, finds confirmation and expansion in their liberty. Man is truly free only among equally free men; the slavery of even one human being violates humanity and negates the freedom of all.
> V. The freedom of each is therefore realizable only in the equality of all. The realization of freedom through equality, in principle and in fact, is justice.

The vision belonged to Rousseau and Hegel and Feuerbach, while the rough way to get there belonged to Bakunin.

The mid-1860s were also the time of his greatest challenge to Marx, when Marx and Engels conspired to disempower him as a dangerous splitter of the cause. It's not the story of Bakunin's ousting from the First International, however, that interests us, so much as how Bakunin could foresee such a system would not bring Russia liberty. He had taken fresh cognizance of Russian difference in the lamentable prison years.

The story of Bakunin's acquaintance, collaboration and falling out with Marx was for so long a cornerstone of the history of international socialism that one couldn't see the bricks for the wall. The comparison pointed up the patience of Marx, his social democratic qualities, and the 'objectivity' of Marxism, and distanced Marx's vision of Communism from the terrorism that, through his idolizing of Nechaev, became associated with Bakunin's name. Yet what it also pointed up was the sheer alienness of Russia in Marx's Western eyes. For most of his life, to repeat, Marx felt that the Russians were hitching a ride on the very idea of the French Revolution while their country showed no revolutionary potential of its own.[32] Engels shared Marx's distrust of Russia and both thought all Russians were nationalists in disguise. When in the 1860s they spread the rumour that Bakunin was a Russian spy they mischievously gave vent to their deep prejudices.

In 1868 Marx noted that 'they [Russians] always run after the most extreme that the West can offer.'[33] They *were* different because of that long history of autocracy. Marx was also right that Russian extremism had fed on what Bakunin's generation learnt in German universities.[34] Marx was moved in the last decade of his life to alter the essence of his economic theory to fit Russian circumstances. But Russia *was* different.[35]

Late in his career Bakunin translated *The Communist Manifesto*, and began to work in 1872 on a Russian version of *Capital*, having ignored it when Marx sent him an original copy five years earlier. He did this work not because he was a convert but because he was desperate for money.[36] *The Communist Manifesto* was printed anonymously in Russia as 'the foundation of a new social order'; but when *Capital* was submitted for publication it was permitted because the censor judged it of no relevance to the country's own situation.[37]

In the end, just as Marx dismissed Bakunin as precipitate and heedless, so Bakunin predicted misery if Russia, with only a vague ethic of brotherhood and peasant solidarity against the tsar, adopted Marxism. The project would eventuate in a country run by social engineers. He wrote:

> According to Mr. Marx, the people not only should not abolish the State, but, on the contrary, they must strengthen and enlarge it and turn it over to the full disposition of their benefactors, guardians, and teachers – the leaders of the Communist party, meaning Mr. Marx and his friends – who will then liberate them in their own way. They will concentrate all administrative power in their own strong hands, because the ignorant people are in need of a strong guardianship; and they will create a central state bank, which will also control all the commerce, industry, agriculture, and even science. The mass of the people will be divided into two armies, the agricultural and the industrial, under the direct command of the state engineers, who will constitute the new privileged political-scientific class.[38]

With the authoritarianism he detected in Marx at the forefront of his mind, and the completely unacceptable idea of the 'dictatorship of the proletariat', Bakunin declared: 'If you took the most ardent revolutionary, vested in him absolute power, within a year he would be worse than the Tsar himself.'[39]

Bakunin accepted that in Russia attempts to organize revolution were likely to be defeated 'by the moral flabbiness, apathy and love of theorizing with which Russian society has infected its youth'.[40] In its weakness it might, like himself, be entranced by a vision of strong central leadership. It might, as he did, glorify the Russian bandit, and use even the bandit to force political change. Still Bakunin's instinctive antipathy to all authority remained and in this circle of contradiction, out of which only a living hero could expect to emerge triumphant and beyond scrutiny, Bakunin lived his life. He did indeed praise contradiction in those terms. It could be justified if it was alive in one man.[41]

Bakunin would be called a nihilist implicitly by both Turgenev and Dostoevsky, and by generations of historians to the present day, because of his hymning of the destructive urge. In fact he was too deeply affected by institutionalized Russian violence to function as a normal man. But Russia wasn't normal either; both were exceptional, and what Bakunin said about his country and his countrymen could be heard as an apologia also for himself:

> The Russian is better, kinder and has greater breadth of soul than the Westerner but the fallout of oppression contorts him. Fear reigns and fear kills the soul . . . The autocracy does not want the enlightenment and elevation of the Russian people . . . let Russia arise and speak . . . and show the world.[42]

When the political philosopher Hannah Arendt came to understand violent dissatisfaction with the unjust and unfair political system in Germany in the early twentieth century, prior to the Nazi totalitarian onslaught, it made her sympathetic not only to Bakunin but even to Nechaev, his passing terrorist idol:

> From Nietzsche . . . to Jünger, Brecht and Malraux, from Bakunin and Nechayev to Alexander Blok [we must not] overlook how justified disgust can be in a society wholly permeated with the ideological outlook and moral standards of the bourgeoisie . . . the 'front generation', in marked contrast to their own chosen spiritual fathers, were completely absorbed by their desire to see the ruin of this whole world of fake security, fake culture, and fake life. This desire was so great that it outweighed in impact and articulateness all earlier attempts at a 'transformation of values' . . . or a reorganisation of political life . . . or a revival of human authenticity [as] in Bakunin . . . Destruction without mitigation, chaos and ruin as such, assumed the dignity of supreme values.[43]

I suspect that if Arendt herself is hard for many outside the German and Central European traditions to understand, it is because she too was formed in the school of German Idealism, with its perennial concern with 'authenticity' and what Bakunin chased after as 'reality' as opposed to the 'fake security', 'fake culture' and 'fake life' of the ruling class or economic system.

But is it so difficult to grasp? Kant and Schiller and Hegel had struggled by means of intricate distinctions to reconcile total personal freedom with the existence of a higher moral authority to point human action in the right direction. The distinction between 'positive and negative determination' in the human heart depended on a committed voluntarism on the part of the individual. But to what authority could it commit itself? For any German Idealist, from Kant to Arendt, from Tübingen to the Soviet Union, there had to be an absolute moral law to refer to, guaranteeing that the experiential life that followed it could never be fake, or deceived. Idealism replicated the Christian idea of choosing, as a free person, to do God's will in Kantian moral law. It was an essentially positive interpretation of human moral capacity to make the right choice and not fall into emptiness and despair. It called on all the world's good citizens to live up to the ideal.

The risk that positive liberty ran in practice was that a strongman would step in and determine the lives of others according to his vision of what they should live up to, and not theirs, and not an absolute law at all, but arbitrary. And so the wiser half of Europe looked to traditions that worked – not 'higher' laws – as it became politically democratic and socially and morally liberal. But did that negate the beauty of the Idealist – now socialist, soon to be Communist – hope for a society in which everything would be *real*, every individual emancipated and nothing *fake*, fake in the sense of spiritually empty?

Bakunin, who in his better self had held that Kantian-Hegelian hope, died, in Berne, in 1876, never having properly recovered from his seven grim years in the Peter and Paul Fortress. In his last hours he read Schopenhauer, whose pessimism comforted him, he praised Beethoven and he diminished Wagner, as a way of sorting what had mattered to him over a fraught life.

7

A Land of Hamlets and Don Quixotes

We are all, in spirit, not exactly revolutionaries but something in us defines our position as either Hamlets or Don Quixotes. Don Quixotes seek salvation in some external object, while Hamlets look inwards. As Turgenev, Russia's third and quite different great novelist, observed the changing Russian political climate, he saw that the rebel and the believer were both versions of a significant life. 'In other words, for each one of us either his own ego is of cardinal importance or something else ranks higher than ego.' Don Quixote believed 'in a truth that is beyond the comprehension of the individual human being, to be achieved only through the medium of self-abnegation and undeviating worship'. 'His own life he esteems only insofar as it can serve his ideal, which is to institute justice and truth on earth.' Were they to meet, the Quixotes of the world would call the Hamlets selfish. 'To live for oneself, to be concerned with one's own ego – this Don Quixote would regard as a disgrace.' But the Hamlets would see the Quixotes as demented. So, as Russia went forward, could there be only one version of the good man? Turgenev's finest fiction was set at this crossroads.

There were deep personal reasons why this rather Schillerian comparison of opposite personality types appealed to Turgenev. One was to be able to reflect on how he was seen, as a private, apolitical man, by his committed contemporaries. Another, and a consolation, was because in the way he thought about it the division soon broke down. Associating himself with the Hamlets, Turgenev considered himself weak with regard to life's cardinal decisions. In his fiction he created many tardy types, unable to grasp the nettle, who, if they were not exactly Hamlets, were faint Russian answers to that other typology of the age: either Goethes or Schillers, either selfish men or moral heroes. The Goethe types were rounded personalities, with healthy impulses that established their success in the world. The Schillers, 'sentimental' in contrast to the 'naive' Goetheans, were crippled by their personal worries.

In actual life Turgenev was a Hamlet-type, in love, left gnawing at his imperfect happiness. The opera singer Pauline Viardot, the indispensable companion of his soul, was married to another man. As a Hamlet he may even have associated his rival in love with the Quixote, for Louis Viardot had recently translated into French Cervantes's epic work when the three first met. On the other hand, did this Hamlet from Russia not love his Pauline hopelessly and quixotically? For the unattainable Pauline Viardot he was ready to forgo his native country and his personal fulfilment. So yes, Hamlet and Don Quixote were a way of looking at things; but they weren't simple opposites. Their relationship was more dialectical, almost a Hegelian thesis-antithesis, with its possible resolution in action. The short stories, like 'A Hamlet of Shchigrovsky Province' and 'The Diary of a Superfluous Man', wanly courted a positive outcome for the emotional outsider.

Hamlet and Don Quixote as a pair of antithetical concepts helped Turgenev think about what the European mid-nineteenth century expected of moral character. Might the age, at its midpoint, be headed towards a philosophy of ever greater self-interest? Or would some vision of collective well-being prevail? The defeat of the 1848 revolutions seemed to show a politically wide-awake generation pursuing extravagant causes and yet having slim chances of success.

> During my life's wanderings I too have encountered individuals giving up their lives for non-existent Dulcineas or for some crude, other loathsome object that became for them the incarnation of their ideal. I have witnessed this, and when those types have vanished from the world, let the book of history be closed, there will remain in it nothing worth reading.

So Turgenev in 1860 paid tribute to his revolutionary friends: Herzen and Bakunin among them.[1] But at the same time he was sceptical.

The wording of the 1860 essay was a model of what the autocratic regime forced upon the Russian literary press. It was poised between the political, the literary and the personal. Though Turgenev's editor longed for it, the nineteen-page text was constantly interrupted over its more than a decade in the making. But then it was finally published in the first week of 1860, when author and publisher could breathe more freely than under Nicholas I. Since the decease in 1855 of the 'gendarme of Europe', and the patriotic clearing-up after defeat in the Crimean War, the climate under his successor Alexander II was more liberal than it had been for 35 years.

> Don Quixote exists (if one may put it so) outside himself; he lives for others, for his brethren, in the hope of neutralizing evil and to outwit those sinister figures . . . whom he regards as the enemies of mankind . . . He does not probe or question; he believes, forever undismayed . . . Hardly a scholar, he regards knowledge as superfluous . . . He knows one thing . . . [he] may at times resemble a total maniac . . . [but he] is the most moral creature on earth . . . [he] is an enthusiast, radiant with his devotion to an idea.

There is more than a hint of anticipation of Isaiah Berlin's famous 1953 essay 'The Hedgehog and the Fox' in these words, comparing the man who knows one thing with the man who juggles many, many possibilities. What one might call the liberal arc, linking Russia's few liberal writers across two centuries, is outside the range of the present story, but it reminds us of the subtle persistence of a Schiller-inspired impulse, since 1793, to analyse human character as a response to and as a prelude to any actual revolution. When Turgenev wrote about that 'enthusiast, radiant with his devotion to an idea', he seemed already to be naming the future Russian revolutionary. He had met him, in embryo, this quiet hero, among his friends. He knew him to be like Herzen's friend Nikolai Sazonov, derided by Marx and instantly forgotten by history, and like Bakunin who, at the time Turgenev's essay appeared, was still under house arrest in Siberia. There was no Russian revolution in sight in Turgenev's lifetime, but much of Turgenev's major fiction would consist in putting the Quixotic streak in his characters to sad and sympathetic test in available revolutions elsewhere. The eponymous hero of *Rudin* (1856) had already fought and died on the Paris barricades to end the reign of the 'King of the French', Louis Philippe; Insarov had committed himself to the pan-Slav independence struggle in *On The Eve* (1859); and while neither of these Russians was totally engaged in the foreign cause in his heart, it came as his life's work to throw himself into *action; for some cause at least*. The Hamlets, by contrast, were such selfish men. They were just how Turgenev might be seen through activist eyes. He was in evident depression over his itinerant, self-exiled, self-centred life just at the time of this essay, which was not so much a defence as a clarification of human possibility.[2]

Hamlet questioned everything. He was always a disbeliever. He probed his own ego, and disbelieved in it too. Still this ego ultimately was what was precious to him, and held him together. 'This is the ultimate position to which he invariably reverts, because his soul does not espy in the world beyond itself anything to which it can adhere.' 'Forever agitated, in regard not to his duty but to the state of his own inward affairs', Hamlet embodied contemplation. And if there were no causes that made sense, was Hamlet not right to hold back from action? On the other hand, 'the book of history should be closed' if men willing to pursue impossible causes ceased to exist.

So far as the Hamlets were concerned, who never did any-thing useful for society, one way to deal with their incarnation in Russia was to say goodbye to them as the 'Idealist' generation. Yet the question was whether a new generation, more down to earth and more materialistic in its philosophical attitudes, less inclined to look to literature and music for consolation, could produce some better result, whether in terms of individual happiness or for a more efficient modern Russia. Given that the country was presently look-ing like a backwater compared with the West, was practical action needed? Was ideological commitment the thing? How could Russia move forward? All this was beautifully explored by a novelist whose supreme gift was to express the tensions of the age in a minor key.

On the cusp of a new age, the 'Hamlet and Don Quixote' essay considered how intellectuals related to the people. It was the Russian problem of the day, but it was also one that had been prominent in Young Germany, and surely it will always arise; the problem of the relationship of the educated elite to the mass of the population will recur until all of us are educated equally. Marxism would claim very dubiously to solve it, but then it would strikingly resurface in

mid-twentieth-century France, when, in the wake of the Nazi occu-
pation, France seemed as much in need of intellectual leadership
as mid-nineteenth-century Russia had done, after an experience of
tyranny. Post-war French intellectuals struggled over whether mem-
bership of the Communist Party was the right choice. The problem, as
it had been felt in nineteenth-century Russia for most of the century,
and as it was felt in post-war France, which inherited that Russian
tradition through Marx, was that intellectuals were not workers, so
how could they know what working-class life was like, or in Russia
the life of the common people? On the scene of 'Young Germany' too,
neither Heine nor Marx had been able to boast real working-class
roots, which had immediately opened up a line of attack from their
critics, for how was it they could claim they knew what the workers
wanted? Bakunin proclaimed the wisdom of the common people,
but he did so as an aristocrat. Marx claimed to solve the problem
for Marxism, and indeed for Marxist-Leninism, by showing how an
intellectual could acquire a working-class consciousness: put him
amidst the workers, there to learn his part, and ensure that the next
generation of intellectuals had an actual working-class background.
Since Marxists believed consciousness was determined by socio-
economic origin, this was their solution. Turgenev's wrestling with
how to get oneself out there in the world and concerned with the
needs of others was much more in line with Hegel's understanding
of alienation. It was psychological. There was a rounding process, a
matter of self-development from within, that every morally ambitious individual must want to go through; but he might fail, just
because he wasn't made strong enough to grasp the nettle.

The truly Russian way to solve the problem was the one shortly to
be proposed by the communitarian Pyotr Lavrov. It was the idea that
the educated person was guilty as such, since the privileges that made
him or her educated were premised on the deprivation of others. It
was a version of original sin and it found favour in nineteenth-century
Russia, as it has done in our own times. Who knows what it meant
in Britain on the cusp of the twenty-first century, when it was part
of a fleeting reworking of socialism, but in Russia in Lavrov's time it
meant that an ethical educated life had to be devoted to the deprived
common people. Bakunin followed a parallel path to Lavrov, when
he declared that the common people knew better, and that the educated class should bow down to them and learn from them.[3] For that,

Lavrov always defended Bakunin. Turgenev, no political activist, may have disappointed his contemporaries, since he had first found fame as a writer through his sympathetic portraits of Russian peasant life. But they couldn't know that his real service would be to notice the various allegiances between intellectual and people, and provide a way to understand the entire age, as he oriented himself in the ideological climate that culminated in the Lavrovian 1860s.

The age that had arrived in Russia was that of 'Populism', a word that meant, at the time, both a devotion to the well-being of the common people and a desire to improve their lot. It comprised both Enlightenment and anti-Enlightenment elements. In Russian terms it was both Westernizing, wanting to see the people educated, and Slavophile, advocating, as Herzen in his post-1848 disillusion put forward, the appropriateness of the ancient Russian peasant community, the *mir*, over other socialist and Communist models from the West. The Russian common people, it was very strongly felt, had an intellectually unsullied, traditionally inflected grasp of how to live.

For a committed European, alienated by the crudeness, cruelty and extremism seemingly inherent in those 'traditions', this view would always be hard to accept. I'm sure Turgenev, one of whose novels was based on the image of impoverished achievements going up in smoke, didn't hold it.

What is clear, however, is that in the moral half-century or so immediately preceding the Revolution, something like Kant's categorical imperative was merged with a peculiar idea of the educated person's original sin to guide Russian intellectual life into a closer alliance with the people, the *narod*, after centuries of alienation. The original sin of birth into a socially privileged situation had to be expiated through service to the people; and that service became the moral as well as the political meaning of a Russian life well led, to be mapped out by a philosophy that was a relic of Idealism. There had to be a different way of seeing the world, a change of consciousness, and to that Romantic vision should be added a rigorous Kantian morality to make sure the intelligentsia were enlisted.

In Turgenev's view, overlaid over this noble, if self-crippling, idea of service to the other – crippling for a Hamlet, at least – was the Quixotic assumption of 'the people' as that object. The Russian people were the focus of an impossible and quite possibly misguided love. The poet Nikolai Nekrasov, in his 1869 epic poem *Who Can*

Be Happy and Free in Russia?, showed *all* classes corrupted and in difficulty. Turgenev suspected Quixotism in Russia's whole headlong enthusiasm for progress, and this despite his own sympathy for peasant life. He knew Hamlet would not have gone down this path. But then Hamlet was a useless man of the past, only concerned with his own soul, so perhaps a new type of man really could come into being:

> The Hamlets on the whole are really nugatory to the people; they impart nothing, they can lead nowhere, for they themselves are astray . . . Besides the Hamlets loathe the populace . . . Hamlet is an aristocrat – not only by right of birth but also by reason of nature.

More importantly, in an age in which the people stood to be politically mobilized, who among them would follow a Hamlet? A Hamlet-type wouldn't inspire Sancho Panza. Only Quixotes will: 'the [masses] follow blindly and wholeheartedly . . . [with] enthusiasm . . . ignoring personal benefits. This is the universal and historic behaviour of the masses.'

Turgenev was trying to work something out in his long-delayed essay of 1860, and the sweetly poetic novel *Fathers and Sons* (1862) was where he arrived. The story of the boorish, 'hairy' young doctor Evgeny Bazarov is a magnificent contribution to our understanding of the Russia of the day. Bazarov was keen to raise living standards and at the same time to make a political statement that he was definitely *not* a man of refinement, and so the perfect candidate to be taken as a new type. The novel then told the story of his tragic waste, in Russia, or anywhere, simply because he was a more complex man than he took himself to be. It was the story of an active and modern man devoted to work that would benefit the community. He was a doctor, and medicine took up so much of his time and interest that he had no time for love. Bazarov believed in a gloriously rational and 'scientific' future for human nature, with dispassionate, disinterested types like himself at the helm. They would not be ideological leaders but practical helpers armed with scientific knowledge. Disdainful of the humanist values of the old Idealist generation, Bazarov didn't boast any particular concern with specifically Russian popular virtues that might now emerge, and this is why he presented himself, and was seen by those around him, as fitting the fashionable term 'nihilist'. But it wasn't that he believed in nothing, rather that he was anti-spiritual. He believed it wasn't emotional commitment to some essentially religious vision of a better society that humanity needed, but a better understanding of physiology. That way fewer lives might be lost, Russian or any other. That way sickness would diminish. There would be less pain and more pleasure. Bazarov was one attempt on the part of nineteenth-century Russia to say goodbye to Idealism completely. The roots of his views lay in the sad materialistic lull in German philosophy from about 1850, and in British utilitarianism, fed into the Russian progressive argument by Turgenev's and Lavrov's contemporary Nikolai Chernyshevsky. Thinking in terms of another arc, Chernyshevsky was a future favourite of another thinker who would apparently bring science to the rescue of Russia, Vladimir Ilyich Lenin.

Bazarov's materialism was no longer Feuerbach's post-Christian religion of humanity, but a science-based utilitarianism for all. For Bazarov and his kind, indeed, Feuerbach was part of the problem, perpetuating the unscientific society. The new men of the 1850s were not mystical *Naturphilosophen* like Schelling; and they were not preachers in love and the meaning of the bodied existence like Feuerbach. They were experts in physics and chemistry.

Bazarov's faith in science made him a universalist. But – and this was Turgenev's message – natural science couldn't account for the inner life he found he did after all possess, when he fell in love; and that was the story of the novel. It showed how this self-same Bazarov, busy dissecting frogs while his older counterparts were reading Pushkin or playing the cello, fell apart the first time a woman stole his heart. In truth he had no way to understand himself, whatever that self was, because he forbade himself to think in inner, soulful, Hamletian terms. He never recovered from that woman's rejection, and in Hamletian-Quixotic fashion wasted his life, and wasted, in fact, the service he might have rendered to improving lives in provincial Russia.

Marx wasn't mentioned in the novel, but the philosopher, physiologist and eventual politician Ludwig Büchner was. To repeat, the background to Bazarov's contempt for the older, 'Idealist' generation of the fathers, and his reliance on laboratory science in the stead of humanist faith, rehearsed that change in emphasis that had swept the German universities after Hegel; not, as we just observed, in order to follow Feuerbach (as Marx had done) but rather to take inspiration from the Jakob Moleschotts and Karl Vogts and the Büchners of the day.[4] It was not now the phenomenology of the mind that was in the forefront of discovery, nor Feuerbach's religion of brotherly love, but empirical science bolstering a thoroughgoing materialism in denial of the human soul. This positivist German reorientation became, bit by bit, part of the Russian pre-revolutionary century, as Russian social democracy arrived, and materialism and atheism became the latest watchwords.

In a scene in *Fathers and Sons* the young Arkady Kirsanov, Bazarov's friend and would-be disciple, takes a volume of Pushkin out of his father's hands and replaces it with Büchner's *Kraft und Stoff* (Force and Matter). Hot off the German presses in 1859, Büchner's work pulsated with Bazarov's mechanistic view of the universe. Büchner was himself a doctor. In the novel he stood for the view that nature had no intrinsic purpose and humanity's place within it entailed nothing spiritual. Büchner was an anti-Idealist and became a popularizer of Darwin. He instrumentalized evolution to promote atheism; and he seemed to his enemies to be trying to reduce the human to a random survivalism. Turgenev quietly took his stand here, in the Hamlet and Don Quixote essay. He saw evolution as reflecting 'a law basic to all human life', in which the conservation of matter and its transformation into new energy vied for dominance. In human terms this amounted to a tension between conservatism and progress, and between egotism and altruism:

> These two forces of immobility and motion, conservatism and progress are the fundamental levers of all existing matter. They are implicit in the burgeoning of the meanest flower that blows; they are the key that will unlock the secrets of evolution; and that give insight into the process whereby the most virile nations have evolved. But let us not dwell on such conjectures, which in any case are beyond the scope of our theme.

Two years later he created Bazarov as a study of those moral forces in competition within the soul of one man. Marriage was represented as conservative bliss, but also to want to be happy in love was essentially selfish, and only minimally imaginative.

The new materialism of the physiologists didn't have the answer to the mystery of love. The self-assured Bazarov's passion for the enticing Anna Odintsova soon turned him into a hopeless Quixote in pursuit of his Dulcinea. His Bakunist desire to destroy humanistic values was routed by her existence. She made a mockery of his nihilism. The relationship didn't look particularly attractive to outsiders. It wasn't sweet, it was rather perilously erotic, and it involved that strange enough entity for the day, an intellectual woman. In a way that added to the mystery. Meanwhile all this faint Romanticism and defeatism invited a response from the other side. Chernyshevsky offered a counter-model in his *What is to be Done?* (1863) the very next year.

Chernyshevsky showed that a new kind of men and women could get together by organizing their lives rationally and serving the cause; and sex wouldn't be the first thing on their minds. But Turgenev's blueprint preserved the perversity of human nature as compared with the simplified rational partnership that Chernyshevsky offered, and the vast difference in artistic skill between the two writers has ever since commended Turgenev's view of the world to humanist readers.

That Lenin admired both writers suggests something even Bazarovian about that future Russian leader who after all had a passionate extramarital affair.[5] But it's not only because of a quirk of Lenin's that it matters to consider these rival stories in terms of the fundamental quarrel over the value of humanity that will play out when Utopia becomes a Russian system. They already show us the clash between the morally simplified revolutionary personality, the future *homo sovieticus*, and the decadence of unreformed men and women. It's a Soviet world-view in the making, with its codification a mere fifty years or so ahead. It looks forward to the moment when under the banner of the golden hammer and sickle on the red flag Russia versus the West will become a competition on a massive scale between altruism and egoism. In a revolutionary society altruism will be presented as the outcome of science, as Marxist-Leninism gains the upper hand over a defunct individualism. The egoism of the West will be a matter of stalled progress in the direction of socialism; a matter not of revolution but of reaction. On to this entrenched Russian moral outlook will then be grafted a Marxist critique of capitalism, and of the decadence of the bourgeoisie that lives by it.

Pride and an unwillingness to submit to each other, and risk being vulnerable, kept Bazarov and Odintsova apart. By contrast, Bazarov's friend Arkady and Odintsova's sister Katya simply got married and at the end of the novel looked set to live happily ever after. Still their conventionality and ordinariness would never help banish the old and energize the new, and here was where Turgenev sympathized with Bazarov. There was a spiritual force in love – and in Quixotism and in some people – that no materialism and no common sense could account for. How they loved was related to their passionate need for life to have a universal meaning outside and beyond themselves. But then again what if that meaning was only really to be found in mortality? Death is the key to our humanity, for we are not rational machines. Bazarov contracts typhus while treating a patient: unconsciously perhaps, but deliberately he hastens his end; and then he is granted his last wish, to die in Odintsova's presence. We'll never know whether he found the meaning in love and death he hoped for.

Turgenev's reassertion of the spiritual *as* the Quixotic will come on the eve of 1917 to seem both part of the Russian Revolution and a revolution of its own, at once against a purely 'scientific' understanding of social progress and in favour of a science of greater spiritual comprehension, reaching back, in fact, to German Idealism. For the Russian Revolution was not just a Marxist-Leninist moment. It was Russia's great moment of self-definition as a modern cultural force, summing up and forcing to a particular summation the conflicting tendencies that had been under debate for the past century. Some of that debate was rational and some of it poetic, some of it humane and some of it bizarre.

One of the obscured lines of Russian revolutionary inheritance was particularly this legacy of the German experience of 1848 when, because of the coincidence of political radicalism and philosophical materialism, the meaning of love and death and the meaning of the universe ranked as revolutionary questions, intermingled with the needs of the common people. The political vision in Central Europe, adjacent to Russia, in 1848 was open-ended, its problematics, despite the appearance of *The Communist Manifesto*, hardly formed. What seemed still to matter more were 'the experiential extremes of everyday life, the authentic moments of meaning beyond the artificiality of institutions'.[6] Such questions, disinherited by the collapse of religious belief, and by Idealist metaphysics, agitated a generation. Some, like Wagner, and soon the young Nietzsche, wondered whether a metaphysics of tragedy could not be reborn, despite the new materialism, for bodied human beings can still have spiritual ambitions and sacrifice their lives for love. Turgenev as an artist working in this climate was like a Russian Schumann to the German Wagner, *Fathers and Sons* no opera of the future but a piece of delicate pianism exploring the same boundaries of the human.

After the Emancipation of the Serfs in 1861 Russia was only very slowly reaching out towards social and political change. Setting his novel either side of that date, Turgenev showed social relations becoming less formal, love becoming freer, women becoming feminists. On the question of how to bring progress to Russia, which was a socially conservative and only quasi-European backwater, the spread of scientific attitudes and the arrival of new tools and machinery was indeed a tentative answer. Bazarov *was* a better doctor than his father, who was merely an amateur practitioner of homeopathy. So, perhaps science would help Russia modernize. But, to come back to what 'Hamlet and Don Quixote' suggested, if modernization must also entail some kind of ideological commitment, in Russia, what kind of men and women would be capable of it, and at what price? When Sartre a century on asked how Frenchmen could live up to their liberty he came to the same conclusion as Turgenev. It would be about choice; but about choice in the face of absurdity – Quixotism – because no one could go on believing in the higher law and the categorical imperative that solved the problem of commitment for Kant. Only Marxist-Leninism would claim to have a non-sceptical answer to morality in the post-Christian nineteenth century and it would do that by insisting that revolution was a rational and objective goal ordained by the way of History. And so Marxist-Leninism replaced the moral authority of Christianity, while marrying it to a materialist world outlook.

Marx and Engels argued that history favoured progress in a certain direction, because capitalism was bound to collapse; thus commitment to the Communist cause was not a moral gamble, but a matter of rational insight, the fruits of which the intellectuals must pass on to the workers. A whole world in the making would believe that, and new heroes would step forward to honour it.

What originally turned Turgenev away from the philosophy he was studying in Berlin and inclined him to become a superb writer of fiction was probably a two- or three-fold thing. As they went out of fashion the subjectivism of Schelling and the phenomenology of Hegel seemed less gripping, and developments in experimental science reduced the pantheism of *Naturphilosophie* to a private poetic comfort, no longer in contest as knowledge. Feuerbach on love and death, and Wagner's music, were last ventures in late, late, too late, German Romanticism. Turgenev learnt his Hegel from Professor Karl Werder and that also made a difference. Werder was the most prominent Berlin academic of Turgenev's day, and a socially welcoming and popular figure around whom the Russian students in particular rallied. But he was also himself a writer and poet, and while his job was to teach Hegel, he felt that his real task was to encourage the appreciation of what was beautiful in art.[7] His passion for theatre and his studies of *Hamlet*, amongst other plays, may well have inspired Turgenev to make the crucial half-turn from philosophy to literature. It was, according to the journalist Karl Gutsgow, the case that many artistic and creative writers of the latest day had turned to Hegel, because he gave the kind of inspiration that had previously come from Goethe and Schiller, both philosophical writers. And so Russia too developed a strongly philosophical artistic culture, as the nineteenth century, through great figures such as Turgenev and Dostoevsky, continued to assimilate the German heritage through literature, and through cultural-historical modes of thinking rooted in Idealism.

One tendency was to expect moral and political lessons from literature. When Turgenev returned from Berlin in 1842 and in 1845 reviewed the latest Russian translation of Goethe's *Faust* for one of the fat journals, he reported to Russian readers that Goethe was these days typically considered an egoist, and that this had political ramifications. In fact an earlier critic, Wolfgang Menzel, had used the different personalities of classical German literature's two greatest figures to establish the moral preference of Young Germany. Goethe's disdain for the French Revolution became notorious three decades after the event, and Schiller's enthusiasm, however brief, was exalted without further qualification. An age passionate for humanitarian reform in the despotic German principalities of course needed Schiller as a politically and morally engaged figurehead. Menzel's views were translated into Russian and published as early as 1829. In fact neither Turgenev nor Herzen, both of them of aristocratic birth, was convinced. Herzen wrote three separate versions of the Schiller/ Goethe story, in which he struggled to dismiss egoism and finally endorsed it as importantly bound up with ethical individualism.[8] Turgenev, at the same time as he too reminisced over a foreign-learnt, stillborn individualism in Russia, resisted the political morality that was replacing it.

As the two great values of the Idealist generation, Personality and Art, were expressly simplified, and as scientific positivism, itself a popular, anti-authoritarian force, introduced new goals into both domains, so the tendency increased to make propaganda out of literary characters; because, after all, literature had a great readership. The tendency passed both into Marx's own political writing and into Russian literary concerns, so that it would not be difficult one day for the two to converge. A supreme example was the use of the trope 'Robinsons', meaning 'Robinson Crusoes', which passed from Marx to Russia and still appeared in the Soviet press in the late 1970s. It became a way of attacking souls alienated from a socialist society because they were inclined to the capitalism that developed in England in the eighteenth century, or because they were, in fact, ethical individualists.[9] Literature itself became a battleground, between those who believed in complexity of form expressing a subtle humanism, and those who would simplify the novel, above all, to teach basic, ideologically correct, social lessons.

A critical landmark was Chernyshevsky's *On the Aesthetic Relations of Art to Reality* (1855), which effectively proposed replacing Schiller's bourgeois aesthetic idealism with a theory of art suited to the needs of the common people as viewed through the eyes of the committed radical intelligentsia. The opposite of Idealism, it subordinated art to reality and asked how it could be useful to convey information and otherwise out-of-reach experience, like visiting distant parts.

In the characters praised and characters attacked by critics in the Russian 1860s we can almost see the seeds of an eventual people's ideology sprouting. Lev Tolstoy would praise the intangible infectiousness of art; but otherwise he would grow these populist attitudes in his anti-modernist, anti-elitist *What is Art?* (1897) until Western lovers of art for art's sake felt them to be choking weeds. Meanwhile, in the age of Turgenev and Marx, both born in 1818, an ideology became established in Europe after 1848, insisting that the bourgeoisie and its fancy tastes were the ultimate obstacle to progress. Marx found Schiller to be a bourgeois Idealist, great in his time but whose latter-day dramatic influence had degenerated into mere windbaggery. Marx hurled abuse at the latter-day Schiller imitators of this world, full of fine phrases but no action.[10] In the same moment Turgenev wrestled over the world's leftover Goethes. Leaving aside his culpable lack of sympathy for the French Revolution, Goethe was universally identified with the character of Faust, and Faust's individualism was now politically and morally despicable on a progressive view. Still Turgenev demurred from the simplifying, moralizing habit himself. Only around the time of the 1845 *Faust* review, in an early story, 'Andrei Kolosov', did he create 'an almost Soviet type of hero'.[11] Ever after, in exemplary fashion in his 'Hamlet of Shchigrovsky Province', and in the severe late tale 'Enough' and the magnificent 'King Lear of the Steppes', he wrote stories at once sympathetic to obscure lives and grateful for the insights that could be deflected on to them from the most profound creations of great European writers of the past. Turgenev suggested unnamed individual lives were still truer than the heroes and villains, and positive and negative lessons for the future, of simplified contemporary Russian debate.

The step that Marx made, attacking the present-day bourgeoisie as too concerned with its own well-being to engage in a radical politics that would help the working class, Bakunin had also taken in his capacity as a European revolutionary.[12] But as a Russian he too knew the home situation was different. 'Russian social life is a chain of mutual oppressions; the higher oppresses the lower, the latter suffers, does not dare complain, but he in turn squeezes the one who is still lower . . .'[13] A revolutionary loathing of the bourgeoisie never rang true in pre-revolutionary Russia, at least not until a distinct monied middle class emerged in the last decades, and perhaps even then only to the extent that this class was associated with the morally decadent West. In Russia it was the autocracy that stood in the way of a liberated, egalitarian and fraternal society, and no personality but the Quixotic was likely to try to tackle it.

Turgenev was neither anti-bourgeois nor anti-aristocrat. His obvious affiliation was with a kind of Russian upper middle class, with some land and a few serfs rapidly becoming servants and personal friends. But because the autocracy had so distorted and maimed Russia, as Bakunin put it, Turgenev as an enlightened soul existed in

a social vacuum. His condition was the equivalent of Hegelian alienation. His kind, who by their very experience of the West wanted
reform in Russia, still only read of improvement in books, and the
more they read the more their lives seemed cut off from immovable
Russia, while they did not belong to the burgeoning West either. The
possibility of a Russian leading a fulfilled life – 'Who Can Be Happy
and Free in Russia?', to repeat Nekrasov's title – was confined to the
sphere of personal relations. In fact, as we noted before, the publication in 1852 of Turgenev's *Sportsman's Sketches*, evoking peasant life
with such sympathy, actually had contributed to the passing of the
1861 Emancipation Act. But what did that mean for him? As with so
many writers, it was his own creativity, his own powers of observa-
tion, that allowed him to transcend the norm, not some intentional
act of commitment.

Turgenev didn't hate anyone on behalf of his failed protagonists.
He didn't have Marx's contempt for the bourgeoisie because he
didn't know a bourgeoisie in Russia, and he counted as a bourgeois
in Europe. Equally he lacked Bakunin's hatred of all authority. What
he did believe in, encouraged by a reading of Schopenhauer, was
Art, in the broad European sense of the word. Human experience
could never be perfect. Only Art could gesture at perfection. He was
a lingering Idealist, who conjured delicately with Art and ideas, and
an Art-worshipping pessimist. After he moved definitely to Western
Europe in 1854 his faith in Russian life dwindled ever more.

Turgenev was a White Russian before his time; an exile from a
future revolutionary state. He lived in a between-world of writing
and music and the unattainable beloved; in a mixture of languages
(French, German, Russian, English), cosmopolitan and perilously
peripatetic. With his art linking him back to Goethe and forward
to Henry James, he was a Robinson Crusoe of the mind who wrote
about other Russians who failed to find a place in Russian society,
and who often felt that German Idealism had misled them about their
own and their country's prospects. He was a man prepared, inwardly,
to live on his own island, alone.[14]

8

The Chattering Classes and the Moment of Grace

Back in 1842 the novelist Nikolai Gogol had pictured a moment of fabulous national synergy, when the troika rose into the sky. This country could transcend its weaknesses and become great, the end of his novel *Dead Souls* suggested. A generation later Dostoevsky captured the same energy as a twitching and twinkling and sparking among chatterers. Multiple minuscule live elements in the ideological cosmos flickered with potential answers to the Russian future.

Take any of Dostoevsky's three last novels. Each was a fictional omnibus showing something was 'going about' in this nation fringing Europe. Not yet the Communist spectre, but it was certainly powered by philosophy. And yet always the picture was ironic: ironic about intellectual fashion-following and the capabilites of the human heart.

In *The Devils* (1871) the minor character Shigalyov was invited to a provincial birthday party. He and other would-be local activists were happy to raise a glass, and soon discussion fell on what was to be done. Important-seeming men from the capital arrived, although, if their presence promised new input and guidance, that hope was soon dashed. The conversation remained vague, repetitive and comic. The virile Rogozhin kept his concerns to himself, while Stavrogin, a complex, intelligent man, also barely spoke, and the kindly, self-sacrificing Kirillov was silent. The only event was when the would-be believer Shatov found himself once more confronted by the manipulative and violent Peter Verkhovensky, Dostoevsky's Bakuninesque Peter Supreme. Furious, the seeker after God denounced the scoundrel and got up and left. The other partygoers were mostly concerned with getting their own point of view across.

If ideology was about instrumentalizing simple ideas to arouse mass action, Peter Verkhovensky showed how the potential sources might be coordinated. He challenged the local crowd to take themselves seriously as social activists. Did they intend to form a cell? How did they know that someone in their midst was not an informer? Above all, whatever their disparate beliefs, how exactly would they step over from theory into practice? With at its centre a pointless thuggish murder the whole novel witnessed how vividly Dostoevsky discerned the emerging patterns of conspiracy and obedience, amorality and cruelty, in Russia's pursuit of Utopia.

What was the problem to be overcome? A character with long ears and an air of desperation placed a notebook on the table. One 'solution' to mass society, he said, would not be revolution but to administer a paradise on earth. Deprive 90 per cent of the people of their freedom and let the remaining elite run the country. Or make it simple and cull the mass numerically. Shigalyov, 'a superb caricature of the doctrinaire',[1] laid out his plan and waited. But no one rebutted him. No one really said anything. Except after a while a lame teacher mused: 'A mysterious index finger points to our great country as the country most suitable for accomplishing the great task.'[2] But Dostoevsky explicitly made this speaker *lame*. Meanwhile the metropolitan intellectuals hastened off to another meeting in another place.

Shigalyov declared himself to have arrived at unlimited despotism as the answer to unlimited freedom. The pending freedom of Russia's masses hardly boded well. For Dostoevsky the shadow of despotism hung over Russia, like vice over Christendom, the curse of birth into an imperfect world. What form would or could democracy take in Russia? Shigalyov's mental journey was one possible, prophetic, version of a totalitarianism that would link Kant's moral law to absolute *un*freedom. As all the mystery, the hope, and the latent terror of Russia's later nineteenth century unfolded, absolute *un*freedom was one possible version of the utopian arc carrying forward German Idealism to the Russian Revolution.

It is clear Kant never meant his absolute moral law to be fused with the autocratic state or the power of an autocratic Church. In his post-Rousseauan world the citizens were free, and how to use and retain their democratic freedom in post-feudal society was a noble and inspiriting question for a modern humanity. But the danger was that this new idea of freedom, wrenched from divine gift and given by man to man alone, would just as quickly be taken away from him by an all-powerful state; or become fused with absolute truth on earth, which might amount to the same. Call that freedom? Men would live like ants in an anthill.

The question, just a firework in Dostoevsky's tinderbox mind, of what linked the Kantian moral life with totalitarian politics, would become vastly important to twentieth-century Western philosophy after 1945, when Continental philosophers began to look back on how Nazism and Stalinism happened.[3]

Sixty years earlier Shigalyov had simply not known what to do with his theory. Looking for a guiding idea for the Russian future, he had to ask himself, did he believe in 'man', like the would-be Kantian Kirillov? Surely not. But also not in God. Gloomy by temperament, he had simply got hold of a theory that appealed. Like the spiritual strugglers Kirillov and Shatov, Shigalyov belonged to

> those idealistic Russians, who, struck by some compelling idea, immediately become entirely obsessed by it for ever. They are quite incapable of mastering it, but believe in it passionately, and so their whole life passes afterwards, as it were, in the last agonies under the weight of a heavy stone which has fallen upon them and half crushed them.[4]

As for Dostoevsky himself, he rejected absolute worldly authority, as Ivan Karamazov's toying with 'The Grand Inquisitor' showed. If there was freedom, that famous episode suggested, it could only be freedom in Christ. But who could say what that meant in political and practical terms?

If the solution was not Christ, perhaps it was beauty. The idea that beauty would save the world so possessed Dostoevsky that together *The Idiot* (1869) and *The Brothers Karamazov* (1880) devoted two thousand pages to that escatological search. It's true that many of those pages were 'ironic'. Still they throbbed with nervous excitement. A beautiful personality – Jesus Christ, or Schiller himself, or a Schillerian hero (recalling how Bakunin too constantly saw others, and himself, in those terms) – would transform the nineteenth century. One form that Schiller's aesthetic idealism took was to imagine 'the beautiful soul': *krasnodushie*, the condition of having such a soul, was a trope vividly alive in nineteenth-century Russian literature. The dual version in Dostoevsky of how beauty might bring about revolution was especially interesting because it spanned two potential solutions from the two poles of his spiritual life: one from secular German Idealism and one from Russian Orthodoxy.

Nineteenth-century Russia saw Schiller as the inventor of characters who offered potent moral-political allegories to the contemporary world. Karl Moor in *The Robbers* was a beautiful soul corrupted by despotism and deceit. *Wilhelm Tell*'s eponymous hero was a leader of the people. He was himself a moral lever. Even more than as a philosophical Idealist, as which as a writer and thinker he was known to a tiny intellectual minority, Schiller himself radiated an idea of human purity. A generation before Dostoevsky Madame de Staël and Thomas Carlyle both felt it, that Schiller's innocence was a new kind of holiness. That moral vision in turn seized Dostoevsky, who created in the monk Alyosha Karamazov yet another attempt to embody spiritual truth in Russia.[5] Beauty was always a bold vision and always unstable; for who, even Plato, could quite say what it was, instantiated in a personality or a work of art? Alyosha Karamazov, a creation of German *Geist* who was also an Orthodox priest, had a particular kind of foolishness about him.

'Didn't you say once that beauty might save the world?' asked Ippolit Tarantyev of the comparably 'idiotic' Prince Myshkin.[6] Just as in *The Devils* with Shigalyov's theory of absolute despotism, Dostoevsky again had a minor character bring an important idea to the reader's attention. *Mir spasyot krasota?* Mr 'Tarantula' asked, at once formulaically and far too casually. No answer. But then the Prince recalled how once when his soul ached with the beauty of the world, still he felt he couldn't be part of it. To help the reader understand that 'ironic' feeling of alienation, just as the Prince finishes speaking Dostoevsky has appear one of the two beautiful women the Prince loves. Her name means 'light'. But Aglaya is a worldly beauty destined for ruin. Nor does the fiery and flawed Nastasya Fillipovna promise redemption on earth. And so, until and unless beauty can be incarnated in a different kind of character, irony triumphs in the perfection-seeking Prince Myshkin. As the reader is about to witness, irony also prevails in the young student Tarantyev who shoots himself but then the gun doesn't go off.

Irony is alienation; it is lack of community, and it is lack of spiritual authenticity. Its symbol is the ugliness of the tarantula that the young Ippolit sees in a nightmare. Irony is *nasekomost*, best known to us from the buzzing of the fly around the murderer Raskolnikov. Can the moral claims of Idealism really hold? Irony is also the problem of human mortality. It puts a brake on human dreams.

Its fictional debacle notwithstanding, beauty was still Dostoevsky's purest contribution to the revolutionary cause, when he was engaged in the *thinking on*, as opposed to the picturing of, the power of beauty.[7] His 1861 essay 'Mr —bov and the Question of Art' was his direct answer to the socialism and utilitarianism that had overtaken the nineteenth century, and it was what took him back over and over to Schiller's 'all that was lofty and beautiful'.

It is worth picturing the moment in well-known painterly terms to understand Dostoevsky's position in pre-revolutionary Russia. In paintings by the German Romantic artist Caspar David Friedrich (1774–1840), single tiny figures were dwarfed by a sublime cosmos, but each was thinking nobly of the nature of man. Dostoevsky's fantastic beauteous crusade, whenever it could wrench itself free from irony, was like a multiplication and transplantation of Friedrich's tiny figures to a busy, urbanizing Russia. Contrast this vision with the realism of the Russian painter Isaac Levitan (1860–1900), in which a pallid, passive Russian nature was littered with broken wheels and rotten fences and roads leading nowhere. The Romantic German vision still most beautifully answered those inseparable questions: How can we change the world? How can we be better people? But it was still not clear how it could make something happen in Russian reality.

Perhaps it could only ever figure as an appealing but ultimately alien philosophical vision appearing to the denizens of a quite different world. If for Schiller and Kant morality and art were special kinds of knowledge in which a new secular spirituality showed up; and if for Hegel spirit itself was unfolding in the name of all human progress; now Dostoevsky said, yes, it *is* a better kind of philosophy for us than English utilitarianism, or the latest German materialism, but still we have to adapt it to our own ends. It was a kind of Hegelian triad starting in the mid-century he had in mind. German Idealism would show up the shallowness of the new materialism now spread abroad in Russia; and out of that conflict would come a third way, a

Russian path, to inspire the seething and doubting modern Russian Christian.

Dostoevsky was, for all but a few years of his life, passionately anti-socialist, because socialism took a materialist view of the universe. Further it trivialized and instrumentalized art; and finally it reduced the communal social vision to the anthill, precisely because it disregarded the freedom of the spirit. Idealism became new again in Dostoevsky's hands. Where, historically, it had preceded materialism and socialism, and had seemed to have been swept away, Dostoevsky restored it to relevance.

In 'Mr —bov and the Question of Art', he spelled out why he preferred a metaphysical view of life. It was because Idealism did justice to the kinds of ideas, and ideals, that really made people act in 'some cause' and allowed them to act freely. 'Art can be of help to some cause by rendering assistance to it, for it comprises enormous means and great powers,' but not directly and propagandistically, he wrote. To view art as a tool, campaigning directly for social justice, was simple-minded. Not only was the ideological approach ineffectual, it was also coercive. It left readers and viewers with no freedom of response; whereas under the influence of great art men made up their own minds. Once again the threat of a new absolutism loomed, from the secular left, against which the free mind and the roving soul had to defend themselves. With Russia's progress in mind, but rejecting the simple idea of mass propaganda which had become fashionable with the first generation of Russian social democratic thinkers, Dostoevsky, like his favourite Germans, preferred art to direct political action.

He held a metaphysical theory of art, which believed Art could speak to the Human Soul:

> Who knows, perhaps a kind of internal change takes place in man at the impact of such beauty, at such a nervous shock, a kind of movement of particles or galvanic current that in one moment transforms what has been before into something different, a piece of ordinary iron into a magnet?

Someone may engage in significant social or political action because he once experienced a beautiful work of art. 'Who knows whether it was [his impression of the Apollo Belvedere] made him act one way and not another, unconsciously?'[8] Dostoevsky, writing in 1861, Russia's most liberal year on record, the year of the Liberation of the Serfs, was reawakening classical aesthetics to serve a new utopian praxis. But instead of politics he had in mind an alchemy of the soul and a process redolent of the transubstantiation of the body of Christ.

He marvelled at the power of artistic beauty to guide human life:

> We believe that art has an independent, inseparable, organic life of its own and hence also fundamental and unalterable laws for this life. Art is as much a necessity for man as eating and drinking. The need for beauty and creation embodying it is inseparable from man and without it man would per-haps have refused to live in the world ... man accepts beauty *without any conditions.*[9]

A world balanced in favour of ugliness would be an outrage. If beauty didn't prevail then we should refuse to live in the world. (Later this argument would be fused with the proposition that if no God pro-tects the innocence of children then we should 'return the ticket'.)

In fact we crave beauty because we are increasingly uneasy about alienated modern life:

> And why does [beauty] become an object of worship? Because the need for beauty is felt more strongly when men are at variance with reality, in a state of disharmony, in conflict, that is to say, when they are most of all alive, when they are searching for something and trying to attain it; it is then that they are overcome by a most natural desire for everything that is harmonious and for tranquillity, since in beauty there is harmony and tranquillity.

Beauty in art evokes such a powerful response that it heightens our desire, 'in a time full of aspirations, struggle, vacillations, and faith ... a time of highly active life' to be reconciled with the world. 'Beauty is harmony ... it is the embodiment of a man's and of mankind's ideals.'[10]

Hegel thought beauty had been dying out for the past century or so and that Reason was the predominant feature of modern cul-ture. But Dostoevsky clung to beauty as the specifically Russian principle. 'It does seem to us that this universally human response is even stronger in the Russian people than in all other nations.'[11] In short, 'the faculty that is indelibly part of human nature, creative ability, the foundation of all art', will lead Russia on. It will determine 'clearly and incontestably' what to do.[12]

Yet we remember that Dostoevsky had a view of his country's sacred potential ill-matched by its present condition. Good energies existed, but grotesque half-forms were born of them. Good men were never quite good, or quite stable, which amounted to the same thing. The way Dostoevsky doubled his characters and overlapped and debased their beliefs and showed up their gestures as inauthentic undermined the hope of pure Kantian motives existing on Russian soil, and would have totally destroyed them, had he not, himself, in meta-comments on his own work, tried to retrieve the situation. In *The Diary of a Writer*, through the 1870s, Dostoevsky struggled to square his apparently negative view of the Russian people with hope for the future. In the end he singled out the *narod*, the simplest folk. Replying to a critic who had accused him of absurd inconsistency in his visionary pronouncements, he wrote:

> In fact, I said just the opposite: 'there are true saints among the *narod*, and what saints they are: they give off light and illuminate the way for us all.' They do exist, my respected commentator friend, they truly do exist, and blessed is he who is able to discern them. I think that here, that is to say in these particular words, there isn't the least bit of ambiguity. Besides, ambiguity does not always come from the fact that the writer is unclear but sometimes from quite opposite reasons . . .[13]

The omission marks rounding off this piece of verbal sleight of hand were Dostoevsky's own. Although 'the same *narod* in which Dostoevsky saw . . . Christianity . . . also taught him the outer limits of willfulness and debauchery in the hearts of human beings,'[14] he thought Russia was special. He did not know where that *Sonderweg* (special path) would lead, but it would have some recognizable religious and moral content.

If, meanwhile, *The Devils* was a true history of the revolutionary movement,[15] as Dostoevsky had asserted to the Tsar himself, the potential disappointment of the utopian vision was too painful to sort out. On Russia's behalf, Dostoevsky really wanted to find the true inclination in himself; he *wanted* to be committed to Beauty, Truth and Goodness. But the evidence to convince him was not there. Ideals existed galore, but reality traduced them evilly. There was a terrible example in a contemporary newspaper, which he picked up in his *Diary of a Writer* (and had separately recounted by Ivan Karamazov), of a peasant brought to trial for whipping his wife. As Dostoevsky embellished the account with his own speculations, he painted a picture of spectacular brutality and depravity.[16] Something in this Russian peasant soul violated every idealization of the feminine in Western culture, and since Dante the feminine had led the Western mind to higher things. Set against Goethe's exaltation of the Eternal Feminine, the way of the Russian peasant was a lowly insult and a degradation of the human. And yet there was a truth in this Russian soul, Dostoevsky insisted.

Dostoevsky had to 'ironize' the Russian situation, in fact, and not only because Russia did not match his Western reading, but also because he recognized deviant traits in himself. They ran as a leitmotiv through his fiction, that above all he himself was possessed by a vileness that spoilt everything; as if he himself were the insect. It was the viciousness of his 'Underground Man', the nameless protagonist of the infamous 1864 novella, and of Dostoevsky himself, which cast the world in such a nasty light. What was to be done about that?

Dostoevsky's embellishments to his telling of the peasant beating, which results in the wife hanging herself, were particularly sadistic. He imagined the loose floorboard in which the woman's legs are wedged and the violent sexual gratification that comes the way of her strap-wielding husband as he inflicts ever more pain. 'The wildness pleases him. The animal cries of his victim intoxicate him like liquor . . .' Can we really take this as an illustration of the stupidity but also the unselfconscious holiness of the Russian peasant soul? Dostoevsky wasn't fit to dream the nation's moral dream and he knew it.

A Western critic writing at the height of the Cold War judged that

> The nightmare of disfiguration is all but triumphant in Dostoevsky's journalistic sketch [of the punished wife]; in his novels however, the form of beauty, the moral and spiritual attributes of the Russian Gretchen, constitute an antithetical dream, a dream of purified spirituality.[17]

But can we really accept that reading on behalf of a Russia waiting to be transformed? Dostoevsky's totally 'ironized' view of Russian potential meant that beautiful Western dreams, dreams on paper that were slowly transforming Western society, were constantly and miserably traduced by a monstrous insect living in St Petersburg.[18] Dramatic scenes, such as Fyodor Karamazov's rape of 'Stinking Liza', a Holy Fool, in *The Brothers Karamazov*, pointed up the baseness of humanity. Schiller, Dostoevsky's ultimate source for the imagery surrounding his *rejection* of humanist faith, lingered on in that moment in the 'Ode to Joy' when the German Idealist imagined even the worm redeemed. But Dostoevsky, translating Schiller's worm into an insect, following the poet Fyodor Tyutchev, couldn't accept this possibility. Humanity was often base, and he, the great writer, was also guilty.

Dostoevsky's personal story has been told many times. He had a depressive and suspicious character. Aged seventeen, he had noted how in his troubled mind everything serious crumbled into 'satire':

> I don't know whether my melancholy idea will ever subside
> ... It seems to me that the world has taken on a negative
> meaning, and from elevated, refined spirituality there has
> emerged satire.

His sense of himself as the outsider undermined the very existence of a coherent social whole that he might otherwise long for:

> If a person who shares neither an effect nor an idea with
> the whole, in a word, if a total outsider should wind up in
> this picture what will happen? The picture is spoiled and
> cannot exist![19]

He had this nervous tendency to see the world as nasty and debased. The letters of 1846–9 catalogue his nervous desperation and culminate in 'I have a vile, repulsive character.'[20] Meanwhile in that year 1849 reactionary Russia incarnate dealt him a blow from which he never recovered.

He was flirting with revolutionary terrorism, aged 28, when he was arrested. First the mock-execution after eight months in prison, and then four years' Siberian detention in the company of violent criminals and scoundrels punished him so severely his spirit died, and then it was reborn, as eventually he had the chance to write to his brother:

> What happened to my soul, my beliefs, my mind and heart in those four years I can't tell you. It would take too long to tell . . . One thing: don't forget me and help me. I need money and books.[21]

He requested 'the Church fathers and the history of the Church', Kant's *Critique of Pure Reason* and '*Hegel*, especially Hegel's *History of Philosophy*'.[22]

Meanwhile the confession of what he suffered and how it changed him, how it was still affecting him in military service in remote Siberia, came slowly:

> There's only one thing to fear, people and tyranny. You can wind up with a commander who takes a dislike to you (there are such people), who'll pick on you and wear you down or kill you with duties, and I'm so weak that of course I'm incapable of bearing the whole burden of soldiering. 'All the people there [in Semipalatinsk] are simple folk,' I'm told encouragingly. But I fear a simple person more than a complicated one. People are people everywhere, however. Even in prison among brigands I, in four years, finally distinguished people. Believe it or not, there are profound, strong, marvellous personalities there, and how delightful it was to find gold under a coarse crust. And not one, not two but several. You couldn't help respecting some of them, and others were absolutely marvellous . . . What a wonderful people. All in all the time hasn't been lost for me. If I have come to know not Russia, but then the Russian people well and as well as perhaps few people know them. But that's my petty vanity! I hope it's forgivable.[23]

Four months later, in July 1854, he was inward-looking, as of old, but hinting that he had been transformed by a new faith, or fatalism:

And as for my soul, heart and mind – what has grown up, what has matured, what has withered, what has been cast out along with the weeds – you can't convey that or tell it on a scrap of paper. I live here in solitude; I hide from people. Moreover, I was under guard for five years, so it's the greatest pleasure for me to find myself alone sometimes. All in all prison took a lot out of me and implanted a lot in me. I've already written to you about my illness, for instance, strange attacks that resemble epilepsy . . . please do me the favour, however, of not suspecting that I am the same melancholic . . . as I was in Petersburg in those last years. Everything has absolutely gone away, vanished, as if by magic. Everything comes from God and is in His hands, however.[24]

Another eighteen months later his knowledge of the *narod*, and his sense of religious predestiny, had caused him to open his arms to the pan-Slav movement, he told the poet Apollon Maykov:

I have always been truly Russian, I'm telling you frankly. What is there new in that [Slavophile] movement that has taken shape around you and of which you write as though about some sort of new direction? . . . I share with you completely the patriotic feeling of the *moral* liberation of the Slavs. That is the role of Russia, noble, great Russia, our holy mother . . . You write that society seems to have awakened from apathy . . . but whoever concluded that it lacks energy? Explain an idea well and appeal to society and society will understand you . . .[25]

Apologizing for his own socialist years, when 'sober-minded people, who set the tone for everything, viewed French ideas from a learned angle,' Dostoevsky reinvented his idea of Russia's exceptionality. 'Indeed I share with you the idea that Europe and its mission *will be completed by Russia*.'

I assure you that I have everything Russian so much in my blood that not even convicts frightened me – they were the Russian people, my brothers in misfortune . . . I could understand [the soul of a bandit] because I was a Russian myself. My misfortune allowed me to learn a great deal in practice . . . I found out in practice as well that I had always been a Russian in my heart.[26]

As this national and religious feeling filled him with new hope, above all for a return to a European Russia where he could resume his writing career, he reflected that 'the mercy of our Angel-Tsar is boundless.'[27]

It's difficult to discern how much Dostoevsky's inner life was a microcosmic instance of the horrible political macrocosm that was tsarist Russia, and how much was mental self-flagellation out of deep disturbance. Two years after his release from prison he lucidly analysed the course of the last nine years that had changed his life:

> Before [his arrest and trial] . . . I had been ill for two years in a row with a strange, psychological illness. I fell into hypochondria. There was even a time when I would lose my reason. I was too irritable with the susceptibility developed by the illness, with the capability of distorting the most ordinary facts and giving them another form and dimension.[28]

He should have 'confessed' this illness at his trial. On the other hand, 'although this illness had a strong inimical influence on my fate, it would be a poor justification and a debasing one':

> Imprisonment began for me – four years of a grievous, horrible time. I lived with thieves, with people lacking human feelings, with perverted principles . . . But I swear to you there was no suffering greater than when I realized my errors, realized that I was cut off from society, an exile, and could not be useful to the extent of my energy, desire and capabilities. I know that I was condemned justly, but I was condemned for dreams, for theories. Ideas and even convictions change, a whole person changes too, and how painful it is now to suffer for what no longer exists . . . to be doing at least something for the redemption of the past uselessness and – to languish in inactivity.
>   . . . The Monarch is kind, merciful.[29]

Needs must, he accepted the Christian benevolence of the ruler. This, the marriage of autocracy and Orthodoxy, was the basis of

Russian exceptionality. Bowing before it, he could redeem his past uselessness and get back to Petersburg.

A key trope in the letter to Apollon Maykov was the moral crime of uselessness on the part of the Russian intellectual. He had to fear it and had to be punished for it. 'I realized my errors . . . I knew that I was condemned justly.' This letter would have read well at a 1930s show trial, in the worst years of Stalin.

Both before and after the 1849 landmark, moreover, whenever Dostoevsky suffered he felt that suffering allowed him to pay his dues to 'Holy Art' and furthered his self-overcoming. Self-purification was at stake, and the mission of Christianity in art. God, Tsar, People and Art: it was a formula for a transformed, creative self and a transformed future.[30]

Behind it lay seemingly incontrovertible facts endorsed by experience. No Russian could be effective as an outsider. European socialist ideas were too theoretical for Russian reality. Meanwhile self-overcoming through writing was always going to be difficult for a man of his unstable temperament, and even to resort to art he had to be allowed to leave military service and Siberia.

And yet one might ask, somewhat differently: did the perversity of his soul reflect an ongoing political situation neither he nor his nation could escape, and into which ever new generations were inducted by cruel institutions? Was Dostoevsky not thrown up by Russian reality as its most accurate reflection *ever*? To the extent that he felt that congruence, he interwove his two great transformation projects. But even then he doubted his capacity to contribute to the national cause. Unlike Maykov he could never conjure with 'an unprecedented tribe of giants' to define the nation and defeat its enemies.[31] Instead he had an art into which he poured his characteristic mixture of hope and indecision, utopianism and irony, beauty and cruelty.

From the would-be writers Devushkin and Ordynov of the early fiction to the priest Alyosha Karamazov, Dostoevsky's alter egos were either feminized and unreal, or consumed with passive aggression. They struggled with passivity and timidity. Furthermore, in his fictionalized Russia, as sexuality came to function as an index of Utopia, either the act was never consummated or brutality took over. With extreme impotence and extreme aggression equally useless to any cause, the 'Underground Man' was, in fact, unwanted. Indeed, he seems today more like a prototype for a fascist conspirator – an Andreas Baader or an Anders Breivik – than a revolutionary socialist.

Dostoevsky struggled with the very idea of a good action, let alone his part in actually bringing about social revolution. While like Nietzsche he responded to images of upheaval that swept the crowd along in fear and unknowing – he took note of the fire in St Petersburg in 1862 and those set by the Paris Commune eight years later[32] – the would-be transformational moments in his fiction came down to epilepsy and hallucination and murder. These testaments to his 'ideological eschatology' were not moral choices.[33] He was fixated on punishment and rebirth, as if in cowering need for a power greater than himself to intervene.

Like Nietzsche, Dostoevsky yearned for the transvaluation of all values from deep within his own sickness. But this had nothing to do with a political process. Nietzsche was also not motivated by guilt, nor was he tempted to believe in a personal God. Against the cruelty and violence in *his* imagination, however, Dostoevsky longed for redemption and, after the torment, grace.

So one might say that while he struggled in vain to imagine himself as a good revolutionary, it's clear he had no faith in Russia's intelligentsia to achieve that revolution. These 'superfluous souls' were so well known for their alienation from the *narod* that it became a fashion with those even stupider, who imitated the intelligentsia's alienation, and desire to overcome it, to wear peasant clothes in solidarity:

> I heard recently that a certain present-day landowner, in order to blend with the people, has begun to wear truly Russian dress and to go to peasant commune meetings in it; as soon as the peasants see him they say to each other, 'What is that masquerader doing here?'[34]

On the other hand, just because they were unconvincing, should educated, even half-educated Russians live as recluses? 'There are no half-ways – either live with everybody or be an absolute recluse.'

As he struggled, the options narrowed. Eventually the craving for redemption drove Dostoevsky into the extreme reactionary camp. It was 'Those simple Russians whose name is fifty million', who resisted Western manners, that attracted him. The *narod* had sustained a simple Christian faith through the ages, and even in their deviousness and brutality they were capable of compassion.[35] They were stupid, but the venal petty bourgeoisie and the corrupt intelligentsia were not better. This was the faith that came to him in prison and filled the *Writer's Diary* of his final decade.

So finally, in the simplicity of Orthodox faith, kept alive through the ages of autocracy, this great Russian writer found a Russian answer to a German demand to retain spirituality in modern life. So finally Dostoevsky, a Russian, found a programme that compared to the young German Idealists with their First Systematic Programme in Tübingen. It felt in both cases like an answer to the secular iconoclasm of the French Revolution. Dressed up as a national spiritual revolution, the Russian reaction against 1789 was wholly bound up with pan-Slavdom. It belonged to an imperial politics, and was supported by a wholly instrumentalized Christianity. Dostoevsky was involved in the project of a great modern Russia: in the emergence of Russia as superior imperial power.

Something in this newly emergent version of Russia's worldly power did disturb him. He wrote in a letter after his Omsk prison experience, and later gave the same view to Ivan Karamazov, that he preferred faith in a non-instrumentalized, entirely compassionate Christ to any truth on earth.[36] It was, therefore, a kind of Russian inwardness he was cultivating, to safeguard the Russian soul from political authority. For worldly 'order' was always a Russian spiritual worry, bound up with political manifestations and uses of 'reason' in Europe that seemed repellent. Reason, as order, had already, by Dostoevsky's day, made its impression on the nineteenth-century Russian mind as a prison.[37] Dostoevsky himself rejected bourgeois orderliness as 'colossal internal and spiritual regimentation'. Meanwhile he sympathized with the Frenchman who felt a similar aversion to the 'community' foisted upon him in the name of socialism. In short Dostoevsky was an anti-utilitarian irrationalist in his efforts to define the otherness of Russia.[38] His Russian inwardness was different from the German inwardness of the Idealists and the Romantics, perhaps precisely because of this fear of order; but it was akin.

It doesn't get him off the hook. Reading the *Writer's Diary* comprising journalism and short fiction written in the last eight years of his life, one might well ask how in the guise of a spiritual revolution an alternative imperialism grew.

Perhaps that post-Omsk craving for Hegel was the answer. Under German tutelage Dostoevsky's thinking about Russian spiritual identity became historicized and available as a political tool. He achieved what the Russian Romantics of Hegel's day had first begun to long for, the *bogatyr* as the saviour who would lead Russia antithetically through the best of what France and Germany had to offer and on to synthesis and new originality.[39] In particular his thoughts about psychology, nationality and modernity fed into a widespread search through the nineteenth century for a new kind of man, starting with Lessing's and Schiller's re-education of the human race. As Schiller put in the *Aesthetic Education*:

> Reason has accomplished all she can accomplish by discovering the law and establishing it . . . How is it then that we still remain barbarians? There must . . . be something in the disposition of men which stands in the way of the acceptance of truth . . . The majority of men are far too wearied and exhausted by the struggle for existence to gird themselves for a new and harder struggle against error . . . the development of man's capacity for feeling is, therefore, the more urgent need of our age . . .[40]

The secular search for the New Man passed from Idealism into European social democratic thought, and the likes of Herzen would have wanted to belong there.

On his first visit to Europe, however, Dostoevsky, so steeped in Schiller and yet so unable to accept the fullness of his humanist faith, concentrated on how capitalist bourgeois society repelled his Russian soul. The West was repugnant because it was individualistic. He pondered

> the individualistic basis of the whole Western world and the necessity of finding some way to live together, of finding some way to fashion a community and set up house all in the same anthill; it may only be an anthill, but we had better get organised without devouring each other, or else we'll become cannibals!

This was Shigalyov's problem about how the mass of people could coexist freely. If socialism was one possible answer, Dostoevsky now felt, it would never work in Europe. Socialism in Europe would be coercive and artificial, because that individualism would have to be repressed by rules. 'There is Utopia for you, gentlemen!' he wrote ironically.

Socialism paradoxically stood even less chance of succeeding in the West than in Russia, because the West's entrenched individualism denied the very possibility of fraternity. Worse still, when the Western-style socialists tried to persuade people to adopt a socialist principle of community on rational grounds, rather than out of the warmth of comradeship, all they could create would be anthills of sameness.[41]

The Russian, by contrast, would do better setting up a more fraternal and egalitarian way of life for the new masses because fraternity was natural to him and community spontaneous.

Now in the forest of contradictions it was surely *this* hopeful aspect of Dostoevsky that prompted Anatoly Lunacharsky, the first Soviet Commissar for Culture, to hail him as a fellow of the Bolshevik Revolution.[42] That view would not go forward as the orthodoxy of Soviet outlook. But it's worth remembering that the Soviet socialist order would always claim to be a voluntary brotherhood, organized by the Party. Dostoevsky thought that the natural fraternity of Russians guaranteed them freedom and difference, whereas Western reason, imposed on the living body of life, created prisons; and it is piquant to reflect on that mirror image of what, from the West looking East, seemed to be quite the opposite case. Dostoevsky, often called a prophet, foresaw at the very least, in matters political, that the twentieth century would witness two different socialisms side by side, with an idea of individual freedom keeping them apart.

And on he travelled, from St Petersburg to Paris and Paris to London, and all the while there was the sense that if he could pin down the essence of the Russian nation he could transform it. Unlike the Western bourgeois, debased by money-grubbing self-interest, the Russian could still respond to beauty.

Another chain of thought had it that Russians at least resisted being 'finished Europeans' – finished in the sense of finessed:

> Lord, what kind of Russians are we? . . . Why does Europe hold such a powerful, magic, compelling appeal for every one of us? . . . I am speaking of our privileged upper set . . . How is it we have not been transformed into finished

Europeans? That we have not been metamorphosed? I believe everyone will agree, with some rejoicing, others, of course, with disgust, that we have not matured enough for this metamorphosis.

It was a kind of Rousseauan thought, that the 'wild' Russian was in the end nobler than the over-cultivated Westerner; and of course he had been a reader of Rousseau in his youth.

But then what is this matter of national identity? How can we talk of the French way and the English way and so on? For a moment he was self-questioning about his Russian messianism:

> Can there perhaps be a kind of chemical combination between the human spirit and its native land, so that you cannot tear yourself away from it? . . . How difficult it is to make things clear from the start, even to one's self! Three generations may fail to elucidate some vital, mighty thought . . .[43]

But if there was a moment of critical constraint, it quickly fell away under pressure of the real experience of being abroad. Dostoevsky speculated on the metaphysics of national belonging in the same way he believed in the power of beauty in art to change the world. 'The West, that jewel of Humanity: what kind of idol was that?' In the self-destructive and apocalyptic scenes Dostoevsky witnessed in heaving, sooty, overcrowded, drunken London, where early capitalism triumphed like an Old Testament falsehood, he looked forward to a superior communal truth coming out of Russia.

Dostoevsky's content would never fit any actual modern political ideology, least of all the Soviet. It was either religious-messianic or anarchic, or primitively communal, nothing that a socialist *state* could build on. His utopian thoughts, both politically and psychologically, focused not on that fairness that a sympathetic Westerner would take to underlie socialism and Communism, but on power. And power he respected for so long as he could not overwhelm it in some ultimate struggle between good and evil that would be the moment of reckoning for autocratic Russia.

So again what did the first Soviet commissar for education, Anatoly Lunacharsky, have in mind in 1920 when he called Dostoevsky 'the dreamer who cast the spell of Revolution on Russia'? Surely it was this interim readiness to define some hitherto elusive Russian spirit for effective political use. If the revolution, or one great concealed spiritual element of it,[44] was the long-awaited explosion of self-expression of the Russian people after centuries of repression, then Dostoevsky's philosophical art was an essential part of it, showing the 'deep' Russian soul under construction.[45] Part of that soul was a mysterious elusiveness that was, in fact, entirely opposed to worldly power. In the view of the great critic and Dostoevsky scholar Mikhail Bakhtin, a mere decade or so into the post-revolutionary era, the chattering, 'dialogical life' of the people, no sooner harnessed politically, would be newly driven underground, because external order was always unwelcome. But the other part of the Russian soul as Dostoevsky constructed it seemed to be pure Schillerian longing. The Marxist critic Georg Lukács long ago argued that Schiller, and we might venture German Idealism as such, liberated a certain 'latent' content in Russia's self-awareness; and Dostoevsky became the prime spiritual vehicle for that other, moral, Russia also seeking revolution.

9

'The Triumph of the Movement which is Dear to Me'

I t was like finding the one book that provided the answer. A man born in 1856 took a book off a shelf and the world changed. Georgy Valentinovich Plekhanov read Marx and knew what to do.

His reading passion in his youth dismayed his military-minded father. 'Take more exercise, boy!' Plekhanov senior cried, but then *he* had a character said to resemble a Prussian king, and surely that wasn't the future of Russia. Russia didn't want militaristic German rigour and even found it ridiculous.[1]

Plekhanov junior retained his father's self-discipline, but his personality was softened by his mother's compassion. He became a philosophically informed political organizer and commentator. He had a moral conscience and an aristocratic bearing. Sympathetic liberal contemporaries, Russian and foreign, liberal in the sense of accepting the French revolutionary premises, admired a man who was noble and decent. Tomaš Masaryk, the future founder and first president of a left-leaning, internationalist Czechoslovakia, was among them.[2]

Plekhanov developed spiritually, and then anti-spiritually. First he accepted the Christian thesis of humanity, and then denied it in the name of human freedom, the way German philosophy had done fifty years earlier. This acknowledgement of Feuerbach, in effect, happened when he was still at school. His mother had brought him up in the Orthodox faith, but his questions in the Holy Scripture class were found to be unacceptably disruptive.[3]

Again, just as when Feuerbach turned on Christianity, when the young Plekhanov abandoned the Bible he discovered his social conscience. That conscience became filled with images from the poetry of Nekrasov. Nekrasov, famous for the question asked in his picturesque epic verses, *Who Can Be Happy and Free in Russia?* (1869–77), briefly overtook Pushkin in popularity in the two socially minded decades after the 1861 Emancipation.[4] Plekhanov and his aristocratic friends, who otherwise knew nothing of peasant life, read his verses aloud and had their eyes opened. With Nekrasov they made a genuine move on the road to socialist revolution. 'You do not have to be a poet/ But you are obliged to be a citizen,' Nekrasov told them. Again it was what European political radicals had experienced two generations before. Just as early German socialists in 1844 had learnt of the plight of the Schleswig weavers from Heine; and just as Engels had in that same year published a whole, still astonishing, book on working-class misery in the Manchester factories and London slums; so it was now, in Russia, Nekrasov's poetry of compassion that lamented child labour in factories. But Nekrasov was equally concerned with the everyday brutality, cunning and cruelty of Russian peasant life, and with the meanness of spirit and the money obsessions he found in all her social classes. *Komu v Rusi zhit' khorosho?*, an all the more devastating title in Russian because it was so simple, asked coruscating questions about a system that, as Bakunin and Herzen had observed before him, gnawed away at the good intentions of *all* its people, whatever their social position. So one might say that when the emergent Russian Populist conscience caught up with English and German socialism of thirty to forty years earlier it did so thanks to Nekrasov with a peculiar Russian tweak. What was inhumane about that country was not one social class but the whole configuration of society, from top to bottom.

In his second year at university, Plekhanov began to imagine a changed system that would give Russia and its people justice. The goal was at once revolutionary, to remove the tsar, and traditional, to revive and encourage the embedded ways of Russian peasant Communism. In his praise for the peasant *mir*, Plekhanov was hardly alone. The great Russian publicist-philosophers abroad, Herzen and Lavrov, also idealized it, as did the Populists at home, with their goals voiced by Nikolai Mikhailovsky. With Plekhanov on the revolutionary side meanwhile was Bakunin, constantly reminding the European public of the ills of Russian autocracy and agitating from afar for the abolition of the Russian state. Plekhanov joined the Land

and Liberty wing of the Populist movement that was prepared to contemplate violence against the tsar's own person. The future assassin of Alexander II in 1881, Vera Zasulich, was a fellow member. Yet within a couple of years Plekhanov realized how irrational was that Russian mass in whose name he and his fellow intelligentsia reformers were risking their lives. Students had gone out into the countryside but the very people they wanted to help, the *prostoi narod*, had called the police. If Russia was to be happy, Plekhanov decided, alluding to Nekrasov, there had to be a *rational* political solution.

The rational solution would be an objective and necessary explanation of the way the world was, to which Russia might be induced to conform. Objective and necessary meant that no sane person could question the truth of the way ahead. It would have the authority of science. The solution would not therefore be Russian peasant Communism but the a priori tenets of Marxism. Marxism was an objective science that discerned the way in which history was bound to unfold. 'The great scientific service rendered by Marx lies in this, that he . . . regarded man's nature itself as the eternally changing result of historical progress, the cause of which lies *outside* man.'[5]

Unlike the Populists Plekhanov was not in love with the idea of the common people, the *narod*. The Russian peasants were a disappointment because they only wanted their own enrichment vis-à-vis the landowners. The peasants loved the tsar and, therefore, perversely, 'the system'. Their non-revolutionary potential and their human banality caused Plekhanov to switch decisively, aged 23, to Marxism as the infallible way to a better world.

All the yearning for the right combination of expansive dynamism and social harmony that Hegel had packaged for the progressive Prussian *Weltgeist* Plekhanov took over in its Marxist form for Russia. Philosophy, as a testament to the unfolding world spirit, explained and anticipated the optimum human path.

The utilitarianism of the previous generation had laid the foundation for so much political faith being placed in science. Turgenev's Bazarov had so much wanted to be useful, which was why his Russian generation had abandoned their German Idealism for the laboratory. In fact Plekhanov had a strong literary bent, but chose mining studies for his university degree, because of the strength of his faith in science to bring about social and moral change. His first-year marks at university were excellent; his second year he was expelled for non-attendance. It was as if Turgenev had already anticipated part of Plekhanov's personal story. And yet this real-life hero of the next generation wasn't dissecting frogs. In between those two university years he first sheltered an anti-tsarist activist and then threw himself actively into the cause; after which there was no way back. A good man risking violence and criminality, Plekhanov might have earned himself a place in another brilliant novel capturing Russia's progress towards revolution, Joseph Conrad's *Under Western Eyes*. Inspired by events in the 1880s, Conrad's novel of 1911 looked back to the decades in which, also in terms of human psychology, and through evolving social and political patterns in a newly urban and activist Russia, Russian Marxism became possible.

The kind of life Plekhanov would lead from the age of 23 almost until he died aged 61 in 1918 was decided in those two tumultuous years 1875–6. He helped free a colleague from prison, escaped, was rearrested and finally was involved in the murder of an agent pro-vocateur, for which he had no other recourse but to flee abroad. For a time he led a cross-border cloak-and-dagger existence under a false name, working as a teacher in south Russia until his identity was discovered. He engaged in similarly clandestine fashion with factory workers in St Petersburg. But then his fellow agitators were plotting to assassinate the tsar and finally Plekhanov demurred. 'You cannot establish a house of parliament at the point of a pistol,' he declared.[6] What was needed was to 'find the correct formula for the manufacture of revolution'.[7] The very word 'manufacture' was important. It belonged to a time of ever-increasing industri-alization on mainland Europe, and in Russia, and it pointed to a technological solution bound up with it; this at a time when Marx was already speculating as to when the proletariat would seize the means of production.

Thereafter, exiled by his criminal status, and seeking political shelter in Geneva and Paris, Plekhanov spent his time reading Marx and Engels on the right economic conditions for revolution, and Darwin, on secularism and human progress, and trawling through swathes of history and across the sciences, in pursuit of that formula to suit Russia.

It was a difficult but intellectually industrious life in which he mentally reorganized a whole vast country from an impoverished base abroad. For Plekhanov the philosophy he read every day, in the university library in Geneva, and sometimes as far afield as the Bibliothèque nationale in Paris, was at once the foundation of the good life and the 'science of sciences'. He also read widely across the sciences.[8] On the one hand, scientific and technological advance would lead to a better social future for the mass of people everywhere; on the other, philosophy would guide its hand. Into a vision of social and spiritual progress designed by Hegel went the scientific positivism that swamped the latter half of the century, and a kind of Darwinian optimism that socialism was unfolding as part of an evolutionary process.

There was something unreal about this recreation of the German *Vormärz* in Russia forty years later, precisely because it was so theoretical. In 1844 Marx castigated the Germans for delaying revolution precisely through their attachment to philosophy. 'Just as the ancient peoples lived their pre-history in their imaginations, in *mythology*, so we Germans have lived our would-be future in thought, in *philosophy*.'[9] At least in France they conducted actual revolutions and didn't just think about them indirectly. Marx would have been absolutely right to extend this criticism to Russia forty years later. Plekhanov was the latest example of two, now nearly three, generations of thinkers trying to find concepts to argue for change; not to carry it out. But as we have seen, he drew back from activism, because he felt the Russian populace would never support revolutionary action, unlike the French bourgeoisie of 1789.

Plekhanov's experience of Russia, on the one hand, and of Marxism on the other, anticipated the complicated Russian 'progressive' future. It would be a selective reincarnation, on Russian soil, of France in 1789. Marxist-Leninism would stop certain aspects of progress happening – namely liberty – while making others – equality and fraternity – possible. What had to happen was that a socialist intelligentsia

> must become the leader of the working class in the projected liberation movement, must explain to it its political and economic interests, as well as the connection between these interests, must prepare it for an independent role in the social life of Russia. It must with all its forces strive so that in the first period of constitutional life in Russia,

our working class can come forth as a special party with a definite social-political programme.[10]

Plekhanov read Marx but then after Marx he read Hegel. It was from Hegel that he 'learnt many of the basic patterns of his way of thinking'.[11] And those patterns precisely made it possible for him to believe that with the dialectical materialism of Marx and Engels philosophy had arrived at the richest, most developed, most concrete stage in its history, just as the mass of mankind was coming into its own.[12] Dialectical materialism, 'the theory of the development of the world with its interconnections, contradictions, leaps',[13] was the great achievement of Western philosophy and justified the rise of the proletariat to take charge in a post-capitalist world.

Dialectical materialism, 'diamat', was a theory of material and therefore economic change leading to social and political change. It claimed, as a description and prediction of those processes, to be scientific and objective like the experimental disciplines Evgeny Bazarov and his positivist generation worshipped. But it also, in almost Fichtean fashion, delivered the promise of a new politics. It was nourished on a deep, non-rational Romanticism, with 'the working class' substituting for Fichte's 'nation'. Viewed as a phenomenon of the imagination, it was what Kant would have called the illegitimate projection of an 'exemplary necessity' into the world; and the projection grew with the aesthetic power of its own images. At the heart of diamat was that sense of opposite phenomena clashing and sparking energy to produce forward movement that was so evident in the young Marx alone, the brilliant young thinker unable to stop the industrialization of the age from sparking unconscious as well as conscious connections. Diamat was philosophy as a combustion engine to carry the last great Western vision of Utopia to its realization in Russia. All the practical improvements that Bazarov wanted to bring to humble Russian life, and the education that Chernyshevsky wanted to give to the common people, to make them politically aware and turn them into democrats, could be loaded onto its moving wagons. It was the Iron Way of nineteenth-century philosophy, solid, secular, mechanical; and yet at the same time, in spirit, a historicized Christianity which claimed to show infallibly how the equivalent kingdom of God would unfold on earth. It's hard to overestimate how convincingly scientific the dialectic seemed, and how it could persuade intelligent men. Plekhanov felt only a Don Quixote would not act in accordance with the course of historical inevitability; and that Quixote wouldn't be an amiable hero, he would be ludicrous.[14]

Something else was going on in the mid-nineteenth century as the hold of Christianity weakened and yielded to science. That yielding, and the consequent justification of materialism, was the real, very general, impact of Darwin, and one of its components was the emancipation of the body. The human body was on the Western philosophical agenda in its own right, and with it those questions of pain and pleasure which religion had transposed to a supposed other plane. If the body was, it now turned out, the clue to our human existence in the world then the philosophical mind had simply been in error for as long as human physicality had been repressed. Otherworldly perfection no longer mattered. The body was the ultimate equalizer; and why shouldn't there be bodily satisfaction for all in this world? the working class that exhausted its strength generating profits for the owners of industry might well ask. The spirit had been overthrown in philosophy, Hegel stood on his head, but the working class was still abject, its claims to that full and equal life forcefully held at bay, because of capitalism. Marx had articulated this parallel, between the emancipation of the body from Christian repression, which was happening, and the longed-for emancipation of the worker from capitalist exploitation, still to come, in a stunning metaphor:

> *Philosophy* is *the head* of this emancipation, its *heart* is the *proletariat*. Philosophy can't come into its full reality until the proletariat is no more and the proletariat can't come to an end before philosophy becomes what it really is.[15]

One had to imagine a world in which neither the working class nor philosophizing about their condition would any longer exist; indissolubly tied up with the other, dialectically intertwined, both would have been solved.

Some of this rejoicing in the liberation of the body would explain, for instance, why the Bolshevik Revolution would in its early years preach free love; and why part of the Marxist inheritance was the idea of the Party eventually withering away. But it wasn't that aspect of dialectical magic based on the complete collapse of the gap between mind and heart, and full of longing for a world in which philosophy would no longer be necessary, that ultimately concerned Russia as a nation. What made Russian Marxism was something much simpler: the idea of a great cosmic historical force compelling Russia in a new direction.

Plekhanov faced opposition in Russia, just as Marx himself did, because Populism was the more instinctive position for a Russian *intelligent* to take up. A woman like Vera Zasulich saw the suffering of the peasantry, and the resistance of the landowners to the 1861 Emancipation, and the deviousness of the tsar, who appeared to make concessions to liberty while making freedom impossible. She knew which critical cause to join. She had to defend the people. Populism was also the more instinctive cause because it helped *define* the *Russianness* of the Russian people. It wasn't an internationalism but belonged to Russia's national emergence, and was part of its programme of self-help.

The Russian situation, in the 1880s, when Marxism and the forging of a Russian national identity through an image of peasant life were both critical options, was therefore unique. It meant that an intellectual like Plekhanov had to re-live a conflict between Enlightenment emancipation and Romantic nationalism that Hegel thought he had solved. All the time the Western idea of progress was growing, and spreading in a Marxist form to Russia, Russia itself was playing havoc with the Western calendar of that growth. It was drawn, as it awoke, to believing itself on a special path. A negative view of the progress of the revolutionary idea in the West fed that conviction. After the failed revolutions of 1848 the Western bourgeoisie was after all growing from strength to strength. Now, for a Russian Populist, that pattern of development played straight into the hands of the autocracy, whose aim was equally to grow a European-style capitalist economy in Russia. Populism was anti-capitalist, and revolutionary. So was Marxism. The crucial difference was the specific identity of Russia.

It was when Zasulich and her friends murdered Alexander II in 1881 in the name of liberty that the orderly, decent Plekhanov reverted to Enlightenment internationalism. He got off the Populist/ Bakuninist/German Romantic train and reverted to Marx.

Plekhanov wanted law, and he couldn't find it in a Russian civil context. Who could live well in such a country? Nekrasov had intimated. Against that Plekhanov saw law embodied in the scientific discoveries of Hegel and Marx. For them history itself had its laws:

> Marxism represents a complete and rigorously materialistic world-view . . . A complete world-view differs from an eclectic one in that each of its aspects is connected in the closest way with all the others . . .[16]

Plekhanov's sole anglophone biographer speaks of the sublime self-confidence of his philosophical beliefs, which were self-taught and sincerely held. He truly embodied the strengths and weaknesses of his country.

The great impulse of nineteenth-century Russia was to pursue self-help as a nation. Once it realized that it was at once historically disadvantaged but in other respects admirably young and different it also realized that it had huge potential. But somehow it couldn't get there without philosophy, conceived as the science of sciences, and thus philosophy as ideology was poised to become a substitute for the rule of law which Russia had always lacked under the autocracy; and there would have to be a revolutionary party, with a Marxist intelligentsia in its vanguard, to teach the right outlook, because the people themselves were not philosophers.

The text in which Marx mentioned 'dream-history' was not known at the time,[17] but if Marx was right about Germany in 1844, then he might be right about Russia around 1894, that a body of dream-history expressed as philosophy would carry the country forward towards revolution.

How do you make philosophy real and get beyond the dream? You take philosophy into the streets and offer it there as an empowering tool. Plekhanov, almost uniquely among the Russian intelligentsia of the day, sought direct contact with the factory workers and had some success securing their loyalty to the Marxist cause. In that year he was active incognito, he campaigned at the factory gates, and then ever after he was active in his writing. What the workers felt was his real achievement was movingly reflected at the end of his life when, courtesy of the revolution of February 1917, he could at last return to his native country. He didn't have long to live and there is a wonderful photograph from 1918 of his funeral cortège stepping soberly through revolutionary Petrograd, as if to Chopin's Funeral March, with workers holding banners aloft: 'He Died – He Lives. The Office of the Authorized Representatives of Factories and Industrial Plants of the City of Moscow.'

Plekhanov's Russian Marxism is obvious to us now as a fantasy, but at the time the necessity it entailed was just what Russia needed. It was the law of philosophy as an alternative to autocratic perversion and caprice and the first step to philosophy changing the world in a moment of its own ultimate fulfilment. Dialectical materialism might mean a detour and a delay, while capitalism was developed in Russia in order to be overcome, but for Plekhanov, whose greatest ideological insight had been the utter irrationality of the peasants, and thus of the unworkability of the peasant commune as a modern political idea, it was the only decent answer to Russia's future.

He had another legacy. He was very much interested in the interplay of revolution and art. A belief in Art, in the Continental sense of literature and poetry and painting and music, had stayed with him since before he had made that abrupt turn towards mining, in his second year at university, in order to be more useful to the people; since the days of his aristocratic education and his poetry reading with friends. By the mid-nineteenth century, as we have seen, Russia was engaged in a fierce polemic about the status and value of art. Was a positivist attitude to literature the right way forward for a progressive people? Or was art's transformative power essentially a matter of the metaphysics of beauty, as Dostoevsky had recently argued? Chernyshevsky in his 'The Aesthetic Relations of Art to Reality' had demoted and popularized the very idea of the spiritual power of the work of art, the great achievement of Kant's Idealist aesthetics, by insisting that it was subordinate to reality. Art was valuable because it served the real need of informing the people, not because of any intrinsic qualities, said the mid-century Russian reformer. Plekhanov, mindful of this controversy, devoted some of his best later energies to literature.

Art, he wrote in 1900, should reflect class conflict:

> I hold that social consciousness is determined by social being ... art ... expresses in itself the striving and moods of a given society, or ... of given social class ... Literary critics ... must first of all elucidate precisely what aspect of social or class consciousness is expressed in the work.[18]

Social awareness was the essence of Russian creativity in the nineteenth century. Art was bound to draw attention to the injustices which more 'spiritual' ages had passed over in devout silence, and reflect a better real world to come, when socialism would resolve capitalist economic and social contradictions.[19] But the new emphasis on class consciousness, really an import from Marx's obsessional dislike of the bourgeoisie, introduced severe constraints and encouraged a condition of ideological warfare. 'As an apple tree must produce apples and a pear tree pears, so the artist who adopts a bourgeois standpoint must be against the working-class movement.'[20] For the artist, 'Party spirit' was required.[21] You couldn't create the wrong kind of art out of the wrong kind of human material. Art had to serve as a source of positive social models.[22]

This was already the dominant strain in the Russian literary tradition. Positive social models were central to Belinsky's founding school of Civic Art criticism in the 1840s, and Plekhanov was a great admirer of Belinsky, his distant relative. That Russian literature was full of types, like the superfluous men of the older generation and the new men of the first social democratic age, was indeed another way of sorting out what types the ideal society of the future wanted, and which it rejected. But in an authoritarian society in which self-help teetered on the brink of self-punishment, Marxist aesthetic theory in the post-revolutionary Soviet era would pose a severe personal danger to the wrong kind of artists.

As it was, the spirit of positivism hung over Plekhanov's 1900 essay. He thought art criticism should be objective and scientific, 'like physics'. The effect was to turn what had once been a morally and aesthetically oriented humanist discipline of interpretation into a mechanical sociology. Plekhanov's Russian Marxism sought practical help from every cultural phenomenon to speed the mending of a so long mistreated society. But it was also inevitably *dirigiste*. With the Marxist idea that art was only an epiphenomenon of the social, the way was created for the political sphere to dictate what art should say.

Versions of a better Russian future were still in open competition on the cusp of the twentieth century. Would it be a Marxist materialist paradise, with art as its servant, or would it be the outcome of that transcendental striving that Dostoevsky represented with his metaphysical views on beauty and the nation? In 1900 Lenin was well aware of what had to be suppressed if the Marxist view was to prevail.

He saw the biggest threat to a new Russian secularism in the spiritual doctrines of Vladimir Soloviev, the religious philosopher who had recently died, and he asked Plekhanov to write an article to counter Soloviev's influence on the younger generation. Plekhanov seems not to have taken up his pen, but fifteen years later Maxim Gorky went on the attack, ahead of Lenin once in power banning Soloviev's work altogether and banishing his disciples abroad.[23]

Plekhanov's aesthetics were a halfway house. He didn't – couldn't, in his political position – approve of negativity and abstraction. The 'petty bourgeois environment' into which Ibsen was born, for instance, for all that Ibsen struggled with it to make his great plays, 'precluded Ibsen's advance beyond negation to a positive, concrete, social ideal'.[24] Plekhanov probably took from Chernyshevsky the idea that art should be about 'the living man' as a positive character. His commitment to Russian Marxism made him simplify human nature. Sometimes he acknowledged an 'instinctiveness' to the human, a matter of true creativity and spontaneous moral action.[25] But then it clashed with his more prescriptive view. Plekhanov was in fact split between what he was as a lover of literature and art and what he had chosen to be politically. When he was 'inwardly free' he could judge, and enjoy, art and literature according to classical criteria of form, content and effectiveness. He never reconciled his two approaches to art.[26] He believed that art was both an emanation from historical material circumstances and a free play of imaginative creativity. He wanted to be a Kantian and a Russian Marxist at the same time.

The same contradiction, between freedom and prescription, also lurked in his ethics. Lenin, who began by adoring Plekhanov, having turned the corner into the twentieth century had less and less time for the master's increasingly qualified views.

A philosopher on whom Plekhanov alighted almost as an alternative to Marx was Spinoza, who was also a 'monist', which meant his universe was also one substance, not afflicted by a mind/body split. In Plekhanov's day, when it really did seem as if 'the end of philosophy' was nigh, with social progress in full march, Spinoza was a way of hanging on to the theoretical realm, and with that a measure of freedom to contemplate theory, to think for thinking's sake, and not only concern oneself with the practical. Spinoza suggested nature itself was not inert but had a purposeful engine, like a living entity, and that purposefulness fitted in a rational universe.

Plekhanov thought it easy 'to do as did Feuerbach and free Spinozism from its theological lumber'.[27] Precisely because it offered One Truth, a Spinozist modern materialism, like Marxism, would have to be policed for fear of alien ideas entering and diluting it. Materialism was a complete world-view, and not an eclectic mishmash in which anything goes. But it had a great deal to offer.[28]

Plekhanov's Spinoza episode was at once odd and telling of his late worries. On the one hand, there had to be a monism, for Russia: a philosophical harness. On the other hand, Spinoza left more scope for individuals to orient themselves in that rational order of things. Certainly a few late renegades in the Soviet 1920s would think so.

Other aspects of metaphysical systems based on One Big Idea lent themselves to an imposed future conformity in Russia, and because they came out of the German Idealist heritage they blended better than Spinoza. Leibniz supplied the idea that affected all the Goethean generation, who in turn passed it on to Hegel and the German Romantics, of a universe comprising 'unity in diversity'. Every part of the universe, however tiny, mirrored the whole, as microcosm to macrocosm. As with the stick of rock which always contains the same lettering wherever you bite into it, so God's mind runs intact through the whole diverse universe. Leibniz's idea of a perpetual pattern repeating itself in endless diversity but never losing touch with the whole was a theological response to that modern emergency, a changing, sometimes suddenly and violently changing world, with which this story began. A century later, Marxist dialectics revelled in change, but temperaments concerned with order shrank back. What could eternity signify, if change was the clue to the world's meaning? This *was* Hegel's question. Dialectic in Hegel was meant to make a provisional non-eternity bearable. In Marx one of its functions was to make present contradictions, for which read suffering, bearable in the name of the better future.

The Utopia that was now just around the corner for Russia at first included all the influences that affected Plekhanov, as it were as variations on a theme. But then it narrowed the options down to make its citizens conform to One Vision.[29] So let's imagine reversing the process, to see what of the revolutionary story was forced underground. Even though Plekhanov's direct influence was felt less and less, what carried over from his involvement in the last free debates before the Revolution was a kind of Platonic Utopia where the social ideal was tough, austere and communal, but not Leninist. It merged with what Chernyshevsky taught Russia in *What is to be Done?*, that there could be a class of individuals devoted to the rational improvement of society, prepared even to sacrifice themselves.

No intelligent person should be a Don Quixote and get left behind on the tide of history, Plekhanov insisted.[30] Sartre said it fifty years later; Plekhanov said it now: the socialist intellectual should make the *free* choice of a man who believes in determinism. He should aim for 'the triumph of the movement which is dear to me'.[31] He should rouse passions in the people; but they would have to be 'lawful passions'. The people would have to learn that lawfulness from philosophy, and to force them to do so would not be out of place.

What would be a good passion? Well, Kant had idealized individuals who would not exploit each other. Marx wanted to institutionalize that ethic on behalf of the working class, but couldn't show *why* the working class should behave that way, other than that they lacked practice, as the exploited class throughout history. But it was really an ethic for Russia's intellectual leaders that Plekhanov was after. His closest friend in exile for 25 years, Pavel Axelrod, came up, early in their relationship, with a definition of what was wanted:

> He who wishes to work for the people must abandon the university, forswear his privileged condition, his family, and turn his back even upon science and art. All connections linking him with the upper class of society must be severed; all of his ships burnt behind him; in a word he must voluntarily cut himself off from any possible retreat. The propagandist, so to speak, must transform his whole inner essence, so as to feel at one with the lowest strata of the people, not only ideologically but also in everyday manner of life.[32]

And so Marxist Russia, inspired by Plekhanov, planned severe, self-governing Kantians to lead the people into the promised land.

Marx himself had wanted a type possessed of 'the breadth of soul that identifies itself, even for a moment, with the soul of the nation, the genius that inspires material might to political violence, or that revolutionary daring which flings at the adversary the defiant words: I am nothing but I must be everything.'[33] Right at the end of the nineteenth century, when Karl Bernstein proposed a revision of Marxism,

Plekhanov and Akselrod were in outright distress at the prospect of socialism being robbed of its heroic and idealistic character.[34] There could be no scepticism and no relativism; only the one goal.

Standing Idealism on its head was always doubtfully coherent, if that move was supposed to retain absolute commitment to the moral law. For Kant and Schiller the human individual was morally free, but only because there was a moral law to choose to follow. An inner moral signpost was part of the spiritual human make-up, and, believing that, they could commit themselves to building a good and beautiful future. Take away individualized spirituality, however, and the imperative to duty either had to come from some worldly or religious authority outside, or it didn't exist. In Russian Marxism it was supposed to come as a directive from the intelligentsia, and where did they get their authority but from a style of philosophy which was 'a complete and integral body of theory embracing all the main questions of philosophy'?[35] Either you believed in (the) philosophy or there was nothing. Readers of the post-Soviet novels of Victor Pelevin will know what a nightmare 'philosophy' had become by the time the Marxist-Leninist system collapsed.

Despite being Russia's ideological captain for a decade, '[Plekhanov] sometimes appeared to remain "inwardly free".'[36] It was a great tension within a man who had simplified his heart in order to serve his country, between how to account for collective and for individual moral behaviour, and it came to a head in the crisis surrounding the First World War. He realized that class war might have to be abandoned for the defence of the nation, and that historical materialism alone could not guide the moral individual. It was a kind of *Darkness at Noon* moment, his earlier system taking on the aspect of a closed box, like a prison, but now with rays of light penetrating through the cracks. In fact a lifetime of reading and searching had liberated him and rendered him genuinely devoted to seeking, rather than finding, ultimate truth. He realized that Marxism was essentially a moral worry and a moral choice for individuals in their relationship to the working class; but that with that individualized worry the oneness and the ideological uniformity were lost.

The truly successful totalitarians would push Plekhanov aside.

10

'We Want All to be Fulfilled at Once': The Great Uprising of Art and Creativity

D ostoevsky had written in 1861, a year that seemed to see a Russian revolution from above, that 'In Russian society the call for what is universally human, and therefore also the response made by all its creative abilities . . . is of historic and universal importance.'[1] What transpired, from the Liberation of the Serfs to the Bolshevik Revolution, answered that call. Bakunin through his intellectual existence, but even more so bodily, with his high energy and his exultation, his impatience and his violence, his simplifications and his pyromania, even his 'schizophrenia',[2] showed one way in which a secular Russia was set to turn Romantic concepts into political ideals.

Bakunin's pre-Hegelian days were ardently Christian. His later secularism has been called mystical. And in Russia, right from the time of the French Revolution, reason and faith intermingled, directly and in disguise. Thus in the last third of the nineteenth century a violent and passionate atheism contended with an equally passionate Christology; and both spoke the language of German Idealism. When Hegel pursued the harmonious overcoming of social alienation and Schelling rediscovered the Incarnation, both were quasi-Hegelian processes of wholeness and harmony restored, one secular, one religious. They imagined progress dialectically, never far out of sight of the three-in-one unity of God, His Son Made Flesh and the Holy Spirit. On the cusp of the twentieth century a secular borrowing from the Christian Trinity was poised to be turned into an immediate doctrine to save the world, as Tübingen neared St Petersburg.

Russian Christology focused on Christ's dual nature and promised that love and sacrifice could surmount worldly conflicts and inadequacies. The poet Alexander Blok urged his fellow intellectuals to 'listen to the revolution' as they respected Christ's commandments to love God.[3]

What role should Art play in securing this great resolution of life's tensions and disparities? The religious thinker Soloviev had a very Christian-cum-German-Idealist-sounding answer:

The perfected content of Being which philosophy grasps as a truth of thought is directly revealed to artistic feeling. If the universe has meaning, there cannot be two mutually contradictory truths – that of poetry and that of science.[4]

So Art, as Schelling had taught, could see through directly to the Oneness of life and help effect a transfigured world. Moreover, Art naturally worked towards the full truth of the Hegelian World Spirit, because one-sidedness was against its nature. Art and creativity '[work] towards that free theocracy in which the Universal Church will reach the full measure of Christ's stature'.[5]

An instinctive Russia hungry to become, contra Nekrasov, a country where people *can* live well would often, contra Plekhanov, dismiss theory, and demand 'Life Itself!' For Blok the revolutionary age was Dionysian, dancing more than thinking its way to fulfilment. On the cusp of 1917 his fellow poet Andrei Bely called 'all abstractions and all material forms' scum.[6] Yet this same future-oriented Russia would go on devouring the theoretical cultural urgings of Bakunin and Chernyshevsky on the one hand and Dostoevsky and Soloviev on the other. A vital Russia might evoke the free spirit of Art, but it might also, inspired by the atheist materialists, harness the letter of Culture, and call on Art to serve the one correct social vision. When Christ appeared to the Grand Inquisitor in the great story told by Ivan Karamazov, Dostoevsky was contrasting the apparent freedom of composite human dwelling in the one Christ, the recurring Russian ideal of *sobornost*, with the threat of dogmatic socialist uniformity. But of course the religious and the materialist views of Russia's future were both total visions, moving along parallel tracks to their goal and each waiting to be endorsed by the right kind of Art.

Conflicting ideas from German Romanticism, Schelling on the intuitive, Fichte on the national, shaded into overtly political questions as Bakunin (1876) and Dostoevsky (1881) neared the end of their lives. Did Russia's future lie east or west? The West meant rules, and reason, and it meant already growing capitalism. Furthermore Populists believed capitalism only played into the hands of the tsar. The East, expressing itself in mystical traditions binding the people to the soil and to the collective, seemed the more patriotic choice. Yet even the simpler Russian Idea had actually been worked out in terms of that pre-modern world Hegel had advocated leaving behind to make progress at all. Change was a threat to a range of Russian thinkers, as it had been to the German thinkers a century earlier, and what Russian Populism contemplated was an actual reversal of the individualism Hegel stood for. The arguments could be artful. If for Soloviev liberty, equality and fraternity were acceptable, that was because they were an unconscious realization of Christ's commandments. Soloviev's spiritual optimism made it possible for an anti-Western religious Russia to be at once never out of tune with the aims of 1789 but also not threatened by revolutionary chaos. God would stop Russia falling into social chaos. 'God then gives chaos its freedom.'[7] Dostoevsky finally settled for a mystical Christian anarchy for Russia, which he envisaged as an alternative to Western rationalism.

It was dislike of the West that made Dostoevsky resist a purely secular future. And in all this, one can see that what Russia was weighing, then as now, was the cost of chaos against the possibility of freedom. If it yearned poetically for an extreme freedom without rules then that might only be achieved as a spiritual goal. The poet Vladimir Mayakovsky, in a poem he worked on for three years from 1917 to 1920, called for 'Fourth and Fifth Internationals of the Spirit', as if he already knew that the Third International of 1919 projecting worldwide Communism would be a spiritual failure.

Russian Christology embraced 'chaos' and 'anarchy' within ultimate faith. Christology was the ultimate, and ultimately fantastic, way of transcending Russia's East–West dilemma. In defence against all the rules and repressions of the institutionalized Church *and* of the state socialism that threatened from the West, the free-spirited Russian Christ was the only deliverance, representing an open-ended, creative love for mankind. Much of the priestly Soloviev's 'philosophy' was a placid encomium for Christ as love. Dostoevsky and Bakunin were more troubled but their goal was not dissimilar. They wanted a higher-level anarchy to guarantee freedom of the soul; a profound non-belonging of the spirit to any existing worldly institution. In an essay in 1906 a minor writer, Georgy Chulkov, together with the poet Vyacheslav Ivanov, summed up that recently received tradition as 'mystical anarchism'.[8]

In all this the Russians were something less than a modern, individualistic Western-style society. They were still affectionately in touch with their feudal past. God as Idea, Word and Presence touched a vital nerve. This is why the battle over atheism mattered so much, and continued to matter when the Soviet state was founded; and why traces of German Idealism could always be found on both sides. Pre-revolutionary Russia sensed its originality and difference and carried its burgeoning spiritual-political-fantastic identity forward in new art forms. When the works of art it created both answered the German inheritance and left it behind this was Russia's triumph, to use the whole German tradition of thwarted revolutionary politics and philosophy and literature as a springboard to land on its own feet artistically. The revolution, in Art, was fabulous.

By the 1870s, capitalism in Russia was allowing painting under private patronage to emerge.[9] The Wanderer painters, a new school of realists inspired by Populism, and the practice of Western *plein air* painters, flourished. They were in theory free spirits. But they immediately committed themselves to a version of Russia, for, as Chernyshevsky had taught them, Art was subordinate to reality and Russian reality was needy. So they went out into the countryside to paint and to use what they saw to interpret Russian reality to the masses who lived in something less than self-awareness. An old form of representation tackled new subject matter, as in early Van Gogh. The peasants responded by smashing the Wanderers' canvases and calling the police. The new painters continued to reflect upon Russia's special destiny, through scenes of nature and peasant life. Their naturalism pushed against the whole weight of the Idealist heritage on behalf of the real lives of real people. Idealism saw Art as the expression of the transcendent world spirit and would find its most obvious Russian counterpart in the Symbolist era to come.

Yet this Russian Populism in Art that marked Russia's entry into the world of modern painting wasn't exactly Romanticism's opposite. Rather it nationalized what had been a late Enlightenment fondness for talking about mankind, and made the cause Russian, while retaining the highest role for Art. To make Art do national service imposed substantial political limitations; it made it didactic. But the Romantics had always thought the artist should show leadership through insight. So the first autonomous school of Russian painting was a kind of answer to the Nature Philosophy of the early century: practical where *Naturphilosophie* had been high-flown, and reflecting the people rather than an artistic elite.

No sooner had it emerged as a modern school than it became an instrument of propaganda; but that was an acceptable way for Art to function for those who loved their country. The twentieth-century experimental genius Kazimir Malevich wrote of his own beginnings that 'in the Wanderers I saw an art of propaganda and a depiction of the powers at work in everyday life . . . I stayed on the side of peasant art and began to paint paintings in a primitive spirit.'[10] The Wanderer interlude was the first stage of the sudden efflorescence of 'The Russian Experiment in Art' now underway.[11] That experiment meant that not only literature but painting and music and drama, and even finally sculpture, were poised to emerge to tell a beautiful unfinished story of Art and Philosophy and the struggle in Russia to find the right formula. Always there seemed to be two tracks for that search. When domestic politics was still short of space and air, but Art could breathe, the first post-1861 generation of reformers took Art out into the countryside to cleanse it of elitism and reconcile it with the people. Then a second generation with similar aims, either side of the Revolution of 1905, reinvented Art in the urban streets. Now the search was religious and now it was secular; now it was national and now universal; meanwhile the urban scene was interpreted with a special quasi-religious intensity. This investment of passion came about because industrialization had happened so quickly, over a mere twenty years, but also because the religious and the national and the way into the future were already inseparable.

Between 1895 and 1922 the cultural scene in Russia was particularly complex, with many strands of political, moral and aesthetic influence interwoven. The 1905 Revolution, when a now politically informed people pressed for their civil liberties, failed to undo tsarism. The creation of the Duma, a quasi-democratic assembly, was a disappointing compromise. But the following year, 1906, brought a constitution of sorts, and with it a remarkable relaxation of censorship with the result that Philosophy and Art redoubled their expressive power and their capacity to mobilize a utopian vision. Russia's Silver Age not only answered Bakunin and Dostoevsky on matters of Russian energy, originality and faith. It put a capital letter on Art in the hands of a brilliant new nation that wanted equality and had an old tradition of fraternity. It defined Russian radical concerns as substantially different to the cultural humanism and political liberalism that were defining the West.

Otherwise the Silver Age remained distant from the organization of labour and issues of class. As I've emphasized here, not least to redress the balance of the long-held view of the October Revolution as only political, liberty mattered to Russia, but in many artistic minds liberty lay in creativity, in Christianity, and in imagination in the service of a long-abused people. Lenin, when he came, was a kind of Westerner; not a liberal to be sure, but a man of reason and rules, who would have to hammer mystical anarchism into submission to secure the apparent takeover by the proletariat, according to the rationality of history.

Against the class issues imported from the West, which could be adapted to suit centuries of resentment of the autocracy, but were not the same, what did matter profoundly to the Russian artists and thinkers affected by the first Revolution of 1905 was the terrible feeling of their own alienation from the people, despite three-quarters of a century of concern. How could it have persisted, that Russia was not one people? What was an intelligent Russian with a moral heart to do? Blok, born of eminent landed gentry, was so consumed by guilt that his poems and essays after 1907 prophesied the revenge of the common people for all that they had suffered over centuries. It was this alienation that more than any other factor would make widespread the intelligentsia's acceptance of Lenin's revolution, as at least an end to the cruel institution of autocracy. Even the religious philosopher Nikolai Berdyaev was in favour; and when Lenin expelled him from the country, he and others like him couldn't understand their enforced separation from a new country where they felt they had just as much work to do as in the old. Lenin in fact was manipulating that old alienation by creating a banished 'Russia Abroad'.

But this is to run on to what happened after 1917, when it became harder and harder to identify the many diverse forces that had stoked the revolutionary momentum. I want to come back to one of them, that 'Life Itself'. It was a German Romantic ideal reworked in the Russian language of *sobornost*: the spiritual collective.

'Life Itself' meant spiritual exuberance. The intensely committed life, which Soloviev called a theurgy, expressed it, and how one arrived at commitment was through seeing the world differently. The religious faithful and the poets, and the Symbolist painters, and the future Marxist-Leninists all believed that the world could be transformed by adopting a radically new theory of knowledge. The Cartesian foundations of a modern Western scientific outlook were never in prospect. It was a more subtly negotiated relationship between the human mind and the external world that German Idealism had offered, and it invited speculation as to a truly perfectible human existence; because the human mind, naturally inclined towards the good, wanted wholeness and harmony with all its heart. That longing that Kant had discovered over a century before transcended the traditional rationalist gap between perception and desire, the world as it is and the world as it ought to be. And Kant's moral-aesthetic longing was now the common heritage of both the Marxists and the religious philosophers on the threshold of the twentieth century. The great revolutionary art of 1895–1922, the work of Malevich and Tatlin, and the Symbolist poetry of Blok, and of Velemir Khlebnikov's reinvention, syllable by syllable, of language and landscape, was great because it hungered after this radical renegotiation of knowledge. Russian revolutionary art would now partner mysticism with engineering to build that world in steel and concrete, colour block and abstract pattern, towering over distant rivers and mountain ranges, and thrusting its way through ever busier, ever wider, city streets, while addressing the conservative Russian people and the revolutionary proletariat equally.

The great enemy of the avant-garde generation, as it had been for Dostoevsky, was positivism. This was the crude idea that empirical science alone could solve the essential human dilemma. Positivism amounted to the narrowed, materialistic vision hostile to the worlds of sentiment and faith. It was the anchor Turgenev's tragic Bazarov had tried so hard to hold on to, with a more efficient – who cared if soulless? – Russia in mind. Positivism inspired the 2+2=4 formula that Dostoevsky's Underground Man rejected. Mathematics, Euclidean, pre-Einstein, was the wrong model for Russian society. In fact it reminded Berdyaev, reading Bely's 1916 novel *Petersburg*, of how cruelly tsarist Russia had been administered, by an unfeeling and abstracted bureaucracy. It wasn't lost on this poetic generation that Euclidean science was itself dying after 1905, when Einstein's theory of special relativity displaced two hundred years of mechanics. The history of physics and the history of Russia were as one.

Dostoevsky, a spiritual libertarian of dangerous intensity, like his Underground Man, cultivated a ferocious anti-positivism. Soloviev, of sweeter temperament, patiently spelled out how the positivist West had taken the wrong path. The West simplified and banalized the human question. Similar sentiments would be expressed by the writer Dmitry Merezhkovsky and, again and again, by the poet, classicist and cultural essayist Vyacheslav Ivanov, as revolution approached. In 1892 Merezhkovsky attacked the 'rude materialism of dogmatic forms' and the 'suffocating, deadly positivism' that threatened to imprison and putrefy Russian culture too. For Ivanov looking back from 1919, in 'The Crisis of Humanism', the human person had never before been 'so closed and walled-off within his selfhood, so cold of heart' as under the influence of positivism.[12]

Commenting on Bely's *Petersburg*, Berdyaev said the power of 'bureaucratism' to strip out the real life of the people and impose upon it 'straight lines, cubes, squares ... the geometric method' was simply evil.[13] Presumably Berdyaev would have seen that Malevich's free-floating geometry, and the whole impetus of Suprematism and Constructivism, was to reflect a different kind of science, which Russian artists immediately interpreted as more magical and more visionary. In its last years of freedom the Russian revolutionary generation was helped by an ardent anti-positivist, Friedrich Nietzsche. There would be Nietzschean themes in both the religious-philosophical and the Bolshevik ways of figuring and furthering early twentieth-century Russia's passionate desire to 'live dangerously', in order to live a free and creative life at all. But of course dangers lurked there too, of a maximalist kind, Lenin and Nietzsche having in common the desire to philosophize with a hammer.

It was surely both because of and despite positivism that this generation fell in love with dialectical materialism as an alternative kind of science. Diamat, transformed by Marx and Engels but not totally divorced from its origins, was the last great inheritance from German Idealism, and it too, like Soloviev's theurgy and Malevich's Suprematism, was destined to change the world through embracing the internal contradictions inherent in all natural phenomena. The contradictions were 'Life Itself'. Engels's most recent biographer in English, Tristram Hunt, calls the dialectic 'an inspiring mystery'.[14] But then with relativity science had indeed rediscovered the improbable and the invisible in the cosmic process.

In the beginning, Schelling had wanted a philosophy of nature that was dynamic and creative for the same reason as did the Russian artists and religious souls who carried his tradition forward a century later. He knew that the creative participation of the individual – the very opposite of the positivist tape-measure approach – was needed to know, as it were, real reality. At the heart of God's Creation, as Schelling had first glimpsed it as a Tübingen seminarist, was a living symmetry which meant that the human mind and the mind of the world were in a reciprocal relationship, reinforcing each other on the road to perfection. The fact that this relationship was 'living' was taken to guarantee it from falling back into the falsehood of 'dead' philosophy. True philosophy had to breathe and twitch and grow like the total organism to which it belonged. It constantly strove to express that living totality.

Schelling's Identity Philosophy had reworked Leibniz for a (neo-) Romantic age sceptical of clockwork but still wanting the grand plan of all things. And now a generation excited by non-Euclidean geometry – Kandinsky's generation, to mention yet another great Russian artist, albeit semi-exiled, in its grasp – reworked Schelling. Often the crusade against positivism expressed itself in the search for the perfect neo-Schellingian symbol.

In the work of the philosopher Sergei Bulgakov, and in the early paintings of Malevich, the Idealist theory of knowledge was transformed into a theory of work which was itself a symbol. Labour conditions were always a practical topic for a Marxist, and a Marxist-Leninist, but surely there was also a symbolic component on the German side too. Along with the Marxist view that capitalism showed up the unfairness of exploited labour went the Idealist view that work was actually an extension of artistic activity and thus another aspect of what can overcome our existential conflicts and root us in a world, and a society, that we can call ours. Work for Marx was about humanity going to work on nature. It established the relationship between subject and object, like knowledge itself. It was, in Marx's rather blunt hands, the blood, sweat and tears equivalent of Schellingian intuition and Hegelian self-making, that you go out there and apply yourself to the materials given in this world you're thrown into. Work overcomes alienation. Work fulfils us at the highest philosophical level. In Russia on the cusp of revolution the analogy travelled the other way. The worker was the artist, or part of the same world as the artist, creating symbols of a Social Oneness and a Unified World Spirit with his labour, as Philosophy blessed a new age. The need to pioneer new industries and harness new energies, the very notion of building a modern society brick by brick, was transformed by Russian Symbolism into a fulfilment of the truths of *homo faber*, man the maker, that German Idealism had explored.

Hegel and the young Marx had laid down the hope that labour could retain a spiritual and communal meaning even while, in Marx's case, the worker struggled with capitalist profiteering. In a country that for twenty or thirty years still thought it could bypass capitalism, the Russian peasant commune expressed a parallel wish. Again in Russia the ideal was *sobornost*, where every individual would work as if in a choir. The collective form was nothing to be afraid of. Malevich projected the Russian village into the timeless by flattening his surfaces and freezing his figures, so that what he seemed to be painting were new-style icons. His peasants went about their work like *bogatyrs* resistant to and more powerful than the mere modern. Each one stood for the many. These giants of magnificent physical stature were de-individualized but eternally graceful in their iconic roles. Grouped like the saints, infectious in their static majesty, they presented the tangible and joyful aspect of a mystery beyond expression. Van Gogh and Gauguin laid the foundation for his fondness for peasant themes and encouraged his rich palette, but Malevich was a Russian painter, the most outstanding and the most capable of capturing a world audience since the actual medieval icon painter Andrei Rublev. He was himself that *bogatyr* who would draw out the best of German and French culture to make Russia a new transcendent cultural force, a hope first expressed in the 1820s and now come to pass. Not the *bogatyr*, though, but the Man-God, or the God-Builder, according to a group including the younger Maxim Gorky. Looking back, Gorky relished the spirit of Symbolism married to the needs of the new social and political state. He thought that 'romanticism that provokes a revolutionary attitude to reality, is an attitude that changes the world in a practical way.'[15]

Malevich, and also Mikhail Larionov and Natalya Goncharova, in their pre-1917 Cubo-Futurism and Suprematism, opened up that fantastic artistic vision of a new kind of world, one in which, in fact, in contrast to the subjective and the Romantic, there was an increasing desire for objectivity and artistic anonymity. It seems to me possible to see how the arrival of new technology for building a real paradise on earth suggested to the mind of Malevich that, like Kant, he should set out the tools available, and sketch their scope. As the old, Utopia-inspiring theory of aesthetic imagination passed into a new age of engineering, Malevich's tectonic paintings were a dazzling statement of what a new world had at its disposal.

Real Russian politics, however, the brutal reality of power over the masses and supported by the masses, thought modernist art was going way beyond revolution's needs. It was like the conflict between Marx and Bakunin played out in aesthetics. How much open-endedness, uncertainty, creative anarchy, anti-politics could be tolerated? Gorky in another breath had attacked 'the creator of the black square'.[16] In a country that so depended on Art to sustain the prevailing order, its practitioners had become too free. Lenin, and even more his Petrograd henchman Grigory Zinoviev, were disapproving, and it was in just their flat-footed, brutish spirit that an anonymous critic in 1918 shouted in the direction of a sharply chiselled Cubo-Futurist statue of Bakunin, 'Get Rid of the Scarecrow!'[17] In other words, our revolution is not going to be accompanied by art like this.

As the Revolution bedded in, Malevich would also be forced to change his style. Because the new Russia in the making was always dependent on philosophy to work out the way forward, and because that philosophy was an Idealism attributing to Art supreme powers of insight and leadership, Art had to matter. It was a topic on which Marxism itself presented a doctrinal problem. Did Art arise out of the prevailing socio-economic conditions, in which case the artist could be accused of coming from or siding with the wrong class if he or she produced unacceptable work? Or was Art part of the economic base, essential to the engine? Plekhanov inclined to believe in the active role of Art, whereas the Lenins of the future remained firm. Art was subordinate to reality.[18] At stake over and over again was creative freedom versus total control.

In the battle for what might or might not happen in Russia in the name of Utopia, one common factor prevailed: the appeal of that total answer. In the sphere of Art it led to the feeling that now was the time for Russia to realize its own version of *Gesamtkunst*, Wagner's own early utopian dream.[19]

Where did this dream of totality originate? At the beginning of our story the German Idealist wanted to transcend his own singularity. He wanted

> to break out of the ego trap in which he found himself, and which never allowed him to escape from contradictions, and to do this in two directions, aesthetically-speculatively and mystically, and by this route to reconcile the individual with 'true life', so that he himself could live truly and essentially, i.e. in 'love' and 'freedom'.[20]

Wagner for his part fused elements of his reading of Schiller and Feuerbach, Hegel and Schopenhauer, into that cycle of operas which he projected as the great Art that a political revolution would make possible: *The Ring Cycle*. Wagner's artwork of the future was to be seen in the context of 'The Oldest Systematic Programme of German Idealism' that the Tübingen seminarists had drafted in 1796, and where they declared that

> ideas had to be made aesthetic, which was to say mythological . . . mythology must become philosophical . . . and philosophy must become mythological . . . [then] eternal unity will reign among us . . . Only then can we expect equal development of all powers, of each individual as well as all individuals . . . This new religion among us will be the last and greatest work of humanity.[21]

In fact Wagner's ambition was to restate in music Hegel's system, there to reconcile opposing forces and unite them in a culmination of the spirit. 'Wagner's artwork of the future was designed to help the consummation of the world spirit come true. In doing so it would constitute the musical culmination of the whole history of mankind.'[22] Wagner's immediate model for the fusion of all the arts was Greek tragedy. The age of Goethe and Schiller and of Hölderlin, in effect, had nourished his sense that modern civilization was a sad falling away from the Greek ideal, and needed to be rediscovered.

Vyacheslav Ivanov took up this theme and restated it for Russia's
Silver Age. The symbol and the symbolic drama ushered in an artistic
revolution that was ready to catch up with Wagner's 'Total Work
of Art', but on its own terms, which ranged from the pageantry of
the Ballets Russes, with music and dance and hand-painted sets,
to the synaesthetic experimentalism of Kruchenykh, Khlebnikov,
Matyushin and Malevich's fabulous part-mimetic music drama,
Victory over the Sun. The experimentalists created not so much
middle-class entertainment as they took the neo-Athenian public
space of tragedy by storm with their politically agitated biomechanics.
The poets Kruchenykh and Khlebnikov wrote the text, the composer
Matyushin the music while Malevich devised the Cubo-Futurist cos-
tumes. The stage was a force field as the actors danced their message
across it. The 'transfigurator', a Futurist Wotan with a black square
over one eye, bellowed in the Prologue: 'The spores of Futureville
will fly into life.' The chorus in the 'First Doing' proclaimed 'The
Laws of Nature have changed.' A contemporary Russian production
shows the sun captured, bound in ropes, eerily reminiscent of how
the tsars paraded their domestic enemies, but here making a pageant
out of the old Copernican – and humanist – enslaver now enslaved.
The message sounded perverse, not humanistic at all. 'Hail darkness!'
'We have opened fire into the past. Is anything left? Not a trace.' But
it was about the moment of physical breakthrough. 'Now we can
become intimidating and strong.' 'With risk but without remorse.'
'Remember the past full of sorrows and mistakes.' 'The breaking and
bending of knees, let us remember!' The spirits of the Dionysian
Nietzsche and Einstein moved the action as the cry rang out from
the chorus: 'Liberated from the heaviness of universal gravity we can
organize.' 'There will be futurian countries.' A production has been
in the repertory of the Stas Namin Theatre, Moscow, since 2013, and
has travelled to Basel and Paris.[23]

The artist Pavel Filonov responded to the Russian age of
Gesamtkunst with a theory that once more hailed 'Life Itself':

Through our theory we have taken up life as such in painting,
and it is clear that any further conclusions or discoveries
will proceed from this, because everything emanates from
life and not even emptiness exists outside of life. From now
on the people will live, grow, speak and think in paintings,

and they will return to the mysteries of the lives of the great and miserable people of the present and future, whose roots, and the eternal fount as well, lie within us.[24]

Because of the German Idealist roots of both Wagner's Total Art and Marx's total vision in *Capital*, the connection between the two enterprises has become plain. Hegel inspired Wagner to imagine a totally redemptive, revolutionary form of music-drama for the fragmented modern soul. Marx, nurtured by that same Hegelian Idealism, perceived the worker's growing alienation caused by capitalism and responded by imagining the total transformation of economic conditions to make the worker whole again. And so yes, *The Ring Cycle* expresses the contradictions of bourgeois capitalism.[25] But the Russian works in Wagner's mould do something different.[26] Unlike, say, Mussorgsky's *Boris Godunov*, a work belonging chronologically to the Populist period, and which magnificently captures the realities of autocratic power, Symbolist Russian disciples of Wagner incline to the transcendent-phantasmagoric:

> The individual shatters and is scattered in his pursuit of moments. The integrated individual gathers the gold of his noontides, and life pours out of them into a heavy ingot; but our life is cut from the fabric of fleeting visions. The ingot of days is full-weight and impenetrable; the fabric of moments is illuminated by an other-worldly mystery.[27]

Unless, indeed, they are inspired by Wagner to step out into the street, when, once again, the Russian Art of the immediate pre-revolutionary years comes into its own.

When Russian art took to the street, when not the novel, which had been the great Russian art form of the nineteenth century, but drama and music and poetry carried the revolutionary message to the people, *sobornost*, that matter of being together, experiencing together, worshipping together, as if in a cathedral, finally found its artistic home. Russian music and drama could now express with Dionysian exultation the single great moving passion of the Russian soul, to be exalted and delivered as one body: not like the West, said Ivanov, because 'We are curious, anxious and – we can see . . . Avid, we want "all to be fulfilled at once," so far are we from the passion of individualism, the passion of rejection, discrimination and one-sidedness.'[28] *Sobornost*, long the name for the projected national reconciliation between the philosopher-artist and the peasant-worker, was now instantiated in the Bolshevik Festival, while the distinction between Art and Action dissolved.

If its time had not been so short-lived, and its representatives not so quickly dispersed by starvation, political repression and exile, one would feel this was a time of wonder in art, reprising the two European revolutions that were its model: France in 1789 and the German lands in 1848. The French Revolution was when music came out on the streets, and the high art of Beethoven met the spirit of the people; and when the painter Jacques-Louis David at once painted the Revolution, organized the festivities for the National Convention and mobilized the citizens to celebrate the second anniversary of the storming of the Bastille. Now, amid similar happenings in Russia, Wagner's own reaching out to the people, however bourgeois by comparison and compromised by the actual founding of the Bayreuth Festival, helped inspire the agitprop chorus on the eve of 1917.

Ivanov fondly imagined, using the term *sobornost*, that even Schiller, to go right back to the German beginning, had always predicted a triumphant return of the individual to the collective.[29] That wasn't true, but there was a sense in which this extraordinary Russia was showing the Aesthetic Idealists of a century earlier, stuck in their remote German duchies, what a national dramatic art really might become in the service of radical change. Dostoevsky in one breath put the religiosity back into Kant, in another reminded the world that Corneille and Racine, the two geniuses of France's neoclassical stage, had had their impact on 1789, and his own work was setting up Schiller for a similar role.[30]

Soldiers and sailors loyal to the Bolsheviks stormed the Winter Palace, the temporary seat of the Provisional Government, on 26 October 1917. Afterwards the Dionysian people poured in and there was much looting and mass inebriation, thanks to the tsar's wine cellars. Perhaps it was the French precedent, or perhaps it was due to the sheer drama of the occasion, involving that grand building, that it was felt to be as much an artistic-symbolic as a political event. And so it was restaged three years later in 1920, a masterpiece of celebration and propaganda, lit with operatic chiaroscuro, and with a chorus that improved on reality by suggesting that the people had rallied spontaneously from the streets.[31] Schiller had foreseen the moment, indeed, when the world seen through Russian eyes became a stage not in Shakespeare's sense but to carry forward a vision of German Idealism, when all men can 'fraternize here in a universal sympathy ... and come nearer their heavenly destination. The individual shares in the general ecstasy, and his breast has now only space for one emotion: he is a man.'[32]

Afterword:
'The Unity of Great Ideas and Strong Feelings'

The beautiful story of the Russian Revolution spans 127 years, if it is counted from the year Kant's *Critique of Judgement* appeared. It reckons with Kant as both a critical philosopher and one speculating on how wonderful are the ways of the humanist imagination. He tells us how joyful it is that we can reimagine our troubled and fractured world as a harmonious and beautiful whole; but also how easily we can be misled by our yearning to create actual beautiful forms, not in Art, but in Life. In Life Itself.

Kant has been seen as wanting to compensate, or at least imaginatively fill out, a world which Hume had rendered too prosaic, and it is a view with which I wholeheartedly concur.[1] At the same time, Kant needed to find a basis for the moral and the beautiful in a world that couldn't, unlike the British, rely on custom and tradition. And so he set in train a German Idealism that would, mostly, horrify the British, except for their poets, but fascinate the Russians, and also the French, and would remain an aspect of the European ideal, carrying forward the philosophical implications of 1789 to the present day.

The Russian response was not a simple borrowing but an extraordinary reworking. It did to Kantian Idealism implicitly what all the world could see it did to Marxism. It created the philosophy it needed to haul itself out of feudal inadequacy and become modern.

The arc of Utopia is the other image in my title, tracing the trajectory of that borrowing. It would touch down at its far point when Marxist-Leninism promised peace to the world and equality for working men and women worldwide, and the freedom to become something, after centuries of deprivation.

It is a story that needs images, for to wonder how the phantasmic Soviet world came about that followed the October 1917 Revolution is to watch how it was captivated by the strange power of metaphysics: the metaphysics that Kant had begun by examining, with a view to making us optimistic, but also cautious, about our powers.

Dialectic, the dynamic interplay of matter and form in our thinking, the flickering balance, the free potential, that are human nature and human reasoning at their best, was the most exalted of hymns to that potential. Politically located in a projected dynamic relationship between ruler and ruled, and psychologically experienced by each of us coming to terms with our conflicted individuality, it imagined the sweetest of outcomes; as if God had designed a harmonious universe after all.

> Our party is concerned at heart with the constant enrichment of the spiritual life of Soviet people. Hallowed be the growth of their labour and socio-political activity, and the blossoming of their talents. For this attention to mankind and his spiritual world is determined by the humane structure of the socialist system, its objectives and its requirements. It was inaugurated by Vladimir Ilyich Lenin.
>
> ... The spiritual world of Soviet man is the unity of great ideas and strong feelings, tied up with the interests of the collective, the tasks of our society and communist thinking and convictions. Communist thinking determined the ideas and feelings of our people, and their moral qualities, their love for their country, their comradeliness and collectivism. It gives them a conscientious approach to work, carried out for the general good and the good of the country and progress forwards. It teaches internationalism and a refusal to be reconciled to the enemies of peace and the enemies of the freedom of nations. The characteristics of Soviet man are an awareness of duty and civil responsibility, and a striving to contribute to the solution of social questions. His goal-oriented nature is enshrined in the struggle and the effort to see communist ideals triumph.
>
> ... The communist education of the workers is a complex and lengthy process. It demands, in part, the effective combating of negative phenomena, the overcoming of relics

from the past on the consciousness and behaviour of the people. The task of overcoming fully the relics of private ownership, swindling, hooliganism, bureaucratism and indifference to man demand the united forces of party and social organizations, workers' collectives and state organs.

The efforts of the party are now aimed at broadening the scope of awareness and the organisation of the masses. It is the constant concern of the state to improve workers' use of their leisure, in the interest of the all-round development of the personality, and to further the spiritual potential of this society of ours, which is building communism.[2]

Except for the word 'communism' the spirit of Kant still hovered over the official version of the revolutionary dream less than fifty years ago, long after the Russian people had lost faith in what it had become. To many of those caught inside the dream it was not so much a prison as a metaphysical disappointment; not a reflection of Life Itself.

Men and women from all walks of life and all persuasions had rejoiced to see tsarism destroyed, but there was a philosophical perversity in the Soviet outcome laid over Russian life, already visible to the critic Bakhtin in the 1920s. 'Life', he could see, already had to defend itself against 'the highest Totality of how things are: the cosmos and the final Identity of existence: absolute Oneness'.[3] Bakhtin, himself struggling to survive in that harshly policed new country, would try to reclaim spontaneity as street chatter and 'carnival', locating those ideals as events in predictably anarchic works of literature from Rabelais to Dostoevsky.

The Revolution ushered in a new autocracy, alas. But while it seems that tsarism endured simply too long for Russia to sustain another kind of power in actual day-to-day life, the way Kant conceived of the human imagination, and the way that conception created a blueprint for a revolutionary striving through philosophy, had its only real test in Russia, and that experiment needs to be marked. Hence again this story.

German Idealism in the German mind was essentially a conservative force. It was that brief moment of Romanticism, which turned Kant's critical thoughts on imagination into a national programme for a new kind of living, that affected the Russian transformation a century later. Kant's approach to human capacity was detached and critical; but what he described as the aesthetic imagination so inspired the Tübingen men that they took it as a positive programme for a transformed future.

Kant was not the father of positivism,[4] but the father – in the Russian context the noble and tragic father – of the Idealist dialectic. In an age which under Christian influence still saw the human individual as essentially in conflict with himself, with 'higher' aspirations struggling to resist more basic desires, Kant was trying to reconcile the rational and the imaginative, the abstract and the bodied, ethical necessity and individual freedom, and his answer was that in the realm of the aesthetic, defined as the realm of conjectures which had no direct bearing on the actual condition of reality, but which delivered a high level of human pleasure and inspiration, lay some kind of solution. Schiller imagined that if we all developed our aesthetic capacity, in Kant's conciliatory sense, we might finally be at ease with ourselves as the imperfect personalities but wonderful dreamers we are. From there it might really be possible to imagine the coming to pass of an Aesthetic State.

Dostoevsky, torn between rationalism and spirituality, between bodily viciousness and spiritual grace, was the first to want that Aesthetic State for Russia.

The great task of the age of German Idealism had been to retain a meaning for the spiritual and the eternal in the face of transient human practice. Hegel found that meaning in the necessary progress of history. Schelling located it as a hope that Art might show the 'wholeness', 'the oneness' and the meaningful 'totality' of all things to be true. Not everyone could see it but artists and philosophers could, and so make it happen. On the eve of the Revolution, with trains of thought that marshalled Marx and Lenin on the one hand and Dostoevsky and Soloviev on the other, Russia relived this passionate questioning of 'objective' and 'subjective' paths to truth. Was it with the 'generic subjectivism'[5] of the people, a function of collective existence, or with objective science that its salvation lay? This antagonism is really the story of the dialectic as a matter of history and nation, and it was thought to be resolved in the making of the Soviet Union. That was the country and the people which, objective science showed, was leading the world towards a perfect idea of humanity.

The theory of dialectical materialism, as the official philosophy of a transformed and transformative country, was always a hedging of bets between that collective subjectivism expressing the national interest and the claim that, since Communism was scientific, Communist Russia was only an example that all the world should follow, because it would be proved right.

For Leszek Kolakowski, the great philosophical analyst and historian of the Marxist phenomenon, the history of dialectic lay at the heart of Western philosophy when philosophy was still concerned with systematically explaining the human condition and the cosmos. For as long as it was felt that the human condition was uncomfortably imperfect, and that the normal person should feel guilty or angry or disappointed, and want to change that state of affairs, philosophy's task was to comment, and to explain and to try to heal the malaise. Plato and the Platonists felt it, as did, in a more worldly and less alarmist way, Aristotle. The imperfection was felt, generation upon generation, age upon age, in terms of the isolation of the individual, in terms of existential non-belonging, and of this life being miserably flawed compared with an imagined perfection. The feeling of alienation and the sense of pure accident, pure contingency, welling up in the human mind were so troubling, and so life-destroying, that the soul fled from them in search of a 'higher truth' showing why our pain was necessary. 'The soul's urge to liberate itself from contingency involves Plato who dedicated his life's work to showing how the individual could educate and refine himself to overcome the alienation between the soul and its object.'[6] Hegel reworked that Platonism as a task for the individual to find his or her place in society, and thus help that society expand and become more perfect:

> Whatever makes the world alien and essentially different from me is, by the same token, a case of my own limitation, insufficiency and imperfection. To rediscover myself is to make the world my own again, to come to terms with reality.[7]

Alienation was thus an old theological problem long shared by philosophy and which, early in the nineteenth century, re-emerged as the founding question of a new sociology. How is it when we don't feel ourselves to be masters in our own home? was Hegel's question. Not our home in God's world now, but in immediate society. Marx started afresh. If we don't feel at home we suspect that the very system of the world is against us. Not God's system but capitalism. Nietzsche was still angry with God, and called it *ressentiment*. Theomachia was the term that came to the mind of Vyacheslav Ivanov. Modern man was still engaged in a battle with the old gods.

Hegel's phenomenology of the spirit asked how individuals came to terms with a world outside themselves at all. Dialectic, or looking past all that is limited and conflicted to a day when those conflicts will be reconciled, was a form of hope, and of healing. When we think dialectically we feel the connection with eternity from our position stuck in time; we know what it will be like to be there, from the position of here; from what is and was we know we will move on, one day to become spiritually rich and happy. Historical materialism sees the evidence in our very physical existence becoming more comfortable, that being the most striking experience of peaceful change under capitalism.

Marx, by adapting the dialectic and adding in his own feelings about being a Jewish outsider, arrived at the view that overcoming alienation was a collective, class-determined task, aided and abetted by the prosperity capitalism brought. The fruits of this effort the proletariat would finally seize as its own. Dialectic was the means, with the eventual victory of the project assured by the course of history to come, when the proletariat, a class that never exploited, never alienated others, would run the world. Marx, because he lived in an age inspired above all by science and technology, transferred the whole weight of human discomfort at what was lacking in the world to faith in a new way of controlling the fruits of technology; putting it in the hands of a class he thought necessarily to be good, unselfish, people.

As theology, and as philosophy, the desire behind the dialectic was a hunger for more reality. It expressed the longing of one isolated consciousness for ever greater spiritual emancipation in the perfect oneness of being. When it became Marxism it reappeared in the world as the ambition of the proletariat to cease being the exploited class and through its seizing of the means of capitalist production to offer all the other social classes a model of the morally informed existence beyond the unfairnesses and limitations of capitalism. As Marxist-Leninism it gave Russia a way of industrializing while retaining a religious-collective meaning for society and without losing control of its liberated masses. Everyone could, but also must, belong. One of the first things Russians learnt about Communism in practice was that the carnival of life didn't fit with reason. Philosophy, having established an unalienated society, was supposed to wither away, but it turned into a weapon to control the revellers.

Marx promised each and every worker emancipation 'in a real Absolute – not an Absolute which is merely a signpost to a place that the Mind knows it will never reach, that is to say a place that does not exist'.[8] Plekhanov gifted Marxism to the Russian proletariat. But what the Russian wanted was not this dream of the restless Protestant soul, nor its transformation into a crusade against the bourgeoisie, but to get rid of the tsar.

The German Marxist poet Bertolt Brecht developed his idea of 'dialectical theatre' out of his twin experiences of German Communism and Russian drama. He wrote a poem 'In Praise of Dialectics':

> Who's to blame if oppression remains? We are.
> Who can break its thrall? We can.
> Whoever has been beaten down must rise to his feet!
> Whoever is lost must fight back!
> Whoever has recognized his condition – how can anyone
>   stop him?
> Because the vanquished of today will be tomorrow's victors
> And never will become: already today![9]

The clue was the fifth line, 'Whoever has recognized his condition – how can anyone stop him?' That was Hegel's idea, that we recognize ourselves in others, and in society; Marx took it over as insight into our material condition; and Lenin demanded Russian workers become aware of their interests. After two thousand years of spiritual individualism, from Plato to the Idealists by way of Martin Luther, solutions to the pain of the human condition now became a matter of the solidarity of class consciousness: not I but We. We the disempowered will break out of our oppression. We will heal ourselves. Society will be whole. Society will belong to the proletariat. It was a model of reconciliation. But as such it never seemed particularly relevant to Russia.

Or rather, dialectic had a different potential in that society, to the extent that it really meant healing. In the Russian context on the eve of 1917, as Art in the streets showed, it seemed philosophically especially crafted finally to show the intellectual his place among the people, and, perhaps, for the carnivalesque people to trust the theories of the intelligentsia.

The Revolution in Russia was of course a long-delayed offensive against the tsarist ruling class. But lurking on the fringes of what it embraced was also a desire to make life come good for the timid and the incomplete and the hungry, and not just in physical terms. For poets and writers and thinkers who felt themselves too soft and timid to make a social contribution, there was the message that opening understanding of the human to contradictions, and particularly to sexual anxieties, would equally change the world. Something carried over from the German social reforms around 1848 to this effect when the Russian Revolution called for sexual simplification, demystification, de-idealization. It was a much attenuated answer to the Idealist philosophy of Love, a revolutionary free eroticism, but also another manifestation of freedom and openness that was not allowed to last, in quickly normalized authoritarian and petty-bourgeois Soviet conditions.

The whole utopian journey, meanwhile, from philosophical conjecture to glorious realization to abject self-parody, from 1789 in France, through 1790 in Königsberg, 1796 in Tübingen, Petrograd 1917, and so on, was captured in Art that no one shaped and no one tamed, but which just happened. Herzen remembered how the last generation of Russian Idealists and the first generation of activists, Bakunin, each of these successively were passionate about German music.[10] German music meant Beethoven before it meant Wagner, and in recognition of that arc of influence, from the joyful upsurge of the German creative spirit to the attempt to transplant it into Russian actuality, the music of Dmitri Shostakovich happened.

If already before the Revolution the drama of Dostoevsky's own soul operated a noisy, discordant counterpoint to the utopian story, Shostakovich, born 25 years after Dostoevsky's death, perpetuated it, yet always with Beethoven in mind. Coming of age in a damaged Utopia, and distressed by it through his entire life, this tortured artist wrote music in the same way that Dostoevsky wrote fiction, referring to Beethoven as Dostoevsky did to Schiller, and all the time seeking to define what was now Soviet Russian, now humorously, now with desperate seriousness, in the face of endless spiritual squalor, compromise and shame. The people were passionate but spiritually incontinent. Where had beauty, 'the spiritual world of Soviet man', gone?

A Note on
Further Reading

On Kant there is no substitute for delving first-hand into *The Critique of Judgement* (1790), widely referred to as his Third Critique after *The Critique of Pure Reason* (1781) and *The Critique of Practical Reason* (1788). The Third Critique and the 1798 essay on 'The Conflict of the Faculties' are widely available in English, in print and online. Dieter Henrich's *Aesthetic Judgment and the Moral Image of the World: Studies in Kant* (Stanford, CA, 1992) is meanwhile a specialist reminder of how the German interpretation has traditionally taken a wider view of what Kant meant in his Third Critique than has been prevalent in the last two centuries of Anglophone readings. The German approach I have favoured was established by Ernst Cassirer in 1918 in his *Kant's Life and Thought* (London, 1981). Ernst Cassirer's *Rousseau, Kant, Goethe* (Princeton, NJ, 1945) is equally useful reading.

Cassirer also pioneered an exhilarating approach to Schiller as a philosopher in 'Die Methodik des Idealismus in Schillers philoso-phischen Schriften' (1921). See Ernst Cassirer, *Gesammelte Werke* (Hamburg, 1998–), Band 9 (2001), ed. Marcel Simon. Frederick Beiser, *Schiller as Philosopher* (Oxford, 2005) takes it forward. Schiller's *On the Aesthetic Education of Man in a Series of Letters*, edited and with a commentary and glossary by Elizabeth Wilkinson and Leonard Willoughby (Oxford, 1967) remains indispensable. For the Utopianism of Schiller's Aesthetic State see also David Pugh, *Dialectic of Love: Platonism in Schiller's Aesthetics* (Montreal, 1996).

German philosophical responses to the French Revolution are surveyed in *The French Revolution and the Age of Goethe*, ed. Gerhart

Hoffmeister (Hildesheim, 1989). For specialists, J. P. Erdmann's *Kant und Schiller als Zeitgenossen der französischen Revolution* (London, 1985) is a succinct and subtle comparison of Kant's and Schiller's experiences of the French Revolution, without however comparing it with Kant's experience of natural disaster. G. P. Gooch's *Germany and the French Revolution* (London, 1920) is a still useful classic.

In the last thirty years there has been an explosion of interest in German Idealism in the Anglophone press after a difficult period post-war. *The Impact of Idealism: The Legacy of Post-Kantian German Thought,* 4 vols, general eds Nicholas Boyle and Liz Disley (Cambridge, 2013), magisterially surveys the impact of 'arguably the most influential force in philosophy in the past two hundred years', including on historical, social and political thought. See also Frederick C. Beiser, *German Idealism: The Struggle Against Subjectivism, 1781–1801* (Cambridge, MA, 2002) and Terry Pinkard, *German Philosophy 1760–1860: The Legacy of Idealism* (Cambridge, 2002). Brian O'Connor's *German Idealism: An Anthology and Guide* (Edinburgh, 2006) is a much more useful collection of texts than *German Idealist Philosophy*, ed. Rüdiger Bubner (London, 1997), which is a belated translation of a dated German anthology ignoring the heritage of Kant's aesthetic judgement.

Considering the post-Kantian Idealists separately, Schelling is a difficult thinker to approach and has been subject to radically different critical interpretations. His earlier essays, including 'On Dogmatism and Criticism', relevant to the utopian story told here, are available in F.W.J. von Schelling, *The Unconditional in Human Knowledge: Four Early Essays, 1794–96,* ed. and trans. Fritz Marti (Lewisburg, PA, 1981). The early thought is more approachable than Schelling's later extended attempts to reframe the cosmos to accommodate the Subjective Idealist vision. The best way into Hegel remains the Preface to the ever-astonishing *Phenomenology of Spirit* (1807). The shorter Introduction to the same work is included in *German Idealist Philosophy*, ed. O'Connor, mentioned above. Judith Shklar's *Freedom and Independence: A Study of the Political Ideas of Hegel's Phenomenology of Mind* (Cambridge, 1976) is an outstanding guide.

Friedrich Hölderlin: Essays and Letters, ed. Jeremy Adler and Charlie Louth (London, 2009), introduces the poet as also a writer and thinker in the context of his times. Michael Hamburger's translations in his dual-language *Poems of Hölderlin* (London, 1943), are still models of concision and finesse.

The interaction of the post-Kantian Idealists, among themselves and with their immediate predecessors, comes to the fore inevitably in all of the works on German Idealism already suggested. There is no particular book in English on their early careers at the Tübingen seminary. Their association is very briefly treated by Gooch in relation to the French Revolution, while the 1796 document which Schelling, Hegel and Hölderlin collaborated on, 'The Oldest Systematic Programme of German Idealism', is available in *The Early Political Writings of the German Romantics*, ed. and trans. F. C. Beiser (Cambridge, 1996), and online, while the history of its interpretation is minutely analysed in Frank-Peter Hansen's *'Das älteste Systemprogramm des deutschen Idealismus'. Rezeptionsgeschichte und Interpretation* (Berlin, 1989). D. C. Schindler's *The Perfection of Freedom: Schiller, Schelling and Hegel between the Ancients and the Moderns* (Eugene, OR, 2012) is a more stimulating specialist study and partly an answer to Pugh's *Dialectic of Love*, cited above. Peter Sloterdijk's brief essays on Kant, Schelling and Hegel in *Philosophical Temperaments* (New York, 2013), brilliantly sketch how politics, history and psychology formed a three-cornered approach to a new idea of knowledge and thus a new social reality. Erich Heller's *The Artist's Journey into the Interior* (London, 1966) has remained an unsurpassed introduction to the artistic-metaphysical grip that German Idealism exerted on its admirers and practitioners.

Marx's theses on Feuerbach are commonly held to demonstrate his emergence from the Idealist background. But I have found much more helpful the 1843 essay that situates Marx in the German run-up to 1848 and makes reference to the handful of Russians Marx met in Berlin. Karl Marx, 'A Contribution to the Critique of Hegel's *Philosophy of Right*: Introduction', is available in *Early Political Writings*, ed. Joseph O'Malley (Cambridge, 1994), and also online. As with Kant's Third Critique and Hegel's *Phenomenology*, there is no excuse for not dipping into *Capital*. Meanwhile Roy Pascal's study of Schiller, Hegel and Marx on work, in *Culture and the Division of Labour: Three Essays on Literary Culture in Germany* (Coventry, 1974) offers persuasive evidence of Marx's dependence on Idealism, and on a very spiritual idea of 'labour' as both individual fulfilment and an end to the traditional problems of mind-body philosophy.

Henry Eaton devoted a very useful article to 'Marx and the Russians' in *Journal of the History of Ideas,* XLI/1 (January–March 1980), pp. 89–112. In the vast literature on Marx, the journalist-philosopher who did away with philosophy to create theory, S. S. Prawer's *Marx in World Literature* (Oxford, 1977) provides an alternative perspective on a polemicist of genius who was also a writer and critic. Margaret A. Rose, *Marx's Lost Aesthetic: Karl Marx and the Visual Arts* (Cambridge, 1984), uncovers Idealist and Realist assumptions in Marx and sees them as competing elements that anticipate the aesthetic tensions of the Russian revolutionary age.

Reaching both forwards and backwards at this point, Lea Ypi, 'On Revolution in Kant and Marx', LSE Research Online (12 March 2014), and subsequently in *Political Theory,* XLII/3 (2014), pp. 262–87, is a model of post-Cold War open-mindedness leading to new understanding of the eventual connection between France in 1789, the German Lands in the years leading up to the 1848 revolutions, and the October Revolution in Russia in 1917.

On the Russian side Alexander Herzen's three-volume autobiography, *Byloe i Dumy* (My Past and Thoughts), is a classic of the genre. The second volume, *Ends and Beginnings,* ed. Aileen Kelly (Oxford, 1985), deals with the impact of German Idealism in Russia and among Russians abroad up to 1848. Herzen's essays on Hegel are available in English, and also online, and Kelly, a pupil of Isaiah Berlin, has written some of the best contemporary commentary, most recently in *Views from the Other Shore: Essays on Herzen, Chekhov and Bakhtin* (New Haven, CT, and London, 1999). Berlin's own *Russian Thinkers* (Oxford, 1978) and P. V. Annenkov's *An Extraordinary Decade: Literary Memoirs* (Ann Arbor, MI, 1968) remain indispensable background reading. Vintage monographs on the impact of Schiller, Schelling and Hegel on Russia may be consulted, together with E. J. Brown's *Stankevich and his Circle* (Stanford, CA, 1966), though it should be remembered that the Cold War inclined scholars to focus quite narrowly on what was considered, in the West, the history of Russian revolutionary thought. Victor Terras's *Belinsky and Russian Literary Criticism* (Ann Arbor, MI, 1974) is a book for specialists, impeccably sourced.

Bakunin still stimulates radically diverse interpretations. Kelly's scholarly damnation of a politically wayward mystic *Mikhail Bakunin* (Cambridge, 1982) should be read alongside Mark Leier's enthusiastic

Bakunin: The Creative Passion – A Biography (New York, 2006), with its invaluable specialist bibliography to date. Bakunin's 1842 essay on 'The Reaction in Germany', together with 'God and the State', 'State and Society' and other pieces, is usefully available in *Michael Bakunin: Selected Writings*, ed. Arthur Lehning (London, 1973), and otherwise online at www.marxists.org. *The Confession of Mikhail Bakunin*, trans. Robert C. Howes (London, 1977) has an introduction and notes by Lawrence D. Orton. David Weir's *Anarchism and Creativity: The Aesthetic Politics of Modernism* (Amherst, MA, 1997) forges a much-needed bridge from the political to the aesthetic and all but predicts the explosion of creativity that would accompany the Russian revolutionary age.

Turgenev's German interests have garnered a great deal of scholarly comment over the last century, and although none of the specialist work is in English, his essay 'Hamlet and Don Quixote' and his stories, including 'A King Lear of the Steppes', can readily be found online.

Dostoevsky's novels need no introduction but aspects of his thought are helpfully clarified in Linda Ivanits's *Dostoevsky and the Russian People* (Cambridge, 2008) and Bruce K. Ward's *Dostoevsky's Critique of the West: The Quest for the Earthly Paradise* (Waterloo, ON, 1986). Quotes here are from his *Winter Notes on a Summer Journey* (New York, 1955), with a foreword by a bemused Saul Bellow. Meanwhile the fine essay 'Mr. –bov and the Question of Art' occurs in David Magarshack, ed. and trans., *Dostoevsky's Occasional Writings* (Evanston, IL, 1997). Dostoevsky's *Complete Letters*, 5 vols, ed. and trans. David Lowe and Ronald Meyer (Ann Arbor, MI, 1988–91), are an indispensable testimony to his arrest in 1849, subsequent imprisonment and internal exile, all of which had such a powerful impact on his outlook. Joseph Frank's five-volume biography *Dostoevsky* (Princeton, NJ, 1976–2002) minimizes the perversity but usefully keeps track of the chronology.

Heinrich Stammler suggested rightly many years ago that Prince Myshkin's 'Beauty will change the world' was a Schellingian view; see 'Dostoevsky's Aesthetics and Schelling's Philosophy of Art', *Comparative Literature*, VII/4 (Autumn 1955), pp. 313–23. It is hard to overestimate the influence of Schelling on what during the entire Soviet period was the other, unspoken late nineteenth century in Russia. For Schelling's direct influence on Soloviev see Vladimir

Solovyov, *Lectures on Godmanhood*, trans. Peter P. Zouboff (London, 1948), and the first of three talks by S. L. Frank in *The Listener* (28 April 1949). Jonathan Sutton's *The Religious Philosophy of Vladimir Solovyov: Towards a Reassessment* (London, 1988) is otherwise the outstanding guide. Soloviev's Schellingian reworking of Christianity was so important in the immediate pre-revolutionary era that art historian Noemi Smolik found his very name officially suppressed when she began working on Russian modernism before 1989. See her essay 'Out of the Picture: A Friend of Dostoevsky and influence on Malevich', in *Frieze* (17 September 2009), available at https:// frieze.com.

On Plekhanov, who was by contrast central to the official version of Russian revolutionary thought leading up to 1917, see Samuel H. Baron, *Plekhanov: The Father of Russian Marxism* (London, 1963), and Plekhanov himself online at www.marxists.org.

The Russian Idea garners so many definitions throughout the nineteenth century that the early twentieth century begins to look like a complex balance sheet compiled by poets, painters, philosophers, theologians and many others besides. *A Revolution of the Spirit: Crisis of Value in Russia, 1890–1924.* ed. Bernice Glatzer Rosenthal and Martha Bohachevsky-Chomiak, 2nd edn (New York, 1990) anthologizes the many alternative definitions of the Russian future that were smothered by the one doctrine of Marxist-Leninist materialism imposed by the Soviet state. The extracts from the work of two generations reopen a debate in which many hoped the 'spiritual' and 'the material' in unison would revolutionize the human soul as much as the Russian political system. While not overtly designed to show the German influence, *A Revolution of the Spirit* lays bare Russian metaphysical yearning for individual consciousness to be mystically transformed into the nation's collective self-understanding.

Camilla Grey in *The Russian Experiment in Art: 1863–1922* (1962), revised and enlarged by Marian Burleigh-Motley (London, 1986), showed how that definitive collectivism pioneered new forms of artistic expression in Russia's explosive encounter with Western early modernism. The composer Richard Wagner's idea of the Total Work of Art meanwhile caused the aesthetic spirit of 1848 in the German Lands to be reborn in Russia, and with redoubled interest, when his delayed influence peaked after the 1905 revolution. Rosamund Bartlett maps the transfer of Wagner's musical and philosophical outlook in *Wagner and Russia* (Cambridge, 1995). Peter C. Caldwell's *Love, Death and Revolution in Central Europe* (London, 2009) and Mark Berry's *Treacherous Bonds and Laughing Fire: Politics and Religion in Wagner's Ring* (Aldershot, 2006) widen the context in which that 'revolution of the spirit' can be understood.

Mark D. Steinberg's *Proletarian Imagination: Self, Modernity and the Sacred in Russia, 1910–1925* (Ithaca, NY, 2002) finds a Russian working class wanting to add the cause of 'Beauty' to 'Liberty, Equality and Fraternity' and to pursue revolution with a moral passion. Lars Kleberg, in *Theatre as Action* (Basingstoke, 1993), shows how remnants of Symbolism merged with a politics of praxis to put Art centre stage in the new Utopia. James von Geldern's *Bolshevik Festivals: 1917–1922* (Stanford, CA, 1993) tells the story of Russian music and drama coming out to meet the people in the streets and pursue the new nation through a mixture of artistic and moral enthusiasm. Boris Groys's *Gesamtkunstwerk Stalin* (Munich, 1988), translated in English less meaningfully as *The Total Art of Stalinism: Avant-garde, Aesthetic Dictatorship and Beyond* (Princeton, NJ, 1992), sees this artistic Utopia as inexorably leading to the totalitarian state. The Russian edition of the book, published in 2003, was called *The Art of Utopia*.

The Soviet heritage and the demise of Marxism notwithstanding, the sociologist Krishan Kumar, in *Utopianism* (London, 1991), p. 98, argues that the concept of 'utopia' can still be used to keep alive 'the principle of hope'.

REFERENCES

Introduction: The Arc of Utopia

1 Tristram Hunt, *The Frock-coated Communist: The Life and Times of the Original Champagne Socialist* (London, 2010), p. 215.
2 Aileen Kelly, *Mikhail Bakunin: A Study in the Psychology and Politics of Utopianism* (Oxford, 1982), p. 49.

1 The Wisest Man

1 See Josef Bordat, 'Kant und das Erdbeben von Lissabon' (2007), p. 3, available at http://sammelpunkt.philo.at.
2 Filomena Abador, 'The Causes of 1755 Lisbon Earthquake on Kant', https://dialnet.unirioja.es/descarga/articulo/1090088.pdf, accessed 18 January 2017.
3 'The Contest of Faculties', *Immanuel Kant: Political Writings*, ed. Hans Reiss, trans. H. B. Nisbet, 2nd edn (Cambridge, 1991), p. 188.
4 Ernst Cassirer, *Kant's Life and Thought*, trans. James Haden (New Haven, CT, and London, 1981), p. 52.
5 The range of meaning is taken from *Roget's Thesaurus*, section 513, on 'Imagination'.
6 This is my translation of a disputed section. Compare versions in 'The Contest of Faculties', *Immanuel Kant: Political Writings*, p. 182, and in 'The Contest of Faculties', in *Immanuel Kant: Religion and Rational Theology*, trans. Mary J. Gregor and Robert Anchor (Cambridge, 1996), p. 302.
7 Cassirer, *Kant's Life and Thought*, pp. 99–100; Ernst Cassirer, *The Philosophy of the Enlightenment*, trans. Fritz C. A. Koelln and James P. Pettegrove (Boston, MA, 1955), p. 160.
8 Quoted in G. MacDonald Ross, *Leibniz* (London, 1992), p. 85.
9 Manfred Kuehn, *Kant: A Biography* (Cambridge, 2001), pp. 342–3.
10 'The Contest of Faculties', *Immanuel Kant: Political Writings*, p. 178. This is my translation.
11 Immanuel Kant, *Critique of Judgment*, trans. Werner S. Pluhar (Indianapolis, IN, and Cambridge, 1987), Pt 1, 1st Division,

2nd Book, 'General Comment on the Exposition of Aesthetic Reflective Judgments', p. 132.

12 Ibid., pp. 135–6.

13 Ibid., pp. 134–5.

14 Cassirer, *Kant's Life and Thought*, pp. 91–2, 235.

15 Kant, *Critique of Judgment*, Introduction VIII, 'On the Logical Presentation of the Purposiveness of Nature', pp. 32–3; 'On the Ideal of Beauty', p. 80; 'On Beauty as the Symbol of Morality', pp. 225–30.

16 Kant, *Critique of Judgment*, 'General Comment', p. 135.

17 Voltaire, *Candide*, chap. 6. See also 'From the Enlightenment to the French Revolution. Lisbon 1755: The Earth Shook', www.internationalist.org/lisbon1755.html, January 2005.

18 See Ana Cristina Araújo, 'The Lisbon Earthquake of 1755: Public Distress and Political Propaganda', *e-JPH*, IV/1 (Summer 2006), www.brown.edu.

19 Kant, *Critique of Judgment*, Pt 1, para. 22, 'The Necessity of the Universal Assent . . .', pp. 89–90; para. 40, 'On Taste as a Kind of Sensus Communis', pp. 159–62.

20 Ibid., para. 42, 'On Intellectual Interest in the Beautiful', pp. 165–70.

21 Ibid., para. 17, 'On the Ideal of Beauty', pp. 79–84, and para. 18, 'What the Modality of a Judgment of Taste is', pp. 85–6.

22 Ibid., 'General Comment on Teleology', p. 377.

23 Ibid., para. 19, 'The Subjective Necessity . . .', and para. 20, 'The Condition for the Necessity . . . is the Idea of a Common Sense', pp. 86–7.

24 Ibid., para. 65, 'Things Considered as Natural Purposes are Organized Beings', pp. 253–4, including fns. 38 and 39; para. 80, 'On the Necessary Subordination of . . . Mechanicism to the Teleological Principle . . .', pp. 303–7.

2 Good Men, Drama and Dialectic

1 Jean-Marie Valentin, 'Friedrich Schiller et les écrivains français. Du génie dramatique révolté au chantre de l'humanité', *Revue des Études Germaniques*, 243 (2006), pp. 347–65. Schiller's fellow laureates included Joseph Priestley, Thomas Payne, Jeremy Bentham, William Wilberforce, the Swiss educational reformer Johann Heinrich Pestalozzi, George Washington and the Polish revolutionary Tadeusz Kościuszko.

2 *Friedrich Schiller: Die Räuber: Ein Schauspiel in fünf Akten, mit einem Nachwort 'Zur Entstehung und Wirkung von Schillers Schauspiel "Die Räuber"'* (Stuttgart, 1969), p. 143.

3 In Britain, however, Thomas Carlyle saw Schiller as a rational monarchist.

4 The National Convention had already succeeded the Revolutionary Assembly.

5 *Die Räuber,* p. 143.

6 Letter to Gottfried Körner, 21 December 1792, at www.friedrich-schiller-archiv.de, accessed 20 January 2017.

7 Karl Dietrich Erdmann, *Kant und Schiller als Zeitgenossen der Französischen Revolution* (London, 1986).

8 Friedrich Schiller, *On the Aesthetic Education of Man in a Series of Letters*, English and German facing, ed. and trans. Elizabeth M. Wilkinson and L. A. Willoughby (Oxford, 1983), pp. lxxix–lxxx.

9 Ibid., Letter 27, para. 11.

10 Ibid., Letter 27, para. 12.

11 See Isaiah Berlin's famous lecture 'Two Concepts of Liberty' (Oxford, 1958), which, read in retrospect, so strongly reflected the cultural conflict between the Soviet Union and the West during the Cold War.

12 *Schiller's 'On Grace and Dignity' in Its Cultural Context: Essays and a New Translation*, ed. and trans. Jane V. Curran and Christophe Fricker (London, 2005), p. 152.

13 This interpretation of Schiller was pioneered by Ernst Cassirer. See D. C. Schindler, *The Perfection of Freedom: Schiller, Schelling, and Hegel between the Ancients and the Moderns* (Eugene, OR, 2012), esp. pp. xxi and 29. See also Rüdiger Safranski, *Friedrich Schiller oder Die Erfindung des deutschen Idealismus* (Munich, 2004). Leszek Kolakowski, 'The Origins of Dialectic', in his *Main Currents of Marxism*, I: *The Founders* (Oxford, 1978), pp. 9–80, offers a magnificent conspectus but does not refer to Schiller.

14 Gotthold Ephraim Lessing, *The Education of the Human Race* [1780], trans. F. W. Robertson (London, 1872), para. 80, p. 67. Available at www.educationengland.org.uk, accessed 20 January 2017.

15 Schiller, 'Aesthetic Education', in *On the Aesthetic Education of Man in a Series of Letters*, ed. and trans. Wilkinson and Willoughby, Letter 18, para. 4; see also p. 305.

16 Schiller to Goethe, 1 March 1795, in *Briefwechsel mit Wolfgang von Goethe*, Letter 53, available at www.friedrich-schiller-archiv.de, accessed 20 January 2017. See also *Friedrich Schiller and the Drama of Human Existence*, ed. Alexej Ugrinsky (Westport, CT, 1988), p. 149.

17 'The Stage as a Moral Institution', in *Aesthetical Essays of Friedrich Schiller*, available at www.gutenberg.org, accessed 20 January 2017, translation slightly amended.

3 Excitement in the Seminary

1 Idealism was already so much at odds with the Anglo-Saxon materialist understanding of the world, from Hume to Bentham and Mill, just as Goethe's science was divorced from Newton's, as I have made a point of stressing. But that was also part of Idealism's eventual appeal in Russia, that the German heritage was not utilitarian, that it was proposing a *moral system, but not one based on self-interest, as a political goal*, and that it had the confidence to do so because of its recent closeness to theology. Oskar Fambach, ed., *Ein Jahrhundert deutscher Literaturkritik (1750–1850)*, 4 vols (Berlin, 1957–), vol. IV. See also Emil Staiger, *Der Geist der Liebe und das Schicksal* (Leipzig, 1935), p. 36.

2 This was Schiller's view. See *Hegel in Berichten seiner Zeitgenossen*, ed. Günther Nicolin (Hamburg, 1970), p. 52.

3 To Karl Gok, September 1793. See *Friedrich Hölderlin: Letters and Essays*, ed. and trans. Jeremy Adler and Charlie Louth (London, 2009), pp. 17–18.

4 'To the Young Poets' and 'To the Germans', in *Poems of Hölderlin*, trans. Michael Hamburger (London, 1943), bilingual edn, pp. 108–9.

5 Vyacheslav Ivanov, classicist, poet and cultural visionary, discovered Hölderlin for early twentieth-century Russia.

6 Otto Pöggeler, 'Hölderlin im Schatten der Philosophie', in *Der Idealismus und seine Gegenwart: Festschrift für Werner Marx zum 65. Geburtstag*, ed. Ute Guzzoni, Bernhard Rang and Ludwig Siep (Hamburg, 1976), p. 364. These heroes recurred as heroes of love and friendship in Hölderlin's poem 'Hyperion'.

7 *Hölderlin: Werke und Briefe*, ed. Friedrich Beißner and Jochen Schmidt (Frankfurt am Main, 1969), Bd II, p. 604; *Friedrich Hölderlin: Letters and Essays*, ed. and trans. Adler and Louth, pp. 242–3, translation slightly amended.

8 Hegel, *Early Theological Writings*, trans. Richard Kroner and T. M. Knox, and with an Introduction by Richard Kroner (Philadelphia, PA, 1971), pp. 302–8.

9 Ibid.

10 'Vom Ich als Prinzip der Philosophie oder über das Unbedingte im menschlichen Wissen' (On the I as a Principle of Philosophy, or on the Unconditional in Human Knowledge), in F.W.J. von Schelling, *Werke*, 3 vols (Munich, 1956–65), ed. Manfred Schröter, vol. I, p. 265. My translation. The two 1795 essays are available in English in *The Unconditional in Human Knowledge: Four Early Essays, 1794–96*, ed. and trans. Fritz Marti (London, 1980).

11 *Hegel in Berichten seiner Zeitgenossen*, ed. Nicolin, p. 14. See also *Friedrich Hölderlin: Letters and Essays*, ed. and trans. Adler and Louth, p. 17.

12 *F.W.J. von Schelling 1775–1854: Briefe und Dokumente*, 3 vols, ed. Horst Fuhrmans (Bonn, 1962–75), vol. I, pp. 69–71. German text also at www.zeno.org/philosophie.

13 Judith Shklar, *Freedom and Independence: A Study of the Political Ideas of Hegel's Phenomenology of Mind* (Cambridge, 1976, reprinted 2010), p. 10.

14 Ibid., p. 65.

15 G.W.F. Hegel, *Philosophie der Geschichte* (Stuttgart, 1961), p. 73.

16 Shklar, *Freedom and Independence*, p. 97.

17 See Matthew Bell, *The German Tradition of Psychology in Literature and Thought, 1790–1840* (Cambridge, 2005), p. 163.

18 'On the I as a Principle of Philosophy', Preface to the first edition, my translation.

4 Reason, Fashion and Romance among the Russians

1 If here perhaps was already a Russian tendency to build insitutions
   without substance, from Potemkin villages to Marxist-Leninist
   facades, still this wonderfully serious and atypical generation set itself
   some fine tasks. The nascent Russian intelligentsia had: to master
   Schiller, also as philosopher, for a Russian readership; to immerse
   themselves in Goethe, for the sake of calling themselves educated
   at all; to grasp Hegel and the significance of Reason in History; and
   finally to set 'the strength and subtlety of the German mind, the
   greatest intellectual phenomenon of the recent age', in a perspective
   that included Russia. Alexander Herzen, *Byloe i Dumy* (My Past and
   Thoughts) (1852–68), book 2, pt 1, in A. I. Gertsen, *Sobranie Sochinenii
   v 30 Tomakh* (Moscow, 1954–66), vol. VIII. Quotations are from the
   English translation of Alexander Herzen, *Ends and Beginnings*, ed.
   Aileen Kelly (Oxford, 1985), vol. II, pp. 84–111.
2 Herzen, *Ends and Beginnings*, ed. Kelly, p. 111.
3 Ibid., p. 84.
4 Ibid., p. 86.
5 Ibid., p. 107.
6 Alexandra Richie, *Faust's Metropolis: A History of Berlin* (London,
   1998), pp. 95–6.
7 Herzen, *Ends and Beginnings*, ed. Kelly, p. 86.
8 V. G. Belinsky, *Polnoe Sobranie Sochinenii* (Collected Works)
   (Moscow, 1956), vol. XI, Pis'ma 1829–40, pp. 152–3. To D. I. Ivanov,
   7 August 1837. Text available online at http://az.lib.ru.
9 Ibid., vol. XI, p. 507. To Botkin, 16–20 April 1840.
10 Herzen, *Ends and Beginnings*, ed. Kelly, p. 86.
11 Tatiana V. Artemieva and Mikhail. I. Mikeshin, 'Hume in Russia', in
   The Reception of David Hume in Europe, ed. Peter Jones (London,
   2005), p. 196.
12 *Sobranie Sochinenii*, vol. VIII, p. 83. See also Edward Hallett Carr,
   The Romantic Exiles: A Nineteenth Century Portrait Gallery (London,
   1933, reprinted 2007).
13 Herzen, *Ends and Beginnings*, ed. Kelly, p. 85.
14 Ibid., p. 90.
15 *N. V. Stankevich Perepiska ego i Biografiia* (N. V. Stankevich,
   His Correspondence and Biography), ed. P. V. Annenkov
   (Moscow, 1914, reprinted 2010), p. 594. To L. A. Bakunina,
   24 November 1835.
16 Ibid., pp. 383–4, 446.
17 I. S. Turgenev, *Polnoe sobranie sochinenii i pisem* (Moscow and
   Leningrad, 1960–68), Pis'ma I, p. 156.
18 Quoted in Ernst Meyr, *The Growth of Biological Thought: Diversity,
   Evolution and Inheritance* (London, 1982), p. 339.
19 'Diletantizm v nauke', *Sobranie Sochinenii*, vol. III, 'Dilettantism in
   Science', Introduction, signed 23 March 1843, Alexander Herzen,
   Selected Philosophical Works (Moscow, 1956).
20 Ibid., pp. 456–8.

21 Mayr, *Growth of Biological Thought*, pp. 387–8, 456–8. See Thomas Carlyle, 'The State of German Literature' (1827), repr. in *Critical and Miscellaneous Essays (1838–1839)*, vol. I, pp. 34–83, for a sustained evocation of this difference with the Newtonian tradition.
22 Herzen, *Ends and Beginnings*, ed. Kelly, p. 103.
23 Alexander Herzen, *From the Other Shore*, trans. Moura Budberg (London, 1956), and *The Russian People and Socialism*, trans. Richard Wollheim (Oxford, 1979), pp. 165–8, 179. Russian text in *Sobranie Sochinenii*, vol. VI and vol. VII.
24 Ibid., pp. 175–7, 203.
25 Alexander Herzen, 'An Open Letter to Jules Michelet', trans. Richard Wollheim, in *From the Other Shore and the Russian People and Socialism*, with an introduction by Isaiah Berlin (Oxford, 1979), p. 179.
26 I. I. Panaev, *Literaturnye vospominaniya* (Leningrad, 1950), p. 10.
27 'V. U.', 'Vil'gel'm Tell Tragediya Shillera', *Moscow Telegraph* (October 1829), p. 500.
28 *Moscow Telegraph* (October 1829), p. 508.
29 *Moscow Telegraph* (July 1827), p. 284.
30 *N. V. Stankevich Perepiska ego i Biografiia*, p. 587.
31 *Sobranie Sochinenii*, vol. III, p. 74.
32 Ibid., pp. 83ff.
33 *N. V. Stankevich Perepiska ego i Biografiia*, p. 321.
34 Ibid., p. 645.
35 P. V. Annenkov, *Literaturnye Vospominaniya* (St Petersburg, 1909), XV, p. 79.
36 Arthur. O. Lovejoy, *The Great Chain of Being* (Cambridge, MA, 1936), p. 11.
37 Herzen, *Ends and Beginnings*, ed. Kelly, p. 84.

5 Philosophy as Dream-history

1 The more familiar term is 'Young Germany'.
2 Ludwig Feuerbach, *The Essence of Christianity* (Leipzig, 1841), trans. Marian Evans (London, 1854); Eugene Kamenka, *The Philosophy of Ludwig Feuerbach* (London, 1970), p. 16.
3 Peter C. Caldwell, *Love, Death and Revolution in Central Europe: Ludwig Feuerbach, Moses Hess, Louise Dittmar, Richard Wagner* (London, 2009), p. 6.
4 Kamenka, *Philosophy of Ludwig Feuerbach*, p. ix.
5 Caldwell, *Love, Death and Revolution*, p. 7.
6 Heinrich Heine, 'Zur Geschichte der Religion und Philosophie in Deutschland', (On the History of Religion and Philosophy in Germany) (1834), *Ausgewälte Werke in fünf Bänden* (Munich, 1964), IV [Bd 444], p. 213; 'Die Romantische Schule' (The Romantic School), V [Bd 961], p. 41; 'Deutschland. Ein Wintermärchen' (Germany: A Winter's Tale), IV [Bd 444], chap. XXVII. All texts online in German and English at www.heinrich-heine.net.
7 Nigel Reeves, 'Heine and the Young Marx', *Oxford German Studies*, VII (1972–3), pp. 44–97.

8 'Germany: A Winter's Tale', chap. III, chap. I.

9 Karl Marx, 'Zur Kritik der Hegelschen Rechtsphilosophie, Einleitung', in Karl Marx and Friedrich Engels, *Studienausgabe in 4 Bänden*, ed. Iring Fetscher (Frankfurt am Main, 1966), I, pp. 25, 27. In English see 'Introduction', *Marx's Critique of Hegel's Philosophy of Right*, ed. Joseph O'Malley, trans. Annette Jolin and Joseph O'Malley (Cambridge, 1970), available online at www.marxists.org.

10 Karl Marx, 'A Book of Verse: Epigrams' (1837), in *Karl Marx, Friedrich Engels, Werke* (Berlin, 1956–68), Ergänzungsband [suppl. vol.] I; *Marx–Engels Collected Works* (London, 1975), vol. I, p. 683. Also available at www.marxists.org.

11 'Germany: A Winter's Tale', chap. XXV, chap. VIII.

12 Marx, 'Zur Kritik', p. 24.

13 Friedrich Engels, 'Ludwig Feuerbach and the End of Classical German Philosophy' (1886), available at www.marxists.org.

14 See Leszek Kolakowski, *Main Currents of Marxism*, I: *The Founders* (Oxford, 1978), pp. 92–5, 128; Allan Megill, *Karl Marx: The Burden of Reason (Why Marx Rejected Politics and the Market)* (Lanham, MD, 2001), pp. 100ff.

15 Marx, 'Zur Kritik', p. 29.

16 Friedrich Schiller, *On the Aesthetic Education of Man in a Series of Letters*, English and German facing, ed. and trans. Elizabeth M. Wilkinson and L. A. Willoughby (Oxford, 1983), p. 305.

17 'das praktische Leben geistlos'/ 'das geistige Leben unpraktisch'.

18 Henry Eaton, 'Marx and the Russians', *Journal of the History of Ideas*, XLI/1 (1980), pp. 90–91.

19 Marx, 'Zur Kritik', p. 22. V. G. Belinsky, *Polnoe Sobranie Sochinenii* (Collected Works) (Moscow, 1956), vol. XII, p. 49.

20 Marx, 'Zur Kritik', p. 22.

21 Karl Marx, *Capital*, an abridged edition, ed. David McLellan (Oxford, 1995), chap. 13, 'Machinery and Modern Industry', p. 231.

22 Ibid., pp. 254, 258. See also *Marx's Economic Manuscript of 1864–65*, trans. Ben Fowkes, ed. Fred Moseley (Leiden, 2015), pp. 214ff.

23 Marx, *Capital*, chap. 13, p. 292.

24 S. S. Prawer, *Karl Marx and World Literature* (Oxford, 1976), pp. 346–7, also links Marx back to Idealism by suggesting that 'even in *Capital*, aesthetic considerations were never far from Marx's mind.'

6 Bakunin on Fire

1 Alexander Herzen, *Ends and Beginnings*, ed. Aileen Kelly (Oxford, 1985), p. 84.

2 Ibid., p. 375. Cf. Max Nomad 'The Heretic Mikhail Bakunin: Apostle of Pan-destruction', in *Apostles of Revolution* (Boston, MA, 1939) and available at www.ditext.com/nomad/apostles/bakunin.html. 'Bakunin thought he had found the road to the heavenly Utopia of Anarchy. What he actually discovered was the path to the infernal reality of Dictatorship.'

3 Mikhail Bakunin, 'The Reaction in Germany' [1842], in *Selected Writings*, ed. A. Lehning (London, 1973). Online at www.marxists.org.

4 Aileen Kelly, *Mikhail Bakunin: A Study in the Psychology and Politics of Utopianism* (Oxford, 1982), p. 291.

5 *Ends and Beginnings*, ed. Kelly, p. 110.

6 Karl Jaspers, *Friedrich Schelling. Größe und Verhängnis* (Munich, 1955), p. 282.

7 Friedrich Schiller, 'Über den Gebrauch schöner Formen' (1795), my translation.

8 Peter Scheibert, *Von Bakunin zu Lenin, 1: Die Formung des radikalen Denkens in der Auseinandersetzung mit deutschem Idealismus und französischem Bürgertum* (Leiden, 1956), pp. 148ff.

9 Ibid., p. 149.

10 Ibid., p. 147, in the Introduction to his 1838 translation of Hegel's Gymnasial Speeches.

11 Ibid., p. 156.

12 Bakunin, *Selected Writings*, ed. Lehning.

13 Ibid.

14 S. S. Prawer, *Karl Marx and World Literature* (Oxford, 1976), p. 359.

15 Joseph Frank, in *Dostoevsky: The Miraculous Years, 1865–1871* (Princeton, NJ, 1995), pp. 447–8, calls Peter Verkhovensky 'a true Bakuninist revolutionary' and refers to 'Bakunin–Nechaev propaganda' that inspired the novel.

16 Mark Leier, in *Bakunin, The Creative Passion: A Biography* (New York, 2006), p. 333, is sceptical of the conclusions drawn by, for example, Kelly and Arthur Mendel. But see Mendel's 'Bakunin: A View from Within', *Canadian–American Slavic Studies*, x/4 (Winter 1976), pp. 466–87, and Michael Bakunin, *Roots of Apocalypse* (Westport, CT, 1981). Belinsky's view of a 'marvellous', 'primitive', 'unscrupulous' and 'disingenuous' man with whom friendship was impossible, is quoted in David Weir, *Anarchy and Culture: The Aesthetic Politics of Modernism* (Amherst, MA, 1997), p. 55.

17 Kelly, *Mikhail Bakunin*, p. 291.

18 See Joachim Köhler, *Richard Wagner: The Last of the Titans*, trans. Stewart Spencer (London, 2004), p. 221.

19 Kelly, *Mikhail Bakunin*, p. 112 (Bakunin to Herwegh in 1847).

20 Scheibert, *Von Bakunin zu Lenin*, p. 267.

21 Richard Wagner, *My Life* [1870], ed. Mary Whittall, trans. Andrew Gray (Cambridge, 1983).

22 Köhler, *Richard Wagner*, pp. 229–32.

23 Ibid., pp. 221–2.

24 Wagner, *My Life*; 'The Art-work of the Future', in Mark Berry, *Treacherous Bonds and Laughing Fire: Politics and Religion in Wagner's Ring* (Aldershot, 2006), pp. 35–42, 61, 170–71.

25 Leier, *Bakunin*, p. 153.

26 Wagner, *My Life*.

27 Weir, *Anarchy and Culture*, pp. 34, 39–40.

28 Kelly, *Mikhail Bakunin*, p. 38. See also Rowan Williams, *Dostoevsky: Language, Faith and Fiction* (London, 2008), p. 174.

29 Kelly, *Mikhail Bakunin*, p. 193.

30 Leszek Kolakowski quoted ibid., p. 292.

31 *The Confession of Mikhail Bakunin, with the Marginal Comments of Tsar Nicholas I*, trans. Robert C. Howes (London 1977), pp. 110–11, 90–91. 'The *Confession* to Tsar Nicholas I' (1851), in *Bakunin on Anarchy*, ed. and trans. Sam Dolgoff (New York, 1971), and at www.marxists. org, merges these two, non-contiguous extracts from the much longer original.

32 Henry Eaton, 'Marx and the Russians', *Journal of the History of Ideas*, XLI/1 (1980), p. 91. Marx attacked the would-be Russian revolutionary Nikolai Sazonov, a lifelong friend of Herzen and fellow anti-tsarist campaigner, for adopting a French dateline for his article. The same might have been said of Bakunin's adopting the French pen name Jules Elysard for 'On the Reaction in Germany'.

33 Ibid., pp. 100, 108.

34 Ibid., p. 99.

35 Ibid., pp. 103–6.

36 Ibid., p. 99.

37 Ibid., pp. 98, 100.

38 *Bakunin: Statism and Anarchy* [1873], ed. Marshall Shatz (Cambridge, 1990).

39 Quoted in Daniel Guérin, *Anarchism: From Theory to Practice* (New York, 1970), pp. 25–6.

40 Kelly, *Mikhail Bakunin*, p. 280. These words were actually a defence of Nechaev and seem to show Bakunin making use of Marx's earlier criticism of the Russian Idealist generation.

41 See Leier, *Bakunin*, p. 136. The implication is that 'the [contradictory] life-process of . . . individuals . . . as they really are' is dialectically productive, and particularly in himself, as his biographers show. For a highly partial positive commentary see Paul McLaughlin, *Mikhail Bakunin: The Philosophical Basis of His Theory of Anarchism* (New York, 2002), pp. 86–7.

42 Quoted in Leier, *Bakunin*, pp. 164–6.

43 Hannah Arendt, *The Origins of Totalitarianism* (1951), new edition with added prefaces (London, 1976), p. 328.

7 A Land of Hamlets and Don Quixotes

1 Turgenev was a White Russian before his time; an exile from a future revolutionary state. He lived in a between-world of writing and music and the unattainable beloved; in a mixture of languages (French, German, Russian, English), cosmopolitan and perilously peripatetic. With his art linking him back to Goethe and forward to Henry James, he was a Robinson Crusoe of the mind who wrote about other Russians who failed to find a place in Russian society, and who often felt that German Idealism had misled them about their own and their country's prospects. He was a man prepared, inwardly, to live on his own island, alone. 'Gamlet i Don Kikhot', in I. S. Turgenev, *Polnoe Sobranie Sochinenii i Pisem* (Moscow, 1982), *Soch.*, vol. V, pp. 330–48.

In English, trans. Moshe Spiegel, in *Chicago Review*, XVII/4 (1965), pp. 92–109, and at www.donquixote.com, accessed 26 January 2017.

2 See the letters written to his friend Evgeny Lambert, 1856–9, in Turgenev, *Polnoe Sobranie Sochinenii*, vol. II.

3 Aileen Kelly, *Mikhail Bakunin: A Study in the Psychology and Politics of Utopianism* (Oxford, 1982), p. 188.

4 See Peter C. Caldwell, *Love, Death and Revolution in Central Europe* (Basingstoke, 2009), pp. 57–72.

5 See Stanley W. Page, 'Lenin, Turgenev and the Russian Landed Gentry', *Canadian Slavonic Papers/Revue Canadienne des Slavistes*, XVIII/4 (December 1976), pp. 442–56. Robert Service, *Lenin* (London, 2000), p. 51.

6 Caldwell, *Love, Death and Revolution*, p. 2.

7 *Allgemeine Deutsche Biographie*: 'Karl Werder'.

8 See Aileen Kelly, *Views from the Other Shore* (London, 1999), chap. 2.

9 S. S. Prawer, *Karl Marx and World Literature* (Oxford, 1976), pp. 273–6; Stephen Heymer, 'Robinson Crusoe and the Secret of Primitive Accumulation', *Monthly Review: An Independent Socialist Magazine*, LXIII/4 (September 2011), available online at http://monthlyreview.org.

10 Prawer, *Karl Marx and World Literature*, pp. 224–5.

11 Leonard Schapiro, *Turgenev: His Life and Times* (Cambridge, MA, 1979), p. 47.

12 Mark Leier, *Bakunin, The Creative Passion: A Biography* (New York, 2006), pp. 150–51.

13 *The Confession of Mikhail Bakunin, with the Marginal Comments of Tsar Nicholas I*, trans. Robert C. Howes (London 1977), p. 82.

14 See John Carey, *The Faber Book of Utopias* (London, 1999), p. xx. 'All of these solitary utopians (Thomas Traherne, Tennyson's Lotos-Eaters, Aldous Huxley, Joseph Conrad's Marlow) are Robinson Crusoes of the mind, inventing islands for themselves to inhabit. By comparison with normal, public-spirited utopians they can seem selfish. Or they can seem wiser. For they implicitly reject the utopian belief that happiness can be achieved through better social arrangements, more efficient machines or improved labour-saving devices . . .'

8 The Chattering Classes and the Moment of Grace

1 This 'deep' Russian soul under construction was dialectical in terms of what about the West had to be reversed and what about Russian simplicity had to be retained in a higher synthesis of a truly modern political morality. So a suffering, saintly people, devious and malformed, but capable of religious/utopian transfiguration, stepped forward as the most revolutionary in the world. Irving Howe, *Politics and the Novel* [1957] (New York, 1992), p. 69. Howe calls him 'a superb caricature' because when a murder is called for he doesn't lend his support, his theory having no need of murder.

2 Fyodor Dostoevsky, *The Devils* [1871], trans. David Magarshack (Harmondsworth, 1971), pp. 407–8.

3 See, for example, Hannah Arendt, *The Origins of Totalitarianism* (1951), new edition with added prefaces (London, 1976), p. 222.

4 Dostoevsky, *The Devils*, p. 44.

5 Kurt Wais, 'Schillers Wirkungsgeschichte im Ausland', in *An den Grenzen der Nationalliteraturen. Vergleichende Aufsätze* (Berlin, 1958). pp. 67, 79.

6 Fyodor Dostoevsky, *The Idiot* [1869], trans. David Magarshack (Harmondsworth, 1955), p. 420 [pt 3, chap. 5].

7 'Mr. –bov and the Question of Art', in *Dostoevsky's Occasional Writings*, ed. and trans. David Magarshack (Evanston, IL, 1997), pp. 86–137. The art historian Noemi Smolik, in 'Out of the Future', *Frieze* (17 September 2009), points out that this essay was heavily cut in the standard Soviet edition of Dostoevsky's works.

8 *Dostoevsky's Occasional Writings*, ed. and trans. Magarshack, p. 97.

9 Ibid., p. 124.

10 Ibid., p. 125. Translation slightly amended.

11 Ibid., p. 131.

12 Ibid., p. 135.

13 Fyodor Dostoevsky, *A Writer's Diary*, vol. I, with an Introductory Study by Gary Saul Morson (London, 1994), pp. 387–8 [March 1876]. Linda Ivanits, *Dostoevsky and the Russian People* (Cambridge, 2008), p.192: 'The same *narod* in which Dostoevsky saw . . . Christianity . . . also taught him the outer limits of willfulness and debauchery in the hearts of human beings.'

14 Ivanits, *Dostoevsky and the Russian People*, p. 192.

15 Howe, *Politics and the Novel*.

16 Dostoevsky, *A Writer's Diary*, vol. I, pp. 141–3.

17 Robert Jackson, *Dostoevsky's Quest for Form: A Study of his Philosophy of Art* (London, 1966), p. 180.

18 See George Steiner, *Tolstoy or Dostoevsky: An Essay in Contrast* (London, 1960), p. 225, but the source was Schiller, not Balzac. See Dostoevsky, *The Brothers Karamazov* [1880], vol. I, trans. David Magarshack (Harmondsworth, 1958), pp. 110–14, 121–3.

19 Fyodor Dostoevsky, *The Complete Letters*, 5 vols, ed. and trans. David Lowe and Ronald Meyer (Ann Arbor, MI, 1988), vol. I, p. 39.

20 Ibid., p. 150.

21 Ibid., p. 188.

22 Ibid., p. 191.

23 Ibid., pp. 189–90.

24 Ibid., p. 199.

25 Ibid., p. 232.

26 Ibid., p. 233.

27 Ibid., p. 271.

28 Ibid., p. 251.

29 Ibid., p. 255.

30 Ibid., pp. 142, 256.

31 Ibid., p. 232.

32 Lesley Chamberlain, *Nietzsche in Turin* (London, 1996); Steiner, *Tolstoy or Dostoevsky*, p. 183.

33 Joseph Frank, *Dostoevsky: The Stir of Liberation, 1860–65* (Princeton, NJ, 1986), p. 248.
34 Fyodor Dostoevsky, *Winter Notes on Summer Impressions*, trans. Richard Lee Renfield (New York, 1955), p. 54. Translation modified.
35 *Winter Notes*, pp. 47–8. This was the faith that came to him in prison and filled the *Writer's Diary* of his final decade.
36 Dostoevsky, *The Complete Letters*, vol. I, p. 195.
37 Lesley Chamberlain, *Motherland: A Philosophical History of Russia* (London, 2004), pp. 128–34.
38 See Dostoevsky, *Winter Notes*, pp. 88, 115–16. Dostoevsky himself rejected bourgeois orderliness as 'colossal internal and spiritual regimentation'. In short he was an anti-utilitarian irrationalist in his efforts to define the otherness of Russia.
39 See above, Chapter Four.
40 Friedrich Schiller, *On the Aesthetic Education of Man in a Series of Letters*, English and German facing, ed. and trans. Elizabeth M. Wilkinson and L. A. Willoughby (Oxford, 1983), Letter VIII.
41 Dostoevsky, *Winter Notes*, pp. 115–16.
42 Quoted in Howe, *Politics and the Novel*, p. 69.
43 Dostoevsky, *Winter Notes*, pp. 47–9.
44 *A Revolution of the Spirit: Crisis of Value in Russia, 1890–1924*, ed. Bernice Glatzer Rosenthal and Martha Bohachevsky-Chomiak, 2nd edn (New York, 1990), p. vii.
45 Georg Lukács, *Studies in European Realism*, trans. Edith Bone (London, 1950).

9 'The Triumph of the Movement which is Dear to Me'

1 Samuel H. Baron, *Plekhanov: The Father of Russian Marxism* (London, 1963), p. 5. Ivan Goncharov's novel *Oblomov* (1859) satirized German efficiency in the character of Stolz, the antithesis of the placid, traditional-minded hero of the title.
2 Tomaš Masaryk, *The Spirit of Russia*, vol. II, 2nd edn (London, 1955), p. 341; V. V. Zenkovsky, *A History of Russian Philosophy*, vol. II (London, 2003), p. 739.
3 Baron, *Plekhanov*, p. 8.
4 Nicholas Nekrassov, *Who Can Be Happy and Free in Russia?*, trans. Juliet M. Soskice (London, 1917), available online at www.gutenberg. org. The Soskice edition took its title from the amplified title question at line 120.
5 G. V. Plekhanov, 'The Development of the Monist View of History', chap. v, 'Modern Materialism', available at www.marxists.org.
6 Baron, *Plekhanov*, p. 34.
7 Ibid., p. 25.
8 Ibid., p. 286. See also p. 60 for Plekhanov's rationalist bent after 1879.
9 'Introduction', *Marx's Critique of Hegel's Philosophy of Right*, ed. Joseph O'Malley, trans. Annette Jolin and Joseph O'Malley (Cambridge, 1970), available online at www.marxists.org.
10 Baron, *Plekhanov*, p. 103.

11 Ibid., pp. 288–90. He began a series of studies in 1891 with an essay marking the sixtieth anniversary of the death of Hegel.
12 Plekhanov, 'Development of the Monist View of History'.
13 Leszek Kolakowski, *Main Currents of Marxism*, II: *The Golden Age* (Oxford, 1978), p. 340.
14 Baron, *Plekhanov*, p. 291.
15 'Introduction', *Marx's Critique of Hegel's Philosophy of Right*.
16 Baron, *Plekhanov*, p. 286.
17 'Introduction', *Marx's Critique of Hegel's Philosophy of Right*.
18 Quoted in William Mills Todd III, ed., *Literature and Society in Imperial Russia 1800–1914* (Stanford, CA, 1978), p. 35.
19 Alan Swingewood and Christopher D. Ward, *Sociological Poetics and Aesthetic Theory* (New York, 1987), p. 9.
20 Ibid.
21 Régine Robin, *Socialist Realism: An Impossible Aesthetic* (Stanford, CA, 1992), p. 212.
22 Ibid., p.148.
23 Noemi Smolik, 'Out of the Picture', *Frieze* (17 September 2009); the same in Michel d'Herbigny, *Vladimir Soloviev: A Russian Newman*, trans. A. M. Buchanan (London, 1918, reprinted with additional material, ed. William G. von Peters, 2013), pp. 212–13.
24 Baron, *Plekhanov*, p. 314.
25 Robin, *Socialist Realism*, p. 194.
26 Edward M. Swiderski, *The Philosophical Foundations of Soviet Aesthetics: Theories and Controversies in the Post-war Years* (Dordrecht, 1979), pp. 60ff.
27 Baron, *Plekhanov*, p. 291.
28 Ibid., p. 286.
29 Ibid., p. 315.
30 Ibid., p. 291.
31 Ibid.; G. V. Plekhanov, *Fundamental Problems of Marxism* [1907], trans. E. and C. Paul (London, n.d.), p. 93.
32 Ibid., p. 14.
33 'Introduction', *Marx's Critique of Hegel's Philosophy of Right*, ed. O'Malley, trans. Jolin and O'Malley, p. 9, translation amended; Marx–Engels *Studienausgabe in 4 Banden*, ed. Iring Fetscher (Frankfurt am Main, 1966), vol. I, p. 27.
34 Baron, *Plekhanov*, p. 174.
35 Kolakowski, *Main Currents of Marxism*, II, p. 340.
36 Baron, *Plekhanov*, p. 287.

10 'We Want All to be Fulfilled at Once': The Great Uprising of Art and Creativity

1 Fyodor Dostoevsky, 'Mr. —bov and the Question of Art', in *Dostoevsky's Occasional Writings*, ed. and trans. David Magarshack (Evanston, IL, 1997), p. 131.
2 Aileen Kelly, *Mikhail Bakunin: A Study in the Psychology and Politics of Utopianism* (Oxford, 1982), p. 193.

3 *A Revolution of the Spirit: Crisis of Value in Russia, 1890–1924*,
   ed. Bernice Glatzer Rosenthal and Martha Bohachevsky-Chomiak,
   2nd edn (New York, 1990), p. 291.
4 V. V. Zenkovsky, *A History of Russian Philosophy*, vol. II (London, 2003).
5 *Russian Philosophy*, ed. James M. Edie et al., 3 vols (Chicago, IL, 1965);
   revd paperback edn 1969, reprinted Knoxville, TN, 1976 and 1984.
6 *A Revolution of the Spirit*, ed. Rosenthal and Bohachevsky-Chomiak,
   p. 278.
7 Lossky, *History of Russian Philosophy*, vol. I, p. 507.
8 *A Revolution of the Spirit*, ed. Rosenthal and Bohachevsky-Chomiak,
   p. 175.
9 Camilla Gray, *The Russian Experiment in Art*, 2nd edn (London, 1986),
   p. 9.
10 'Kazimir Malevič: 'Autobiography', in *Kistorii russkogo avantgarda*
   (Stockholm, 1976), p. 18.
11 Gray, *The Russian Experiment in Art*.
12 Martha M. F. Kelly, 'Aleksandr Blok's Other Body', *The Russian
   Review*, LXX (2011), pp. 118–36.
13 See Berdyaev's *Peterburg*, 'An Astral Novel' [1916], available at www.
   berdyaev.com/berdiaev/berd_lib/1916_233.html, accessed 20 January
   2017.
14 Tristram Hunt, *The Frock-coated Communist: The Life and Times of the
   Original Champagne Socialist* (London, 2010), p. 361.
15 Irina Gutkin, *The Cultural Origins of the Socialist Realist Aesthetic,
   1890–1934* (Evanston, IL, 1999), p. 65.
16 Noemi Smolik, 'Out of the Picture', *Frieze* (17 September 2009).
   Jonathan Jones, in 'Grave New World: Kasimir Malevich's Resting Place
   Tells the Story of Russia', *The Guardian* (28 August 2013) compared
   Malevich's *Black Square* with the contemplation of Holbein's Christ in
   The Idiot, of which Dostoevsky says it could destroy all faith.
17 John E. Bowlt, 'A Monument to Bakunin: Korolev's Cubo-Futurist
   Statue of 1919', *Canadian-American Slavic Studies*, X/4 (Winter 1976),
   pp. 577–90.
18 See Margaret A. Rose, *Marx's Lost Aesthetic* (1988), p. 119 (and see
   also note on p. 187): 'although Plekhanov sometimes claimed that
   consciousness was generally determined by social existence, and
   "reflected" in art, he (theoretically at least) left a way clear for
   Constructivist and Proletkult artists in the 1920s, in a Saint-Simonian
   manner, for a place for art in the economic base, and hence in the
   economic reconstruction and production of society. This vestigial
   Saint-Simonian avant-garde element in Plekhanov was, however, to
   be ignored by those Socialist Realists who used his theories to justify
   their aesthetic against the avant garde in the 1920s and 30s.' The source
   for Saint-Simonian ideas in Russia is said to be Feuerbach and German
   Saint-Simonians, chief among them Heine, whose Saint-Simonian
   interest prompted a more materialist reading of Hegel.
19 Rosamund Bartlett, *Wagner and Russia* (Cambridge, 1995).
20 H. O. Burger, *Die Gedankenwelt der grossen Schwaben* (Tübingen,
   1951), p. 16.

21 As quoted in Mark Berry, *Treacherous Bonds and Laughing Fire: Politics and Religion in Wagner's Ring* (Aldershot, 2006) p. 19. Berry's groundbreaking work makes nonsense of the tendency to dismiss the concept of *Gesamtkunst* as virtually meaningless. See Brian Magee, *Aspects of Wagner*, 2nd edn (Oxford, 1988), p. 84: 'The underlying explanation of Wagner's *Gesamtkunstwerk* is not that it was an art-form that combined all the arts but that it was art-form that combined all Wagner's talents.'

22 Joachim Köhler, *Richard Wagner: The Last of the Titans*, trans. Stewart Spencer (London, 2004), p. 293.

23 See www.stasnamintheatre.ru. The performance in Basel in 2015 is available at http://vernissage.tv (accessed 17 May 2017).

24 Sibylle Fuchs, 17 August 2013, review of Bonnefanten Museum Maastricht exhibition 'The Big Change: Revolutions in Russian Painting, 1895–1917', on World Socialist website. www.wsws.org. Filonov, quoted from 'A Manuscript in the Institute of Russian Literature, Pushkin House, St Petersburg'.

25 Berry, *Treacherous Bonds*, p. 8.

26 By contrast, the realities of Russian power are magnificently captured in Mussorgsky's *Boris Godunov*, a work belonging chronologically to the Populist period.

27 Vyacheslav Ivanov, 'The Crisis of Individualism' [1905], in *A Revolution of the Spirit*, ed. Rosenthal and Bohachevsky-Chomiak, pp. 163–73, 169.

28 Ibid., p. 170, translation modified. C. K. translation generally.

29 Ibid., p. 163.

30 Dostoevsky, 'Mr. —bov and the Question of Art', p. 98.

31 James von Geldern, *Bolshevik Festivals 1917–1920* (Berkeley, CA, 1993), p. 201.

32 Schiller, 'On the Dramatic Stage Viewed as a Moral Institution' (1784).

Afterword: 'The Unity of Great Ideas and Strong Feelings'

1 I hope I have answered the origins of the expectation, and suggested how fake philosophy would cover the loss. See Ernst Cassirer, *Kant's Life and Thought*, trans. James Haden (New Haven, CT, and London, 1981).

2 *Pravda* (15 March 1979).

3 H. O. Burger, *Die Gedankenwelt der grossen Schwaben* (Tübingen, 1951), p. 16.

4 I state this as a small but important correction to Noemi Smolik's article, 'Out of the Picture', *Frieze* (17 September 2009).

5 Leszek Kolakowski, *Main Currents of Marxism*, I: *The Founders* (Oxford, 1978), p. 176.

6 Ibid., p. 17.

7 Ibid., p. 12. The text is translated from the Polish and I've made minor changes in the English for syntactical reasons.

8 Ibid., pp. 59, 71.

9 Translated by David Riff.

10 Alexander Herzen, *Ends and Beginnings*, ed. Aileen Kelly (Oxford, 1985).

INDEX